# The Anthropology of Power

*The Anthropology of Power* presents case studies from a wide range of societies and discusses what is actually happening when people talk about 'empowering' others. The contributors question whether power is actually being transferred to the powerless, or whether this is a delusion.

This collection draws on ethnographic material from Europe, the Middle East, Australasia, Africa and the Americas, exploring how traditionally disempowered groups gain influence in postcolonial and multicultural settings, from civil war to new communication technologies, from religious imperialism to transnational mining investments. It surveys the relationships between empowerment and economic development, gender and environmentalism. The contributors confront post-Foucauldian theoretical issues on the nature, distribution and balance of power, and ask whether the rhetoric of 'empowerment' actually masks a lack of change in established power relations.

This will make challenging reading for all those interested in theoretical issues of power in the postmodern era.

**Angela Cheater** is the author of a number of influential books in social anthropology, including *Social Anthropology: An Alternative Introduction* (1986). She has taught social anthropology at the universities of Natal, Zimbabwe, Cape Town and Waikato.

ASA Monographs 36

# The Anthropology of Power

Empowerment and disempowerment
in changing structures

Edited by Angela Cheater

London and New York

First published 1999
by Routledge
11 New Fetter Lane, London EC4P 4EE

Simultaneously published in the USA and Canada
by Routledge
29 West 35th Street, New York, NY 10001

Typeset in Bembo by
BC Typesetting, Bristol
Printed and bound in Great Britain by
Creative Print and Design (Wales), Ebbw Vale

*British Library Cataloguing in Publication Data*
A catalogue record for this book is available
from the British Library

*Library of Congress Cataloging in Publication Data*
A catalogue record for this book has been requested

ISBN 0–415–19388–5 (hbk)
     0–415–19389–3 (pbk)

# Contents

# Contributors

**Madawi Al-Rasheed** (PhD Cantab) is Lecturer in Social Anthropology at the Department of Theology and Religious Studies (King's College, University of London) and the author of *Politics in an Arabian Oasis* (I.B. Tauris, 1991) and articles on Saudi Arabia's history, society and politics. She has recently worked on ethnicity and migration among Arab communities in London.

**Angela Cheater** (PhD Natal) has recently taken early retirement from the chair of Sociology and Social Anthropology at the University of Waikato. She has published numerous papers and books, mostly on issues of development in Zimbabwe, but including *Social Anthropology: An Alternative Introduction* (Unwin Hyman, 1989).

**Colin Filer** (PhD Cantab) has taught anthropology and sociology at the universities of Glasgow and Papua New Guinea, and is currently Head of the Social and Cultural Studies Division of the PNG National Research Institute. Most of his recent publications deal with the social impact of the mining industry and social context of forest policy in PNG.

**Rudo Gaidzanwa** (MA, Institute of Social Studies, The Hague) is Associate Professor in the Department of Sociology, University of Zimbabwe. She has published extensively, particularly on gender issues, including her book *Images of Women in Zimbabwean Literature* (College Press, 1985).

**Ngapare K. Hopa** (DPhil Oxon), who served on New Zealand's Waitangi Tribunal (1989–92), has recently become Professor of Maori Studies at the University of Auckland, having also taught in California and at the University of Waikato. Her research interests and most of her papers focus on property rights, settlement issues and urban Maori.

**Wendy James** (DPhil Oxon), fellow of St Cross College, author of numerous books and papers in the history and anthropology of north-east Africa (including *The Listening Ebony*, Clarendon Press, 1988), and editor of *The Pursuit of Certainty* (Routledge, 1995), is now Professor of Social

Anthropology at the University of Oxford. She has acted as consultant to the United Nations on displaced communities in the Sudan and Ethiopia.

**Sigridur Duna Kristmundsdottir** (PhD Rochester, New York), formerly Member of the Icelandic Parliament for the Feminist Party (1983–7), has been Associate Professor of Anthropology at the University of Iceland since 1990. She has published articles in both Icelandic and English, and *Doing and Becoming: Women's Movements and Women's Personhood in Iceland 1870–1990* (University of Iceland, 1997).

**Robert Layton** is Professor of Anthropology at Durham University. His books include *The Anthropology of Art* (Cambridge 1981/1991), *Uluru: An Aboriginal History of Ayers Rock* (Aboriginal Studies Press, 1986) and *An Introduction to Theory in Anthropology* (Cambridge, 1997).

**Manuel João Ramos** (doctoral studies at the École des Hautes Études en Sciences Sociales, Paris; PhD Hons Instituto Superior de Ciências do Trabalho e da Empresa) is Associate Professor of Anthropology at the Instituto Superior de Ciências do Trabalho e da Empresa, Lisbon, Portugal. His publications are mainly on historical anthropology, including his book, *Ensaios de Mitologia Cristã* (Lisbon, Assírio and Alvim, 1997) on the legendary Prester John.

**Peter Skalník** (PhDr, CSc Charles University), Ambassador of the Czech Republic to Lebanon from 1993-6, now teaches Social Anthropology and African Studies at Charles University, Prague, where he is affiliated with the Institute of the Near East and Africa. He has edited *Outwitting the State* (New Brunswick, Transaction Press, 1989), with Henri Claessen *The Early State and the Study of the State* (Mouton, 1978/1981), and with Robert Thornton *The Early Writings of Bronislaw Malinowski* (Cambridge, 1993); and published numerous articles.

**Andrew Spiegel** (PhD Cape Town), Associate Professor of Social Anthropology at the University of Cape Town, has co-edited *Tradition and Transition in Southern Africa* (Witwatersrand University Press, 1991) and *Violence and Family Life in Contemporary South Africa* (Human Sciences Research Council, 1996), and published papers on migration, poverty, household, housing and tradition in southern Africa.

**Peter Wade** (PhD Cantab) is currently Senior Lecturer in Social Anthropology at the University of Manchester. His books include *Blackness and Race Mixture: The Dynamics of Racial Identity in Colombia* (1993) and *Race and Ethnicity in Latin America* (1997).

**Vanessa Watson** (Masters in City and Regional Planning, Cape Town), Associate Professor in City and Regional Planning at the University of Cape Town, has co-authored books on regional planning, urban markets and local layout planning and published papers on urbanisation and housing policy, household rental and urban restructuring.

**Richard Werbner** (PhD Manchester) is Professor of African Anthropology and Director of the International Centre for Contemporary Cultural Research at the University of Manchester. Among his many papers and six books, *Tears of the Dead* (Edinburgh University Press, 1991) won the Amaury Talbot Award of The Royal Anthropological Institute.

**Peter Wilkinson** (Masters in City and Regional Planning, Cape Town), Senior Lecturer in the School of Architecture and Planning and Director of the Urban Problems Research Unit, University of Cape Town, has published on urbanisation and migration patterns, housing policy, local government restructuring and South African planning history.

**Daniel Yon** (PhD York University, Toronto, Canada) is Assistant Professor at York University, holding a joint appointment in Anthropology and the Faculty of Education. His forthcoming book *Elusive Culture* (SUNY Press, 1998) is an ethnography of diaspora, race, identity and schooling.

# Acknowledgements

The 1997 annual conference of the Association of Social Anthropologists of the Commonwealth was held at the University of Zimbabwe, Harare, Zimbabwe. It was the first time the conference had departed the shores of the UK, and on behalf of the ASA, as conference convenor and organiser, I would like to thank the University and its staff, from Vice-Chancellor Graham Hill through many other staff, including those in catering and transport, who helped make the conference the success it undoubtedly was. In particular, Lucy Fisher, then of the Department of Sociology, helped enormously with organisational particulars.

British Airways offered special discounts on flights, for which Dawn Quinche in Harare and Penny Paterson in Auckland (who organised flight bookings) earned the gratitude of many participants.

Of the two dozen papers presented at the conference, only thirteen appear in this volume. Making that selection was difficult in many ways, and I should like to acknowledge here the valuable and lively debate that the other papers (some to be published elsewhere) provided to the conference itself.

# Chapter 1

# Power in the postmodern era

*Angela Cheater*

'Empowerment', especially when divorced from consideration of what constitutes 'power', seems to be a sanitised buzz-word of the mid-1990s, yet as Wright (1994: 163) has noted, the word itself has been part of the discourse of debureaucratisation for some two or more decades. From just one publisher[1] come the following recent titles: *Empowerment: Towards Sustainable Development; Knowledge, Empowerment and Social Transformation: Participatory Research in Africa; Monitoring Family Planning and Reproductive Rights: A Manual for Empowerment; Empowerment and Women's Health: Theory, Methods and Practice; Women and Empowerment: Participation and Decision-Making; Gender in Popular Education: Methods for Empowerment; World Communication: Disempowerment and Self-Empowerment.* Interestingly, while in the mid-1990s empowerment is associated particularly with women, gender, health, education and development, especially in Africa, it features not at all in recent titles on Asia – presumably not because anyone thinks that these concerns are irrelevant in Asia, but perhaps because Asia's ability to empower itself through the global economy is unquestioned. Asia's economic approach to power may be the most effective argument against Foucault's preference for 'a non-economic analysis' which sees power as 'not built up out of "wills" (individual or collective), nor . . . derivable from interests' (1980: 188), 'neither given, nor exchanged, nor recovered, but rather exercised . . . in action' (1980: 89) in a curiously agentless way within 'an unequal and relatively stable relation of forces' (1980: 200).

This stress on authorless, systemic empowerment, rather than on the manipulative agents of power-building, was not quite what I had in mind when organising the 1997 ASA conference on 'Power, Empowerment and Disempowerment in Changing Structures' in Harare.[2] My own concern was much more old-fashioned, a modernist inclination within the context of changing state powers to understand 'what power is, how it is constituted, and how it works within an allegedly postmodern world in which older rules of authority seem to have decreasing relevance'.[3] I had hoped to attract papers dealing with:

the impacts of policy interventions and opportunities at state, supra–state and extra–state levels – for example, on the ways in which people evade or ignore the reach of the state in constructing economic power beyond state control; the opportunities for and constraints on ethnic, gender and other group or categorical empowerment offerred by institutions such as United Nations agencies and forums, multinational Non-Governmental Organisations, the European Union, the International Court of Justice, the Internet and the global media, among many others; the possibilities for empowerment by manipulating the interstices between local, regional and central levels of state bureaucratic organisation; and issues of 'management'.

As reflected in this book, some conference participants shared my assumptions that power operates at the 'hard surfaces' of stratificatory reality (Geertz 1973) but, emphasising the limits of editorial authority and power (both used here in the Weberian sense), contributors' rather than the editor's choices have defined the final content of this collection.

In the two decades since transactional theory last tried to grapple with such issues, there seems to have been an unvoiced shift away from the Weberian distinction (Weber 1947) between power (as the ability to elicit compliance against resistance) and authority (as the right to expect compliance). This shift owes much to Michel Foucault and postmodernism, and possibly reflects the ongoing loss of state authority to both sub–national and global organisations. Foucault distinguishes between central 'regulated and legitimate forms of power' and 'capillary' power at the 'extremities' (1980: 96), which perhaps refracts somewhat differently Blau and Scott's (1963) older distinction between a 'formal' organisation and 'informal' relationships underpinning its operation. It may also parallel, while differing from, Skalník's (1989, this volume) understanding of power as deriving from the state in contrast to authority rooted in popular approval. People's action, connoting revolt from below against the bureaucratisation of power, and anti–judicial 'popular justice' are positively recommended by Foucault (1980: 29, 34–5) to counter bureaucratised judicial power. Populist authority, in contrast, may initially seem oxymoronic. Yet twice in the past quarter–century, the world has witnessed the dramatic effects of such authority in action, in both cases associated with the deaths of and funerary rites for extremely popular people – Zhou Enlai in China in 1976 (Cheater 1991), and Diana, Princess of Wales in the UK in 1997. In these two very different[4] examples (one national, the other global), popular authority expressed in mass public mourning clearly altered, in different ways, at least the symbolic expression of state-derived (including imperial and monarchical) power. Perhaps the Indian government (with Gandhi's funeral in mind) sensed the dangers of such popular expression in pre-emptively reinforcing its authority by declaring a state funeral for Mother Teresa as a foreign yet domesticated icon of that country's disempowered poor.

Yet if Foucault's conceptualisation of power does not allow for the idea of popular authority, it is by no means incompatible with the constructions of Barth (1959, 1966, 1967), Bailey (1969) and other transactionalists:

> individuals . . . are always in the position of simultaneously undergoing and exercising this power. They are not only its inert or consenting target; they are always also the elements of its articulation . . . the vehicles of power, not its points of application.
>
> (Foucault 1980: 98)

There is also a hint here of that contemporary usage of 'empowerment' which implies the drive by individuals, singly or in combination, to get what they want. Moreover, consonant with transactionalist principles, Foucault (1980: 99) advocates an 'ascending' analysis of power focusing on its 'techniques and tactics of domination' (1980: 102) – which initially seem to contradict any bottom-up analysis.

But such an approach helps us to understand how socially equal individuals (academic colleagues, for example) can exercise power over others and for themselves – and get what they want when they want it – merely by ignoring the normal rules of polite social interaction; for example, by barging into a group and interrupting its conversation in mid-sentence, such that those hamstrung by their own internalised rules of politeness do not even voice their upset at such rudeness, but meekly resume conversing when the interruption withdraws. And of course, were the interruption a child (and therefore not the social equal of conversing adults), this example would be one of domination exercised from below. Perhaps the mid-1990s concern in some British circles with lack of manners reflects precisely such empowerment, by the overthrow not only of (class-defined) *politesse,* but more broadly of collective agreement on socially appropriate behaviour. Changing *habitus* must, by definition, disempower those who operate by the rules of an older habitus undergoing replacement (Bourdieu 1977). Further along the scale from impoliteness, insults absorbed without retaliation likewise disempower their recipients, and come close to an official New Zealand definition of bullying as 'the power . . . to hurt or reject someone else'.[5] While such mundanities of power at the personal level might be thought unworthy of societal recognition, publicising previously suppressed conflict may encourage individual 'victims' to empower themselves, for, as Miller (1976: 127) notes, 'It is practically impossible to initiate open conflicts when you are totally dependent on the other person or group for the basic material or psychological means of existence.'

Returning to Foucault – who might well disagree with the above – he himself is not entirely consistent in his various descriptions of power. 'Power in the substantive sense, *"le" pouvoir,* doesn't exist . . . power means . . . a more-or-less organised, hierarchical, co-ordinated cluster of relations' (1980: 198), despite the fact that it 'is never localised here or there, never in anybody's hands, never appropriated as a commodity' (1980: 98), never alienable or transferable. Foucault rejects what he calls the juridical/liberal/economic view of power as 'that concrete power which every individual holds, and whose partial or total cession enables political power or sovereignty to be established' (1980: 88). Yet he sometimes reifies power as beyond individual or even collective control: 'the impression that power weakens and vacillates . . . is . . . mistaken; power can retreat . . . reorganise its forces, invest itself elsewhere' (1980: 56).

Perhaps for these reasons, many anthropologists interested in applying Foucault's concepts have diplomatically avoided his descriptions of power, and instead concentrated on his idea that power is vested, even created, in discourses of 'truth' or knowledge rather than in any Weberian command of (potential) force.

> [R]ules of right . . . provide a formal delimitation of power; . . . effects of truth that this power produces and transmits . . . in their turn reproduce this power. [M]anifold relations of power which permeate, characterise and constitute the social body . . . cannot themselves be established, consolidated or implemented without the production, accumulation, circulation and functioning of a discourse.
>
> (Foucault 1980: 93)

Many have, therefore, sought to disseminate alternative, non-scientific, local knowledges as one form of exercising power (Foucault 1980: 34): it is always possible that these, too, may become powerful ideas. '[I]t is really against the effects of the power of a discourse that is considered to be scientific that the genealogy [as "anti-science"] must wage its struggle' (1980: 84). In this 'struggle', though, Foucault's shifting conceptualisations of power may be ignored completely and elided into the notion of empowerment through discourse. As Gordon (1980: 245) has noted, Foucault sees discourse as 'a political commodity', and 'the articulation of discourse and power as a phenomenon of exclusion, limitation and prohibition', so the link between discourse and (dis)-empowerment is easily made.

Freely available words and their changeable meanings have thus been shifted to central stage by Foucault and his followers, not as the purveyors of information as any basis of power (Foucault 1980: 34; Edwards 1994: 205), nor as used by *The Good Soldier Svejk* (Hasek 1973), nor as vehicles of 'semantic creativity' in their power to name, define, objectify or translate and thereby impose meaning (Parkin 1982: xlvi), but in ways curiously reminiscent of cosmologies that attribute magical power to words (see, for example, Kendall 1982: 199). The term 'empowerment' as used in the 1990s seems above all to be about being vocal, having a right to 'voice'. The constantly repeated rhetorics of public policy and institutional good practice[6] seem designed to strengthen individual choice within the market, and to weaken dependency, merely by verbal reiteration. Pop singers talk confidently of changing meaning through the words of their songs and the (global) impact these have on the popular imagination. They ignore the point made by Yelvington (1996: 329), regarding flirting, that:

> [in such] contestations over consciousness . . . systems of meaning can . . . be analysed in terms of power relations [which] . . . are . . . constructed in pitched battles to decide meaning and interpretation. These battles are won and lost and the victor gets to determine the terms of the armistice, at least temporarily, when systems of meaning are created and enforced by groups with the most power.

Shifting the goalposts of meaning, then, for Yelvington presumes a prior capacity to make new meanings stick. Similarly, for Parkin (1982: xlvii), 'performative language' as 'being' 'entails questions of personal autonomy, self-definition, and power, which only some in any society can ask and answer'. But for Parkin, speaking is also implicated in the ongoing construction of status and the 'apprehension' of the power of discourse.

Wikan (1993: 206, 193) has also expressed scepticism about words and what they convey: 'wordstuck . . . anthropology's romance with words, concepts, symbols, text and discourse may be counterproductive' in understanding precisely how intersubjective communication of meaning occurs. Not only do words express and reinforce the existing power of representative spokespersons (usually older males) to define what *is*; not only are precise words frequently misleading in their literal meanings; not only do people change their minds and re-word at will, but, above all, Wikan argues, the power of 'resonance' as the fusion of emotion and rationality is what 'evokes shared human experience' (1993: 208) and the transmission of meaning. Conveying meaning, as Kendall (1982: 205–6) indicates, may be indirect, involving encoded or concealed challenges to existing influence in apparently simple messages. Thus relaying greetings also relays knowledge of social relationships with political potential.

Pro-Foucauldian analysis after Foucault seems largely to have ignored, rather than refuted, such points, particularly Scott's observation (1985, 1990) that currently disempowered people subvert dominating structures and relationships and come some way towards achieving their goals precisely by *not voicing* their resistance to hegemonic power openly, but by exercising some other capacity or resource.

> Patterns of domination can . . . accommodate . . . resistance so long as . . . [it] is not publicly and unambiguously acknowledged . . . *voice under domination*. . . [includes] rumour, gossip, disguises, linguistic tricks, metaphors, euphemisms, folktales, ritual gestures, anonymity . . . each oral performance

can be nuanced, disguised, evasive, and shaded in accordance with the degree of surveillance from authority to which it is exposed . . . the particularity and elasticity of oral culture . . . allows it to carry fugitive meanings in comparative safety.

(Scott 1990: 57, 137, 162, original emphasis)

Scott's view of surveillance, as a challenge to be outwitted, thus differs from Foucault's concern with its 'productivity' (1980: 119) as a power mechanism which 'permits time and labour, rather than wealth and commodities, to be extracted from bodies' (1980: 104) through 'social production and social service' (1980: 125). But these differing views of Foucault and Scott are not incompatible: unvoiced, suppressed conflict and indirect manipulation are, according to Miller (1976), the strategies used by women to cope with their gendered dispowerment in modern America, where Foucault's view of their surveillance as subordinates is equally applicable.

A focus on capacities or resources, including social networks, leads to the hard question of whether there is a quantum of power. The liberal democratic view (at once Parsonian[7] and postmodern), of power as infinitely expansible, is that of the free market: when the cake is expanding and empowerment is vocality (through ballot box or communications media), questions of quantum and distribution are more easily fudged. The zero–sum view of power is more likely to be found among those competing for some,[8] whether they define it as based on guns (James, this volume), land and land-based resources (Filer, Hopa, this volume) or access to state-controlled resources (Al-Rasheed, Gaidzanwa, this volume). As Wright (1994: 163) has already indicated, the term 'empowerment', when used in the 1970s with reference to the Third World, was initially understood as 'the development of economic activities under the control of the weakest . . . so that they had their own resources for development'. At least in its zero–sum conception, power clearly implies control of resources rather than – or in addition to – 'voice'.

To those using the zero–sum conception of a fixed quantum of power, a Foucauldian approach is not only unattractive, it is also dangerously mystificatory, and not only because – as Cockburn (1994: 111) has noted – it is totally insensitive to the ways in which power is gendered, racialised, and class-ified. More generally, the very discourse of empowerment itself, particularly but not only in the global context of Third World inequality and development, may obscure the 'real' or hegemonic[9] relations of power linking states, developers and empowerers to poor people lacking resources (James, Filer, this volume) and thereby render the already vulnerable even less capable of defending their self-identified interests. The very language of empowerment, argues James, masks any collusion among the empowering by 'screening off' their power relations from 'public discourse': such screening may be particularly important where the exercise of power is popularly associated with lying (Barnes 1994: 78) and, by their public exposure of such masking, social scientists will themselves intervene in the balance of power.

As state power is reconfigured in the postmodern era, authority has tended to be 'professionalised' as sets of rules known to only one set of the social actors involved in specific relationships. These actors are usually bureaucratically organised and use 'all the mechanisms and effects of power which don't pass directly via the State apparatus, yet often sustain the State more effectively than its own institutions, enlarging and maximising its effectiveness' (Foucault 1980: 72–3) especially through their lawful practice. Such professionals in turn argue that their (statutory) rules empower their advice- and representation-purchasing consumers (formerly called clients) to make their own decisions. Frequently, it seems, such consumers end up quite dissatisfied as a result of their (partial) empowerment by such rules. They do not know exactly how these rules work but consider that their interests – compromised by their own un- or poorly informed decisions – have been negatively affected in the final outcome. The frustrations of such mediated empowerment, for those allegedly empowered, are apparently routine, at least among those in the UK using ostensibly people-friendly law to dissolve their marriages (Collins 1994).

Empowerment, of course, implies that all intervening brokers should be eliminated from the consumer's capacity to choose. Adjudicators, mediators, advocates, advisers and representatives are all, by definition, irrelevant, deprived of their former capacity to control and alienate empowered people and/or their interests. Yet, as Filer (this volume) argues, the devolution of power from state to community[10] may increase rather than decrease the potential for brokerage, not least among anthropologists (among whom there is, of course, already an impressively large discourse on advocacy and mediation). And those who have examined the devolution of development assistance from economically advanced states to non-governmental organisations (the new brokers in direct contact with aid-recipients – state, collective or individual), have been very critical of its outcomes (see Hopa, Werbner, this volume).

The mystifying rhetoric of empowerment as expansible, vocal power is the offspring of an optimistic postmodernism linked to democratic and negotiated organisational structures. These, in turn, are related to rational social preferences arising from individual choices. Yet any such liberal democratic transfer of power from those who currently have it to those who do not, could (and should) be expected, not to slip past unnoticed, but to engender resistance in those whose ability to get what they want is affected by others' access. Conceptualising power as postmodern, warm-fuzzy, expansible not only conceals its hard edges; this cloak of opacity also discourages nasty questions of who benefits and how, and runs the danger of collapsing objectives, processes and outcomes alike into an undifferentiated rhetorical empowerment. Dismantling structures has been a real process as well as an iterative voice, and we have heard little about the power plays involved – except from Cockburn (1991, 1994) and, perhaps, in novelists' explorations of glass ceilings as a contradiction of publicly articulated policy. Hence it is not altogether odd that Gramsci and issues of hegemony and consent (Gramsci 1972) appear very rarely in Foucauldian and postmodernist discourses on (dis)empowerment, even among those who have analysed the spatial, presentational, kinaesthetic, status and ritual components (see Collins 1994; Edwards 1994) of what might be called silent − Scott's (1985, 1990) publicly unvoiceable − power.

So how might (dis)empowerment be achieved? One view seems to be that empowerment can be conferred by some on others. Critics seem generally unhappy with this view: after all, the very conception of the free market on which such a 'free gift' rests, is that there are no free lunches. As numerous anthropologists (e.g. Cockburn 1994; Perring 1994; Wright 1994; Filer this volume) have already noted, devolution of state functions and finance has allegedly disempowered bureaucratic service-deliverers and empowered those previously dependent on such bureaucracies. Rolling back the state has been popular in most liberal democracies (and many other states) over the past couple of decades, allegedly to give consumers greater choice in education, health care, retirement benefits, even penitentiary detention. These authors have also indicated that such empowerment has been, at best, ambiguous. While there is no longer any danger of 'locating power in the State apparatus, making this into the major, privileged, capital and almost unique instrument of the power of one class over another' (Foucault 1980: 72), declining states none-theless remain for the present the self-defined guarantors not only of service-delivery to their citizens, but also of rule-changing empowerment processes.

Self-empowerment sounds more viable; and networking has apparently allowed some previously uninfluential individuals collectively to make bigger waves. But grabbing power (if necessary against resistance, e.g. by publicising hidden and suppressed conflict: Miller 1976: 126) can be a messy business, ranging from domestic violence to more general warfare, and is generally dis-couraged by all who stand to lose by it. Internal redefinition of basic insti-tutional rules (Cockburn 1994) is more acceptable, but involves processes of negotiation that derive from past practice and therefore advantage the power-holders, assuming their willingness not only to negotiate in good faith, but also to withdraw gracefully from their advantaged positions (Chambers 1997). Both techniques of self-empowerment have tended to generate later backlash reactions from those disempowered. And in the final analysis, states still stand as both referees and guarantors of such negotiated out-comes, if not of more Machievellian techniques of self-empowerment whereby rules may simply be subverted (Bailey 1969) rather than changed.

A third possibility is the collectively negotiated construction of (new) social rules based on individual choice. Harking back not merely to Barth (1959, 1966, 1967) and Rousseau (1946), but also to Greek history, this option seems at once teleological and internally contradictory. For if the sum of individual choices, however counted, does allow the *demos* power, why is empowerment of such current concern in liberal democracies themselves? And if adjudication is disempowering, why should rule-enforced negotiations (especially in the absence of complete information among one or all parties) be empowering? Such discursive claims might better be questioned than accepted at face value; for, as (Scott 1990: 2) has already noted, the interests of both parties linked by relations of power may be served by 'misrepresentation' in 'the public transcript'.

Such questions suggest that power remains a difficult, elusive concept, particularly when by definition it is hegemonically embedded in one or other cultural habitus. Nonetheless, revisiting difficult ground is often useful, and the chapters in this collection variously address three major issues. The first issue of the relationship between state power and popular authority is tackled directly by Peter Skalník, and indirectly by many others. Colin Filer examines the local realities of power devolved from the system of state-plus-capital to landowning communities in Papua New Guinea. Peter Wade, Dick Werbner and Dan Yon all dissect state-driven discourses in the immensely varied contexts of Colombian environmental protection, Zimbabwean land-use planning, and Canadian schooling. The power of state and other actors to construct 'otherness' is part of Wade's argument, and central to Manuel Ramos's account of the power relations involved in a little-known and ultimately unsuccessful sixteenth- and seventeenth-century Jesuit attempt to gain a foothold in Ethiopia. Mystifications of the much (ab)used 'empowerment' word, many but by no means all of them produced by states, are unveiled by Wendy James.

In addressing the second issue of changes in the balance of power, both Ngapare Hopa and Rudo Gaidzanwa are concerned with the empowerment of formerly colonised people: Hopa with tribal re-empowerment in New Zealand and Gaidzanwa with individual business-persons in Zimbabwe. Gaidzanwa is also concerned with a quite different state discourse in Zimbabwe – that of indigenisation, with its implicit and disputed racial undertones – to Werbner's scientific one. There are obvious links to be made between these two discourses, but as yet political actors in Zimbabwe have not made these links. Both Gaidzanwa and Hopa pursue James's concern with mystification into 'new class' (Djilas 1957) empowerment through appropriation of the control of resources previously belonging to others, or intended to benefit others. More generally, Filer, Gaidzanwa and Hopa all examine the notion of balance in what have become known, somewhat coyly, as stakeholder interests in empowerment processes. Andrew Spiegel and his co-authors, both planners, situate their attempts to influence housing policy in South Africa against the dramatically altered balance between state power and popular authority in 'the new South Africa'.

Prominent among the causes of changes in the balance of power is the issue of new technology. Backgrounding Wade's analysis is the development of bio-technology. Madawi Al-Rasheed examines the use of information technology in the organisation of opposition to Saudi Arabian state politics, while Bob

Layton plots changes in the balance of power against technological and organisational changes in the French village of Pellaport. He shows how villagers
managed their common lands and dairy production very carefully, while treat-
ing the market as an open-access resource, in ways that advantaged the early
adopters of new technologies. As the (European Community) market came
under quota regulation, those too poor to modernise their production technologies were ultimately forced out of market competition, effectively by
their neighbours who had empowered themselves through domination of the
market through their past technological innovations. Such empowerment
appears systemic rather than personal when viewed from a village perspective.
The outcome may indeed be zero-sum, but no one can sensibly argue that
those who remain farmers have empowered themselves directly at their
unsuccessful neighbours' expense.

Sigridur Duna Kristmundsdottir notes a different systemic threat to the
somewhat fragile new balance of interests and power between men and
women that has emerged fairly recently in certain nation-states as a result of
long political battles: this threat stems from globalising discourses. She argues
that globalising processes simultaneously strengthen local boundaries in some
respects while dismantling them in others, and, therefore, that the now-*global*
discourse constructing women as the embodiment of *local* cultural values and
behaviour threatens once more to disempower previously empowered
women. The implication of Gaidzanwa's analysis of another globalising discourse, that of indigenisation, might also be seen as preventing the empowerment of previously disempowered women, at least in Zimbabwe.

Kristmundsdottir's concern with the balance of gendered power flows
into the third issue which some contributors address, namely paradoxes of
empowerment. Simultaneous empowerment and disempowerment (from
different perspectives) 'in the same moment' are noted by Ramos and Yon.
Thus there may be simultaneous as well as alternating paradoxes of empowerment, both related to discursive constructions of essentialised otherness as well
as to unvoiced assumptions about the reach of discursive power. So Werbner's
plea (this volume) for a post-Foucauldian approach will presumably elicit considerable sympathy. Such an approach might include, in addition to the decon-
struction and public exposure of various kinds of discourse (the overtly
politico-mythological as well as those based on knowledges), an attempt to
distinguish the power of discourse from discursive power, and to relate both
to the construction of power bases by social actors.

If the conference theme elicited fewer detailed ethnographies of *fin-de-siècle*
power and processes of (dis)empowerment than I had originally hoped, nonetheless it seems to me that the papers in this collection do expand our (perhaps
sceptical) understanding of a much abused contemporary mystification. Contrary to some postmodernist arguments, they show that power remains a reality:
while using 'voice', it is in no immediate danger of dissolving into words.
*Caveat discursor!*

## Notes

1 Zed Books, spring 1997 New Titles and Development Studies catalogues.
2 It was the first such conference in half a century of the ASA's existence to be held outside the UK. This relocation in itself seems to have had the effect of 'disempowering' the organisation's own membership, based overwhelmingly in the UK, which comprised less than a quarter of all conference participants. That ASA members contributed half of the papers in this collection, therefore, may reflect its globalising recuperation of power through publication.
3 This and the following are quotes from my conference proposal elected by the 1995 ASA Annual Business Meeting.
4 In both cases, millions of quiet but allegedly angry people lined the streets of their respective capital cities, displaying Canetti's (1973) power of the many. However, temperatures of −10°C in mid-winter Beijing contrasted with a sunny summer day in London; and Beijingers learned of Zhou's death and transportation route not from the popular press, but by word of mouth from a hospital leak. They risked a great deal in making this political gesture of support for rule-bound state authority, embodied in premier Zhou as the 'upright official' of Chinese tradition confronting the disorderly party power wielded - also through mass mobilisation - by Mao Zedong. In contrast, support for Diana was popularly interpreted as anti-institutional, and especially anti-monarchist. It may also have reflected especially female frustration with, if not also disempowerment by, male-dominated institutional practices.
5 Telecom New Zealand/New Zealand Police (1997) *Stop Bullying: Advice for Caregivers* (pamphlet).
6 The Vice-Chancellor of one university at which I worked averred that 'good practice' could itself be institutionalised through 'constant iteration', and repeated this view at every conceivable opportunity, as if the words might effect themselves. Some academics thought the institution had a problem with the Vice-Chancellor's strategy, since 'good practice' would have to be agreed and established before it could be 'iterated' – and that would upset the existing balance of practical power among academic staff!
7 Parsons (1971).
8 Academics' views of managerial roles within university bureaucracies seem to fall into this category, as noted in the famous inverted relationship between the value of the stakes (the small swag-bag allotted to a chairperson of department to protect his/her back from competitive colleagues) and the virulence of the competition for such roles (see also Bailey 1977).
9 As identified by anthropologists and other social scientists.
10 Defining 'community' in such contexts is itself powerfully problematic.

## References

Bailey, F.G. (1969) *Strategems and Spoils: A Social Anthropology of Politics*. Oxford: Basil Blackwell.
—— (1977) *Morality and Expediency*. Oxford: Basil Blackwell.
Barnes, J.A. (1994) *A Pack of Lies*. Cambridge: Cambridge University Press.
Barth, F. (1959) *Political Organisation among Swat Pathans*. London: Athlone Press.
—— (1966) *Models of Social Organisation*, RAI Occasional Paper 23. London: Royal Anthropological Institute.
—— (1967) On the study of social change. American Anthropologist 69, 6: 661–9.

Blau, P.M. and Scott, W.R. (1963) *Formal Organisations*. San Francisco: Chandler Publishing.

Bourdieu, P. (1977) *Outline of a Theory of Practice*. Cambridge: Cambridge University Press.

Canetti, E. (1973) *Crowds and Power*. Harmondsworth: Penguin.

Chambers, R. (1997) *Whose Reality Counts? Putting the First Last*. London: Intermediate Technology Publications.

Cheater, A.P. (1991) Death ritual as political trickster in the People's Republic of China. *Australian Journal of Chinese Affairs* 26: 67–97.

Cockburn, C. (1991) *In the Way of Women: Men's Resistance to Sex Equality in Organisations*. London: Macmillan.

—— (1994) Play of power: women, men and equality initiatives in a trade union. In *Anthropology of Organisations* (ed.) S. Wright. London: Routledge.

Collins, J. (1994) Disempowerment and marginalisation of clients in divorce court cases. In *Anthropology of Organisations* (ed.) S. Wright. London: Routledge.

Djilas, M. (1957) *The New Class*. New York: Praeger.

Edwards, J. (1994) Idioms of bureaucracy and informality in a local Housing Aid Office. In *Anthropology of Organisations* (ed.) S. Wright. London: Routledge.

Foucault, M. (1980) *Power/Knowledge*. (ed.) C. Gordon. New York: Harvester/ Wheatsheaf.

Geertz, C. (1973) *The Interpretation of Culture*. New York: Basic Books.

Gordon, C. (1980) Afterword. In *Power/Knowledge* (ed.) C. Gordon. New York: Harvester/Wheatsheaf.

Gramsci, A. (1972) *Selections from the Prison Notebooks*. London: Lawrence and Wishart.

Hasek, J. (1973) *The Good Soldier Svejk* (trans. C. Parrott). London: Heinemann.

Kendall, M.B. (1982) Getting to know you. In *Semantic Anthropology* (ed.) D. Parkin. London: Academic Press.

Miller, J.B. (1976) *Toward a New Psychology of Women*. Boston, MA: Beacon Press.

Parkin, D. (1982) Introduction. In *Semantic Anthropology* (ed.) D. Parkin. London: Academic Press.

Parsons, T. (1971) *The System of Modern Societies*. Englewood Cliffs, NJ: Prentice-Hall.

Perring, C.M. (1994) Community care as de-institutionalisation? Continuity and change in the transition from hospital to community-based care. In *Anthropology of Organisations* (ed.) S. Wright. London: Routledge.

Rousseau, J.J. (1946) *The Social Contract; Discourses*. London: Dent.

Scott, J.C. (1985) *Weapons of the Weak*. New Haven, CT: Yale University Press.

—— (1990) *Domination and the Arts of Resistance*. New Haven, CT and London: Yale University Press.

Skalník, P. (ed.) (1989) *Outwitting the State*. New Brunswick, NJ: Transaction.

Weber, M. (1947) *The Theory of Social and Economic Organisation* (trans. and ed. T. Parsons). New York: Free Press.

Wikan, U. (1993) Beyond the words: the power of resonance. In *Beyond Boundaries: Understanding, Translation and Anthropological Discourse* (ed.) G. Palsson. Oxford and Providence, RI: Berg.

Wright, S. (ed.) (1994) *Anthropology of Organisations*. London: Routledge.

Yelvington, K.A. (1996) Flirting in the factory. *Journal of the Royal Anthropological Institute* 2, 2: 313–33.

# Chapter 2

# Empowering ambiguities

*Wendy James*

My argument in this chapter is a plea to researchers to take very great care in handling the current jargon of the 'development industry'. There is a 'climate of language' which pervades the genre and can make it very difficult to see the difference between advocacy and analysis, or even to see clearly what is being advocated. Historical analysis, like Megan Vaughan's on colonial medicine (Vaughan 1991), can reveal past forms of the collusion between political interest, the use of language and the representation of human experience. To anticipate my conclusion, I suppose I would like to say that the practice of ethnography and social science should aim to make such forms of collusion more visible in the present, as good history can do for the past.

The new 'democratic' management-style discourse used in the delivery of aid and project assistance, for example, has become so pervasive as to have acquired a kind of autonomy, and almost a monopoly in the representation of social and political affairs in the development context (though not only that). It has become a factor of current history in itself, as so many writings are cast within its frame, and within its frame only. It gives the impression of complete-ness in its current attempts to include the viewpoints of those at the receiving end of projects. But is this a completeness which the anthropologist or other analyst should be content with, any more than the historian can be content with the completeness of colonial constructions as a representation of the past? Even in its currently fashionable style of allowing for 'community par-ticipation', 'empowerment', a 'people-focused approach' and 'listening to the voices of the poor', development discourse rarely engages with the human realities of the situations in which it is employed and applied. It may be that those who are paid to do research under the terms of this rubric have little room for manoeuvre and are constrained to report back and make recommen-dations within the same frame. Notions of sharing power, of stakeholders, of participation and representation and so on seem to refer increasingly to the self-contained world of projects themselves: the existence of external structures of land-holding and subsistence economy which have perhaps been disrupted, of political and military formations which have shaped and still shape the forms of social life in a region, tend to fade from view in the world of development-speak. Within the latter, 'power' seems to have taken on a much less substantial sense, mainly the sense of having a place, a voice, and being represented within an administrative or management system. 'Empowerment' seems to have little more body to it than responsibility delegated from above, or from the centre, to monitor others below or beyond one, for whose activities one has to be accountable. One seems to be 'empowered' to take a share of management responsibility and decision-making, but the contemporary sense of the word does not seem to entail any direct control of resources or scope to join with others at the same level in the structure to pursue collective bargaining with the centre. It seems oddly like the operation of 'Indirect Rule' in British colonial Africa!

The concept of power used to be based, in one way or another, upon the ownership and productive use of resources, or upon the control of people through historically established political formations in which legitimacy was invested and specifically located, often though it might be contested and usurped. It could be argued that even in debates between, for example, advocates of the Marxist, Weberian or Foucauldian positions in political theory, dialogue was possible because of a broadly shared understanding of the notion of 'power' under discussion. It may well be pointed out that this established concept of 'power' has 'modern' or 'modernist' attributes linking it to the idea of the strength of the growing nation-state and empire in the industrial age, theorised as 'domination', and that we should now be attempting to find alternative ways of thinking about social organisation. But how far have things really changed, in the current new world of management-speak? Perhaps we should ask whether this seemingly benign and democratic liberal language does not mask the practical realities of the political and financial decisions shaping relief and development aid today, and helping to shape the structural political realities of tomorrow? A re-reading of George Orwell's essay on politics and the English language is a salutary reminder of past configurations of the seductive ways of representation through the word (Orwell 1946).

On the evidence of the *Oxford English Dictionary* (1971), 'empower' as a verb is in itself not new, but well established, having meant since the seventeenth century 'to invest legally or formally with power or authority; to authorize, license'; or 'to impart or bestow power to an end or for a purpose; to enable, permit'. The sense of 'to gain or assume power over' is classed as obsolete. The noun 'empowerment' comes from the nineteenth century. However, a fairly distinctive cast has been given to this word in modern usage. It has acquired an astonishingly wide currency, partly because several different interested usages have seemed to coalesce, giving it the capacious opacity of other successful terms of ideology. Many people agree to use it, though not necessarily all sharing the same goals or intentional applications.

The sense of 'empowerment' which seems uppermost in current development discourse has perhaps two main primary sources. The first derives from the immediate postcolonial left-wing community politics in the style of Paulo Freire; in his 1970 book *Pedagogy of the Oppressed* he proposed (in the formulation of a recent report by African Rights):

> . . . methods of non-formal adult education designed to make peasants and workers aware of the ways in which they were exploited in a feudal-capitalist system, and of the potential to empower themselves by group action. A diluted and depoliticised version of this prescribes that people just sit together to identify their common problems and decide on joint approaches to solving them. Disappointingly for development workers, when they ask people in south Sudan to do something like this, the result is normally a wish-list of aid supplies.
>
> (African Rights 1995: 29)

However, the term, and the associated political ideas, have bonded effectively with those areas of social research allied with new movements and the advocacy of causes. Peter Harries-Jones, for example, has recently written:

> An advocacy approach is intended to alter both perceptions and conceptions of knowledge and in this sense goes beyond a purely factual cognitive domain to encompass 'consciousness-raising' and 'empowerment'. . . . In my own work I link the analysis of social advocacy to the formation of social movements. This link . . . provided a very broad canvas for an anthropologist, a canvas which must be global in scope if it is to tackle the urgent problems of our day – economic, environmental and military.
>
> (1996: 161–2)

This context of usage is akin to that of contemporary debates over gender and women's rights, as well as various environmental causes and the language of Green politics (see Milton 1993).

The term is also used in current reform movements in the churches. A commentator, recoiling at the style of Mass she attended in a new church in Texas, recently wrote:

> The idea is that the priest should not appear exclusive or in any way elevated above the flock. . . . I was roused at the onset of the Gloria when the congregation began a rhythmic clapping. . . . I have given up trying to explain to the younger generation that we were not mere passive spectators at the Tridentine Mass but deeply involved in the mystery. . . . With all the endless talk of 'empowering the laity', of giving us a 'role in church affairs', we have ended up being treated like witless kiddies. . . . The attitude of the 'reformers' is profoundly insulting, *patronizing* in the worst possible way.
>
> (Ellis 1997: 33)

There is however quite another field of use of the notion. In the 'New Right' politics of the 1980s both in the USA and Britain, there was much talk of 'rolling back government', or taking power away from the state and returning it to the people. This was matched by the new language of management. The business use of the term 'empowerment' is quite clearly illustrated in a mid-1996 article in the British press, headed 'The Power Game: empowerment is a buzzword of management culture. Graham Judge seeks the reality behind the rhetoric' (Judge 1996: 1). The *Guardian* editor asks 'Is it a trendy slogan or an effective executive tool?' (ibid.: 2).

> Managing change in organizations has spawned a series of prescriptions and academic models – the learning organization, the flexible organization, the empowered organization, the open company. . . . But too often neglected is the dimension of change that is about people, either as individuals or team members, not about organizations.
>
> (ibid.)

In the interest of improved efficiency in increasingly uncertain and competitive markets, the calibre and skills of employees make a difference, but they 'need to feel "empowered" – to have have some control over their working lives – a factor essential to the successful management of change' (ibid.).

For some organisations it is a response to competitors or a way to use resources better, and for others 'a way to cut the costs of supervision'.

> Some organizations which consider themselves to be 'empowering', still have many managers who talk in the sort of terms which imply an inherent power differential between themselves and staff. . . . But if an employee is to feel properly empowered, then it is necessary for that employee to feel totally trusted. . . . Empowerment is not delegation. It is about making the most of people's potential.
>
> (ibid.)

One of the organisations looked at in the article was BP chemicals at Baglan Bay in South Wales. In the 1970s, they employed more than 2,000 people, but a series of changes were made, leaving only 350. 'Corrective action teams' were set up in 1991 and the 'empowerment process' grew out of their recommendations. 'Special training was used to give employees freedom to use their own initiative, the aim of which is to invest in the best staff to operate the plant safely and efficiently' (ibid.: 3). The works' general manager noted that as a result of empowerment, productivity had increased significantly and there had been a reduction in the fixed-cost base of running the factory. However, the article notes that in the empowerment process, which has been embraced by quite a range of other organisations, there can be a problem of how to manage the managers who happen to be the ones to lose most from it and are in a position 'to launch counter-offensives or delaying tactics' (ibid.). In other words, if you have to become more competitive, conserve your costs and shed your staff, workers and managers alike, through 'empowerment' policies: you can still keep the best people, give them training for trust and responsibility, and do well. One hopes there is some kind of safety net for the people who lose their jobs in this process.

'Empowerment' is more than a journalist's 'buzz-word'; it has become a technical term in management courses. Thus for example in a 1996 textbook *Key Words in Business: Helping Learners with* **real** *English* we find the relevant entry explaining 'Organizations say that they are eliminating middle levels of their hierarchies so as to **empower** ordinary workers and employees. This process of **empowerment** is designed to give them the authority to make decisions that were previously taken by middle managers.' Contexts of use read '*Empower* your people. Don't command and control. Let them use their own initiative and entrepreneurial spirit.'

> *Empowerment*, an ugly transatlantic neologism which suggests that ordinary workers want, enjoy and benefit from being empowered. Of course, with power comes responsibility, and it is not clear that workers who warm to the former are equally happy about the latter. Also, the empowerment of one group usually means the disempowerment of another group, frequently the former's bosses.
>
> (Mascull 1996: 50, italics and bold in the original)

An exercise for students follows, on 'Radical empowerment', with a case study of Semco, a Brazilian manufacturing firm. Here some 300 employees decide their own working hours, productivity and sales targets, salaries and the sharing out of bonuses. There are no manuals or written procedures, no controls over travel expenses. Some workers earn more than the boss. The firm has survived, though partly because the owner combines this experiment with 'some old-fashioned hard-headedness' in laying off workers, facing strikes and demanding healthy dividends (ibid.: 51).

Thus 'empowerment' in the leftish social activist/Green sense has strangely converged with quite another modern usage in contemporary management theory, and come to be connected with the downsizing of firms, cutting of costs and flattening out of management structures. It definitely post-dates the trade union era in Britain and, indeed, goes with the restructuring policies that follow on from the breaking of trade union power. The idea seems to be that management can gain by shedding unnecessary jobs, and 'empowering' those that remain. It tends increasingly to imply coopting a selected few on the periphery, in the interest of central management. It is not clear that the devolution (shedding?) of reponsibility from the centre always goes with a relinquishing of real control over resources; in fact it is a way of cutting down on costs. This is partly why, outside the business context, the management model of 'empowerment' is very different from the kind of community politics which demands a greater local share of actual resources. The leftish advocates of community politics or Green spokespeople are presumably not comfortable with the kind of 'empowerment' represented by cutting resources to local government, the National Health Service, and publicly funded education in the UK during the 1980s and early 1990s, however that might have been combined with the devolution of budgetary responsibility.

There is nevertheless a kind of 'functional ambiguity' to the idea of empowerment that is helping to give it very wide currency (see Gledhill 1994). In the context of applied social policy in the developed world, the different specific meanings of the term are becoming yoked together in apparent harmony (see the very interesting collection of papers brought together by Craig and Mayo 1995). In the USA there is new legislation, for example, setting up 'Empowerment Zones', to revitalise urban neighbourhoods, through extra funding directed towards community development on the participatory model. There will be earmarked budgets for 'empowerment zone programmes', and no doubt evaluation and monitoring reports which attempt to measure and justify the expenditure in terms of the amount of empowerment achieved. One wonders in this kind of context, which closely echoes that of international relief and development, what link can be maintained with the ordinary English language meaning of the terms cognate to 'power'. Recent commentators on the American 'Empowerment Zones' note

> there are dangers in overstating the potential of the neighbourhood movement. The community development movement is no panacea. At best, it offers a transitional programme to address structural issues of urban poverty and racism and the accelerated marginalization of large segments of the US population. . . . Also, the absolute growth of community development organizations is restricted by their dependence on funding support by traditional sources. . . . The movement . . . can become an industry in the sense of reproducing the conditions for the self-serving maintenance of its professional (entrepreneurial) class of managers.
>
> (Wiewel and Gills 1995: 136–7)

In the developing world, there are parallels. In an overview of current usage, Singh and Titi write that within the 'development' discourse, the concept of empowerment has evolved concurrently with the 'bottom–up' approach and as an alternative to that of modernisation. Within the 'development' constituency, they write, empowerment has been used to imply:

> good governance, legitimacy and creativity for a flourishing private sector; transformation of economies to self-reliant, endogenous, human-centred development; promotion of community self-help with an emphasis on the process rather than on the completion of particular projects. . . popular

participation . . . At a more generic level [it] means strengthening . . . the principles of 'inclusiveness' . . . 'transparency' . . . and 'accountability'. . . . The concept goes beyond the notions of democracy, of human rights, and of participation to include enabling people to understand the reality of their environment (social, political, economic, ecological and cultural) . . . and to take steps to effect changes to improve their situation.

(Singh and Titi 1995: 13)

It 'gives people a true capacity to cope with the changing environment as societies and communities enter the transition towards sustainable development' (ibid.: 18). Through this process (reference is made back to Freire 1970):

individuals, communities and nations obtain collective responsibility for their own future. . . . [It] provides people with the capacity . . . to feel like masters of their own thinking and view of the world, and to achieve the desired level of well-being. . . . Cultural and spiritual empowerment constitute understanding culture and spirituality as the basis of human existence and the foundation of healthy sustainable human societies.

(ibid.: 19)

As one of the contributors to the book wryly notes, the concept has acquired 'a considerable aura' within the vocabulary of development:

but it has not yet acquired a socially agreed content. It is also one of those concepts whose full implications people do not realize when they use it. Lurking under its naivety lies a dangerous 'monster', the monster of revolution, for if the logic of the concept is taken to its full limit then it can only mean equalizing or near-equalizing power, empowering those who do not have power within the system.

(Tandon, 1995: 31)

The IMF, the World Bank and so on (as well as liberal intellectuals) speak 'as if power was for them to give and not for the powerless to take' – as they have done in history, through moral force as Ghandi did, through withdrawal of labour or through armed struggle (ibid.: 33).

Academics, beware this seductive concept of contemporary ideology. Why not listen for the more tangible everyday language of politics, community and power, of bodily life, social relations, action and feeling, into which it is being so persuasively introduced? Some of the current management and development imagery and jargon, ironically, seems to be derived from recently popularised terms of anthropology itself – the term 'culture' is a key one here – and one doesn't know whether to laugh or to cry. But we anthropologists, I feel, need to be critical of what I believe is an interested, and ideological, appropriation of what had been a more direct and even analytical use of language. We should keep a safe distance from some of our cousins in the social sciences and move closer to the methods of those writing good history, literature, and journalism. Terence Ranger (1997) has recently made a plea for the claims of African history as against the current 'presentist' trend in so much that is written about the continent, and I would like not only to endorse this but to add to it: history is still going on in Africa, and we must find a way of writing about it that retains a critical distance from the dominant discourse of the present.

In the area of relief and development, there has emerged a seemingly neutral language of need: of societies in deficit, as it were, and needing to be returned to some prior image of traditional normality. There is a deficit of calories, of blankets, and commonly of male household heads; there may be 'displacement' from home, even victimisation in war, almost another kind of deficit, which could be remedied through resettlement or repatriation. Anthropologists may be engaged to advise on the remedying of these deficits, as medics may be brought in to correct diseased bodies. There is often today talk of 'healing' societies in the aftermath of war. Metaphors and imagery abound, though they are mainly those of the development managers. It is very rare to find any writer documenting the more substantial aspects of social history, the pre-existing structures of economic and political life, let alone listening to the metaphors and imagery of the struggling communities in question, those images which feed memory, and which are likely to be far more powerful than simply the correction of a deficit and a return to some status quo ante of a stable traditional society. And this sense of a community in deficit almost lies behind some current uses of 'empowerment': as though the poor, the displaced, or the vulnerable, are just blank and unrelated individuals, without a history of belonging to any pre-existing social relations invested with power.

## Point of reference: the Uduk refugees on the Sudan–Ethiopian border

Like many other communities of refugees, the core of the Uduk-speaking people who were displaced originally in the late 1980s, have seen at close range various 'power' structures (in the older sense) changing around them. To cut a very long story short, they have been displaced several times in the last few years because of the political changes consequent upon the ending of the Cold War, the collapse of the socialist regime of Mengistu in Ethiopia in 1991, and the rise and then fall, and now arguably rise again, in the fortunes of the Sudan People's Liberation Army. Living originally in a marginal area of the northern Sudan, close to the Ethiopian border, the majority became protégés of the SPLA in 1986-7, and were accepted in a UNHCR camp at Assosa in western Ethiopia. With the changing political/military balance in that country and the weakening of the SPLA they were obliged to move back into the Sudan in early 1990, and then to retreat much further south and back across the border to the big camp of Itang on the Baro River in the middle of that year. A year later, in mid-1991, they were obliged to cross back with all the other refugees into the Sudan, as far south-west as Nasir, where the local commanders of the SPLA used them to some extent as pawns in the relief aid game while they made a bid for the leadership of the whole movement. The Nasir bid failed, and local conditions made the Uduk refugees sufficiently desperate to dash back to Itang in mid-1992, where they were involuntarily caught up in violence and fled further into Ethiopia. Some 13,000 were placed in a transit camp at Karmi, just above the town of Gambela, and then moved in early 1993 to Bonga, even further upstream, where a scheme was planned for them. Throughout this saga, they have seen how local political and military interests have determined their fate, to a much greater extent than the interventions of humanitarian aid. They have seen the lack of communication between the UN agencies and NGOs on either side of this international border, particularly during the Cold War years. They have seen at close quarters the results of the SPLA split and the human suffering it has caused. They have seen power in its most naked forms, and have come to judge harshly the kind of 'government' (they use the Arabic form, *hakuma*) which prevailed at Nasir in 1992. Such 'government' did not or could not listen to the justifiable grievances of the people it protected (arbitrary killings by soldiers were not enquired into, for example). At each place where the refugees have spent a period of time they have sought not merely emergency aid but some kind of access to land and forest which they could use to help support themselves (could one say, to recover some of the powers they used to exercise? – yes, but the expression 'empower' themselves does not seem to stretch to land allocation).

As the years have gone by, marked by successive displacements and distance from home both geographically and socially, the Uduk refugees have been reduced in some ways to raw fodder for the various projects that have been constructed with them in view. However, the refugees in Bonga themselves can see the ironies, for they can see how large and elaborate a structure of specialist employment for Ethiopians goes along with investment in permanent infrastructure; how local labour is paid in wages while refugee labour is supposed to be provided free as evidence of willingness to 'participate', how the UN voice requesting the allocation of a reasonable amount of agricultural land for temporary use by refugees fails to produce results. Of course there are many, many improvements in the life of the refugee community, including medical and educational services, and they are conscious of these and enormously grateful. But my point is that they are not unaware of the general political conditions that make the relief scheme an advantage to various categories and interests more powerful than they are. They suspect that if the power situation changed, they would be left to fend for themselves. After all (and they themselves do not harp on this, but just take it as a fact of life) the UNHCR has lost touch with them twice already. The first time was when the refugees left the Assosa camp, and the UNHCR in Addis Ababa (still during Mengistu's time) could only say that they had returned to the Sudan, officials didn't know what had happened and couldn't do anything about it. The second time was when the UNHCR actually evacuated the big camps at Itang and elsewhere in south-west Ethiopia in 1991, just a few weeks before the fall of the government, leaving the refugees to the mercy of the SPLA (which had now lost its former backing).

In several kinds of situation, therefore, it has been crystal clear to these refugees (and no doubt their experience is widely echoed) that the key powers affecting them have been those of visible, known governments, and of armed organisations opposed to these governments. Even the local representatives of the international agencies are seen to come and go at the behest, or at least with the agreement of, the region's governments and warlords. It is scarcely surprising that the language of democratic development, the empowerment of the poor and underprivileged – presented in individual rather than class terms – and the avoidance of dependency through self-help, sounds fairly hollow to them. The underlying problem is often that these terms refer to schemes and projects, of income generation and so on, set up within the frame of the refugee community scheme itself, and do not tie the refugees in to the local regional economy or society. Meanwhile, they observe the proliferation of trading activities and investment in shops, roads, buildings, etc. which the presence of an internationally assisted community attracts. They see the local trading population, in particular, making money and gaining influence through their presence.

I have now had the chance to visit various communities of the Uduk-speaking people at intervals over the last thirty years, though in many respects they are scarcely recognisable from visit to visit (James 1979, 1988, 1994, 1996). Because of the current civil war in the Sudan all communities have had to move several times, and past days of 'peace' are hardly remembered. In the context of their multiple displacement over the last decade, it is almost inevitable that as a 'landless' community they should be represented in the growing piles of unpublished agency reports or 'grey literature' as poor, weak, vulnerable, and historically silent. Inevitably I have both colluded in, but tried to resist, these images, in a series of reports I have written for various agencies (James 1991a, 1991b, 1992, 1995). The problem with the image is partly that there is no proper context; no time depth; and no listening to what the people may themselves consider as vulnerability, empowerment, self-sufficiency, etc. I was rung up once by the BBC World Service, asking if I was an expert on the Uduk tribe; and was it true they were 'dying out'? There is also the problem of pop anthropology; i.e. a naive kind of cultural relativism which seems to me disturbingly strong in the reports of agencies and journalists. Details are picked up and made to stand for a whole culture. I have always tried to point out, for example, that wild foods are a very important supplementary part of the people's diet, and that they have a good knowledge of these foods – which is true, and has even astonished the aid personnel who see them carting sack loads of wild potatoes from the forest that other refugees don't seem to know about. A Finnish journalist once asked me, is it true that these people have never gone hungry before because they know how to use the forest? I am seriously worried that I may have contributed to an image that has weakened their claims to aid. The survival of a group of a couple of hundred through reliance on wild foods is one thing – this was the historical reality. The demands made on the forest by a camp of 20,000 is quite another.

Partly because there are, I think, some echoes of the better-known situations of violence in north-east and other regions of Africa, I would like to outline a much smaller-scale event that begins to indicate the deep complexity of the relatively 'powerless' situation of the Uduk refugees. They have been for years not only without proper access to adequate productive resources such as land and forest, but also without weapons – in a region where the idea of the need to acquire the means of self-defence is quite strong. This aspect of the local pursuit of power in the classic sense is quite excluded from the discourse of 'empowerment' in the development world, and in a way makes a nonsense of this term. Let me briefly describe an incident when the Uduk refugees took their vengeance, in a limited way, on those they saw at the time as their main persecutors. The international, even the national, agencies were absent as this happened at a temporary transit camp where the bureaucracy of relief management had not yet been set up.

Karmi was a transit camp in south-western Ethiopia, set up primarily for about 13,000 of the Uduk-speaking community when they crossed over from the Sudan in 1992 (for the third time since 1987). Then, as they see it, the Nuer, emblematic of the local leadership of the Sudan People's Liberation Army and their most recent persecutors, started to follow them, and were granted zones for building huts in what seemed like a growing ring around the Uduk camp. A small argument led to quite major rioting in January 1993, in which the Uduk managed to get the upper hand, though they used only sticks, stones and home-made weapons, while the Nilotic refugees certainly had at least a few grenades. Calls for personal courage were calls for the long-suppressed 'anger' in the bodies of the people, as they put it, to be released. There were injuries on both sides, and a small number of deaths among the Nilotic refugees, over which the Uduk expressed only satisfaction in discussing the event a couple of years later (for a fuller account of this riot, and the way it was later remembered, see James 1997). This was certainly a moment in the long story of their displacement when they could have claimed to feel, and to exercise, some degree of 'power'. But this is scarcely what 'empowerment' is supposed to mean, and indeed one could even suggest that this term in its contemporary sense is supposed to neutralise, overcome and even control by 'management' any such impulse to angry uprising.

Later, in the 'safe haven' type of refugee scheme at Bonga in Ethiopia, the Ethiopian personnel running activities were complaining to me that the

Uduk leaders, who had been to some kind of seminar on cooperation and 'community participation', did not understand what participation meant, and that I should help explain it to them. I found this surprising as I have always tended to emphasise, perhaps over-emphasise, their strong forms of cooperation and community participation. But what the social services officer meant was that they had complained about having to work without payment on various projects in the scheme, while locals were employed on the same work for wages. From their point of view, they were being treated as cheap labour – even taking into account the general food rations. From the UN and Ethiopian agency point of view, they did not appreciate that they should work for free in order to demonstrate their willingness to act as partners in setting up the projects. As for empowerment, I did not hear this term at the time, but no doubt it will reach all powerless communities in due course. What I do know is that the refugees, some of whom had served in various armed guerrilla organisations in the recent past, and many of whom even had relatives serving with the Sudanese armed forces, felt powerless because they had no guns. They felt vulnerable on this account, although they appreciated (private conversation in 1994) that if they did accept guns from one or more of the potential sources available, they might well be more open to attack, and this would be dangerous because they had so many children in the community. By late 1995, the whole political balance in the region of north-east Africa had swung again; relations between Ethiopia on the one hand and the Sudan regime on the other had become quite tense; Ethiopia and Eritrea were once more looking favourably upon the cause of the SPLA. The refugees in Bonga were among those openly invited once more to join the military effort, and by early 1997 remarkable advances had been made by an alliance of Sudanese opposition forces in the regions of the Blue Nile and the eastern Sudan. The refugee scheme was still ticking over, and reports were still circulating in humanitarian circles of Bonga as a 'model refugee camp'.

There were however innumerable ways in which the nature of the scheme and the assistance at Bonga were represented, and contested. At the start, the UNHCR wished to describe the scheme as a plan for 'semi-permanent settlement', a category which assumed the gradual ability of the people to support themselves, and a gradual cutting down of emergency aid and thus severing the people's 'dependency' on it. The Ethiopian partner agency, the Administration for Refugee and Returnee Affairs (ARRA), would not agree to the status of the scheme as a 'settlement'. This status would obviously entail the granting of a viable area of land for cultivation, and might make it difficult to foresee when the refugees would leave. ARRA insisted on referring to the scheme as a 'camp', something the UNHCR was reluctant to endorse. Again, while the UNHCR continued to speak of aiming at partial self-sufficiency, ARRA used the language of 'self-reliance', implying skills, training, income generation, voluntary participation in projects and so on. In many other ways, the discourse of relief and development failed to engage with the social relations and understandings of the people. There was much talk for example of income-generation projects for helping women, and questions in the office of UNHCR as to why so many households were female headed. The existing tradition of matrilineal family structure and the relatively high status of women, in terms of authority and responsibility, was not noticed. In relation to skills, it seemed to be assumed that the refugee community was a blank slate, and it was not appreciated how varied the old subsistence economy had been, and how much the people wished to return to something like it. They were indeed reluctant to involve themselves in many of the projects put forward by the UNHCR and ARRA and associated NGOs, projects which seemed designed to remain under the control of the personnel of these agencies. Some of the major complexities and unforeseen ironies, not to mention counter-productive effects, of the administration of 'bottom-up' relief assistance in a war zone are very expertly analysed in a recent report of African Rights on the efforts of the UN umbrella programme 'Operation Lifeline Sudan' as it has attempted to deliver aid to the southern Sudan over a period of years (African Rights 1995). This report is strongly recommended for those who would like to pursue further the theme of this chapter, the background to this case study and the complications that result when international humanitarian discourse is brought down to earth. It shows with clarity how the ideology of aid in theory helps the weakest, but in practice the effects of 'empowerment' are unpredictable, and sometimes serve to strengthen existing elites, regimes, local and national NGOs and warlords. These latter certainly strive to make alliances with the aid-givers in ways which profoundly affect the political and military scene but are not always admitted. As their power grows, they may intensify the humanitarian crisis as perceived by the aid-givers, and the scope of the destitute to handle their own predicament may be further restricted.

What is the use to the aid agencies of an insipid and functionally ambivalent notion of 'empowerment' in a situation of multiple displacement like the one I have briefly described – where, at one point along the long road, people took matters to some extent into their own hands and stoned members of another group to death, with the general encouragement of recognised leaders but without the international agencies being aware (as far as I know)? To demonstrate that there is 'anger in your body' is presumably another way of talking about empowerment. What is the use of a concept of 'participation' that means working without wages, or handing over the money you have collected in some income-generating project to an official, or borrowing money from him that you may find you cannot repay and are blamed for losing? Of a concept of 'self-sufficiency', when you have not been allocated anywhere near a tenth of the land you would require for this? Or of the concept of peace-making, and peace-keeping, sanctioned by the local security authorities, which had the effect of intensifying the use of force within the community? During 1994, there were established within the scheme at Bonga elders' courts, which mostly worked against the interests of women, 'refugee police' who sometimes carried sticks, and two 'prisons', one for men and one for women. I cannot document here all the aspects of this situation, but it seems a good point to make before resting my case that 'empowerment' is an ambivalent word. It is the kind of word that the social sciences should use with extreme care, if at all. In spite of the ideology of 'aid-speak' it is difficult to argue that the current transfer of aid has 'empowered' the refugees in any significant or lasting way; it has rather strengthened a whole range of state and state-related organisations and institutions in Ethiopia, and fuelled the wealth and power of local trading networks and elites which are directly or indirectly living off the presence of the refugee scheme, while the refugees themselves have not been granted sufficient land to support themselves. Indirectly, too, any refugee aid is ultimately of significance to the conduct and trajectory of wars and this case is proving no exception: an aspect of power relations which is screened off from the public discourse.

## References

African Rights (1995) Imposing empowerment? Aid and civil institutions in southern Sudan. Discussion paper No. 7 (December). London: African Rights.

Craig, G. and Mayo, M. (eds) (1995) *Community Empowerment: A Reader in Participation and Development.* London/New Jersey: Zed Books.

Ellis, A.T. (1997) The God slot. *The Oldie* 96 (March): 33.

Gledhill, J. (1994) *Power and its Disguises: Anthropological Perspectives on Politics.* London/ Boulder, CO: Pluto Press.

Harries-Jones, P. (1996) Afterword. In *The Future of Anthropological Knowledge* (ed.) H.L. Moore. London: Routledge (pp. 156–72).

James, W. (1979) '*Kwanim Pa: The Making of the Uduk People. An Ethnographic Study of Survival in the Sudan-Ethiopian Borderlands.* Oxford: Clarendon Press.

—— (1988) *The Listening Ebony: Moral Knowledge, Religion and Power among the Uduk of the Sudan.* Oxford: Clarendon Press.

—— (1991a) Background report and guidelines for future planning: Nor Deng centre for Sudanese returnees, Nasir. UN, WFP/Operation Lifeline Sudan, Southern Sector, Nairobi.

—— (1991b) Vulnerable groups in the Nasir region: update on Nor Deng (Blue Nile returnees) and resettlement proposal. WFP/OLS Southern Sector, Nairobi, 15 October.

—— (1992) Uduk asylum seekers in Gambela, 1992. Community report and options for resettlement. UNHCR, Addis Ababa, October.

—— (1994) War and 'ethnic visibility': the Uduk on the Sudan–Ethiopia border. In *Ethnicity and Conflict in the Horn of Africa* (eds) K. Fukui and J. Markakis. London and Athens, OH: James Currey/Ohio University Press (pp. 140–64).

—— (1995) The Bonga Scheme: progress to 1994 and outlook for 1995. A report for UNHCR on assistance to Sudanese (Uduk) refugees in western Ethiopia. UNHCR, Addis Ababa, 25 January.

—— (1996) Uduk resettlement: dreams and realities. In *In Search of Cool Ground: War, Flight and Homecoming in Northeast Africa* (ed.) T. Allen. London and Trenton, NJ: James Currey/Africa World Press (pp. 182–202).

—— (1977) The names of fear: memory, history, and the ethnography of feeling among Uduk refugees. *Journal of the Royal Anthropological Institute* 3, 1: 115–31.

Judge, G. (1996) The power game. Power to the people. The *Guardian* (Careers Supplement), 11 May: 1–3.

Mascull, B. (1996) *Key Words in Business: Helping Learners with **Real** English*, Cobuild Series. London: HarperCollins.

Milton, K. (ed.) (1993) *Environmentalism: The View from Anthropology*. London/New York: Routledge.

Orwell, G. (1946) Politics and the English language. *Horizon* April; also in *Critical Essays*. London: Secker and Warburg, 1946. Reprinted in *George Orwell: The Collected Essays, Journalism and Letters*, vol. 4. Harmondsworth: Penguin (pp. 156–70).

*Oxford English Dictionary*, compact edn (1971) Oxford: Oxford University Press.

Ranger, T.O. (1997) Africa in the age of extremes. In *Rethinking African History* (eds) S. McGrath, C. Jedrej, K. King and J. Thompson. Edinburgh: Centre for African Studies (pp. 269–93).

Singh, N. and Titi, V. (eds) (1995) Empowerment for sustainable development: an overview. In *Empowerment: Towards Sustainable Development* (eds) N. Singh and V. Titi. Halifax, Nova Scotia, Canada/London: Fernwood/Zed Books (pp. 6–28).

Tandon, Y. (1995) Poverty, processes of impoverishment and empowerment: a review of current thinking and action. In *Empowerment: Towards Sustainable Development* (eds) N. Singh and V. Titi. Halifax, Nova Scotia, Canada/London: Fernwood/Zed Books (pp. 29–36).

Vaughan, M. (1991) *Curing their Ills*. Cambridge: Polity Press.

Wiewel, W. and Gills, D. (1995) Community development organizational capacity and US urban policy: lessons from the Chicago experience 1983–93. In *Community Empowerment* (eds) G. Craig and M. Mayo. London/New Jersey: Zed Books (pp. 127–39).

# Chapter 3

# The discursive space of schooling

## On the theories of power and empowerment in multiculturalism and anti-racism

*Daniel Yon*[1]

In this chapter I examine the limits of the dominant theory of power, and its counterpart empowerment, that structure public policies on multiculturalism and anti-racism specifically in the field of education. I draw on ethnographic research which focuses on the dynamics of race, culture and identity in a high school in Metropolitan Toronto.[2] The larger backdrop for my discussion is official Canadian state policies on multiculturalism and anti-racism.[3] In Canada, as is the case elsewhere, multiculturalism draws its inspiration from an entrenched anthropological tradition of cultural relativism. By emphasising the attributes that characterise social groups and communities, cultural relativism produces reified and bounded notions of culture and identity as inheritable entities. Official policies on multiculturalism and anti-racism, which are premised on this popular understanding of culture, are also framed by beliefs in a dominant culture and the proliferation of minority cultures. The 'dominant culture' assumes dominance precisely because it is unmarked while the 'minority' or 'multi-cultures' are assumed to be neatly marked entities and objects of study.

Significantly for this chapter, minority cultures can only be imagined because of the power dynamic suggested by notions of dominant and minority. Ethnicity is in fact produced within such relations of power. In the field of education, multiculturalism is critiqued for its capacity to celebrate 'cultural difference' while at the same time perpetuating racist practices (Troyna 1987; Brant 1986). It was this realisation that gave rise to the more pro-active theory of anti-racism. Consequently, multiculturalism is caricatured for its preoccupation with 'lifestyles' while anti-racism makes claim to addressing 'life chances'.

As multiculturalism's theoretical successor, anti-racism claims to confront racism as the barriers that work against the advancement of specific cultural and racial groups. As such, while centring concerns with equity, it offers no alternative to the way that culture and identity are theorised because anti-racism also drifts towards beliefs in an absolute nature of ethnic and racial categories (Gilroy 1992). More significantly for this chapter, however, is how power is conceptualised through the discourse of anti-racism. Anti-racist discourse and notions of 'dominant' and 'minority' constitute power as zero-sum and hierarchically held among the different cultural groups. Individuals are either empowered or disempowered depending on the racial and/or cultural category to which they belong. Here, power is reducible to culture, race or class. This essentially Marxian analysis of power has inspired a range of equity policies and affirmative actions which address the effects of years of entrenched racism. Zero-sum analysis emphasises the materiality of power and its social effects, such as deprivation, alienation and the violence of racism. However, while the value of such analysis cannot be underestimated, the centrality of power to discourse cannot be adequately grasped within its framework. If we engage the power effects of discourse and the production and circulation of power in everyday interactions, the epistemological limits of power as zero-sum operating unidirectionally are realised. It is this engagement with power through discourse that I want to take up in this chapter.

In the discussion that follows, I draw attention to the workings of Foucault's (1980) 'power/knowledge' through discourse in order to engage the limits of anti-racist discourse on power. In calling upon discourse theory, I am not suggesting that there is nothing beyond the realm of ideas. To do so, as Laclau and Mouffe (1985) demonstrate, would mean falling into the ideal/realism opposition which would constitute discourse as the pure expression of thought. Rather, by examining how certain discourses of culture and identity may constrain anti-racism I want to acknowledge desires and necessity for 'strategic essentialism' (Spivak 1990) and for social formations around such categories as 'black' or 'feminist' in order to contribute to specific projects (Rattansi and Boyne 1990). At the same time, however, I want to acknowledge with Fine that 'even "for" Others there are growing, stifling discourses that essentialise to make culture' (1994: 72). Consequently my analysis calls attention to how cultural representations and identity categories may be both enabling and limiting. Not only does this analysis complicate power as zero-sum, it also asks us to think about the seemingly paradoxical possibilities for empowerment and disempowerment to be present in the same moment. Drawing on Foucault (1980, 1990), I want to note how power is integral to discourses, or 'systems of knowledge', of culture, identity, community and anti-racism. I also want to consider the place of ambivalence in the effects of these discourses.

## Identity, ambivalence and power

In the closing decade of the twentieth century, the question of identity has come to assume considerable significance in popular and academic discussions. In Canada, where both regional and hyphened identities mark groups and individuals within the 'cultural mosaic', the passion for identity assumes its own peculiar significance. Ongoing concerns about national unity mingle with debates on the merits and demerits of multiculturalism. In populist debates, some view multiculturalism as undermining national unity while others see it as guaranteeing unity and coherence. The perpetual question of Quebec's relationship to the rest of Canada ensures that the subject is kept alive and the recent referendum on that province's future brought the debate into sharper focus. In these times, the media has come to play an important role in shaping discourses of identity and national unity. Thus, from the respected television and radio broadcasts of the Canadian Broadcasting Corporation (CBC) on one hand, to the daily tabloids on the other, the media have been preoccupied with the perpetual question, 'What makes a Canadian "Canadian"?' And, by extension, what makes the province of Quebec a 'distinct society' either within the nation state of Canada or as distinct from it?

Tom Walkon[4] reaffirms populist discourses of what makes Canada different from the United States:

> Quebec's existence helps to express the difference between Canada and the United States. The US is the melting pot; we are the mosaic. The US is monocultural and officially unilingual. We are multicultural and officially bilingual. American Franco-phones are relegated to the bayous and backwaters of Louisiana, and pockets in New England. In Canada we have French immersion.

The structure of the discourse that we see inscribed by Walkon, of reified differences between Canada and the United States, is the same as that which circulates at the more micro level as differences between cultural or 'ethnic' groups within Canada. Here again, difference is shaped by the dominant theory of cultural relativism. This constitutes cultures as the attributes that characterise particular communities and social groups. These attributes are assumed to be relatively homogeneous and stable. The conceptual limits of this dominant trope of culture are multiple: it has difficulty engaging the dynamic, contingent and contextual nature of culture and identity (Yon 1995). It overlooks how individuals may occupy a 'third space' (to borrow from Bhabha 1994) that defies the neatness and rigidity of the attributes and categories that distinguish communities. While it constitutes culture as the hidden hand that guards and disciplines those whom it produces, it overlooks how individuals may also act upon discourse and resist that discipline by taking up a range of contradictory and ambivalent positions in relation to the objects that are made of culture.

The power/knowledge of discourse thus calls attention to the limits of zero-sum notions of power because of what Foucault (1980) talks about as 'power effects' or as 'actions upon actions'. Foucault's contribution is therefore to ask us to consider power not simply as an entity that can be 'held, taken or alienated' (Smart 1983: 81) but also as a problematic of circulation working through and within various channels and everyday networks of social actions. Consequently, if we return to the passion of identity and the question, 'What makes Canada "Canada"'? the knowledge of the nation as composed of reified cultures (dominant culture and multicultures) becomes the kind of power which is exercised over those who know or are produced by that knowledge. The discourse of dominant and minority cultures also becomes the structure of knowledge by which communities are ordered and controlled. Within the same framework, the cultural categories that are seen as constituting the nation become the 'capillaries' of power.

Identification with cultural categories (those capillaries of power such as black, feminist) becomes a means to empowerment in the face of racist practices. However, while such categories might be imagined as fixed, within them 'networks' and 'actions' emerge to ensure that power is not uniformly held. Consequently neither the elusive 'white culture' nor 'the black struggle' are homogeneous entities. Similarly the internal categories of class, gender, age, sexuality, which have been used in recent years to draw attention to differences within groups, are never stable or homogeneous. On a macro level, in Canada these 'differences within' are borne out by the ongoing example of language battles in Quebec. Such battles present themselves as actions to challenge the discourse of difference by which provinces can be distinguished in the first place.

'Ambivalence' becomes central to the complex play of power at the level of micro-politics that I sketch in this chapter because it works in two interrelated ways: it works in the subject positions that are taken up in relation to identity categories or as a reaction to classifications and objectification. Thus we see below subjects embracing the category black while working against its stereotypes at the same time. In this sense, and as Bauman (1990) notes, classification produces ambivalence. But ambivalence does not only work internally as reaction to classification. It also works itself outwards in what Bauman terms a 'war on ambivalence' which comes about as a bid on the part of one section of the community to 'exercise a monopolistic right to define certain sections (of the community) and their qualities as foreign' (ibid.: 158). This double-play of discourse and ambivalence and of 'minimal selves' (Hall 1987) produces its own tension and power dynamics which I explore below by discussing ethnographic snapshots from research in a Toronto high school.

## Schooling as a discursive space

Rattansi (1992) notes that debates on multiculturalism and anti-racism stand to benefit from discussions on culture that ensue in social anthropology as well as from the discipline's focus on the micro-politics of everyday social interactions. My focus here on the discursive practices of schooling challenges popular distinctions between multiculturalism as being preoccupied with 'culture' and anti-racism as concerned with 'structures'. Instead I draw attention to how the structures of schooling are cultural and in this way culture is made central rather than peripheral to the debate. My notion of schooling as a 'discursive space' is significant methodologically. To borrow from Tyler (1986), it enables me to 'invoke' the culture of the school rather than claim to 'represent' it in holistic and coherent ways. The notion of the discursive also enables me to focus on how the structures of schooling are found not simply in the formal curriculum, school rules and policies but also in the actions observed and in the conversations with teachers and students and the opinions, desires, anxieties and indifference which they may reflect.[5] I will call the school in which this research was undertaken 'Maple Heights'. The brief history that I provide is constructed from, or evoked by, my conversations with teachers. Together with geographical details, this is intended to set the discursive context for the conversations with teachers and students that follow.

The founding of Maple Heights shortly after the Second World War co-incided with large-scale immigration from Europe to Canada. From its early days, like many other schools in Toronto, it established a reputation as an 'immigrant reception' school. Today, its location was described by one teacher as 'among the poorest in Metropolitan in terms of socio-income'. This claim might not be borne out by the semi-detached houses and neatly trimmed lawns that face the school. However, the majority of Maple Heights students come not from the homes surrounding the school but from high rise apartment blocks some 5–10 minutes away by bus.

The history of the school that unfolds is open to contestation but what is important for this discussion are the ways that historicity acts upon those who produce it. It emerges as follows: in its early days, Maple Heights became known for its high concentration of Jewish students. Reflecting on this 'fact' one teacher commented: 'So you had this work ethic thing.' Here the Jewish past becomes an imaginary reference point for the 'lack' of work ethics in the present. This is an instance of how standards and achievements become ethnicised and racialised in these conversations. Maple Heights over-looks a Jewish cemetery which appears to immortalise this past. However, in the early 1970s increasing numbers of Italian immigrants moving into the area came to challenge the Jewish dominance. This development coincided with the movement of 'the Jewish Community' to the north-east of the city and away from Maple Heights. This demographic change was described as an instance of 'upward social mobility' but also as a 'common sense' example of 'ethnics attracting their own kind'.

When multiculturalism was formally introduced by the federal government of Canada in the early 1970s there were already growing numbers of different ethnic groups at Maple Heights. 'There was an identifiable black group', claims one teacher. 'But there were also Koreans and Spanish-speaking students and, at the end of the '70s, the boat people began to arrive.' The 'ethnic composition' of the school thus changed from being first predominantly Jewish, then 'mostly Italian' and eventually became 'the 57 variety', as one teacher described it. A familiar pattern in these conversations with teachers at Maple Heights was the entanglement of a discourse of resentment towards what are perceived as the symptoms of multiculturalism and anti-racism. Thus, claimed one teacher, 'the education system overlooks all these groups except blacks who receive all the attention', while another noted that 'it is now the white students who feel the minority'. Such remarks become the signs of a 'battle' for multiculturalism in which there is a perception of winners and losers, victims and victimisers. But to offset possible accusations of partisan positions or worse, to preclude any possibility of being mistaken for being racist, the teacher added 'actually together each group is now feeling excluded'.

In the teachers' narratives of the school's past and present, discourses of multiculturalism are conflated with a discourse in which immigrants, race, poverty and crime are collapsed. 'The vacuum created by the departure of Italians from the area was filled by refugees and immigrants', one of my chief 'informants' told me. Unconsciously calling up a popular discourse that marks immigrants as 'visible minorities', she added that the school population in fact changed 'from being 90 per cent Italian to become 90 per cent immigrant'. Not only do Italians lose their visibility in these descriptions, the discourse also shuts down engagement with a particular history of discrimination against immigrants from southern Europe at the same time. The same discourse of immigration and schooling also conflates perceptions of all kinds of 'social ills': 'There are now more single mothers and mothers who are working. Now you have all these interest groups and all this human rights stuff', I was told. Another teacher explained that the area in which the school is located is 'branded a high immigrant area with associations with welfare, crime and not just the same kind of education'. A third teacher noted that 'the building of high rise government housing in the area, together with the fact that students had to go to school in order for parents to qualify for welfare, meant a major change in the socio-economic make-up of the school'.

The 'observations' articulated in these conversations with teachers are presented not as opinions but as 'facts', as descriptions of what they 'see', of how things 'were', and of what they have now become. But what teachers 'see' became entangled with the fantasies of popular conservatism and the discourses of new racism.[6] The 'observations' are also entangled in populist discourses of 'reverse racism' which claims that the tactics now being deployed in multicultural education disadvantage 'us' (read white Canadian). With respect to curriculum the observations give rise to a series of questions by teachers. 'Why have African History month?' 'Why not Italian History month?' 'Why not set a month aside for dealing with the different areas of the world?' But such questions are double-edged. They are posited not as criticism but rather as mere suggestions as to how things could be made even better!

The shifts in teachers' positions on multiculturalism and anti-racism, whether in their re-telling of the history of Maple Heights or in their descriptions of the present, are also collapsed with a populist discourse of 'political correctness'. Multiculturalism was described by one teacher as 'bothering' because, they have 'gone too far in undermining "what is Canada"'. He further exclaimed, 'I have to change in order to teach the 20 per cent because we are not strong enough to say "this is Canada"'. Then, as often happened in these conversations, the United States was summoned as an example of the kind of loyalty that Canada should be demanding of those who choose to live within its borders. Popular distinctions between Canada and the US (as reflected in the newspaper quote above) circulate but in contradictory ways. Thus in one breath it is claimed that Canada should be more like the United States, while in the next breath Canada is celebrated for being different from that country. Furthermore the same teacher who was 'bothered' by multiculturalism noted that 'we are known for our compassion and kindness as symbolised by the peace-keeping operations that [Canada] is known for; for not beating our chests about how good the country is; for trying hard to be a caring society, especially towards the ethnic thing'. Then, in a reference to a recent court ruling that upheld the right of Sikh members of the Canadian Mounted Police to wear turbans, the 'ethnic thing' is seen as backfiring: 'I feel that out-siders are imposing their beliefs on us, such as the example of the Sikhs wearing turbans.' Here, multiculturalism, summarised as 'the ethnic thing', is seen as alright as long as it can be controlled. As a second thought, however, and illus-trative of what I would call a nuanced ambivalence, the teacher held back, adding 'but maybe I'm wrong'. After holding back, he continued with his critique of what multiculturalism has done to 'the Canadian heritage, the English way' which, he claimed, 'is being taken advantage of'.

Evident in the conversations, and the discourses that structure them, is what Bhabha (1994) describes as a 'double narrative movement' which produces a slide between enunciatory positions. In this slide, Canada can be applauded for being 'good' towards 'its ethnics' and at the same time 'bad' for giving them too much. Sikhs imposing their 'culture' on 'us' (i.e. Canadians, read white Canadians) at one moment is articulated as a 'fact' of multiculturalism but in the next moment, the teacher noted that either he could be wrong in giving this example, or that the example itself might be wrong. In these narra-tives the 'power effects' of discourses of multiculturalism are confronted by the effects of conflicting subject positions. In these confrontations, a kind of struggle for the survival of the fittest results as another side of Bauman's 'war on ambivalence'. This struggle, I suggest, is partly because of the instability of the signifiers that are called upon as attributes of national culture. Appeals are made to stable notions of Canadian identity in the face of fluidity, hybridity and change. As these contradictory discourses are encountered at Maple Heights, multicultural and anti-racist policies are not enacted in coherent and unproblematic ways. Teachers also act upon them with ambivalence and contradiction.[7]

Such contradiction and ambivalence were not confined to the teachers at Maple Heights, and I do not use these terms judgementally or negatively. Students were open to engaging the paradoxical and contradictory situations in which they found themselves. I now focus on a student organisation called the African Queens and on my conversations with one of its members named Ann. 'African Queens' was the category of empowerment that was adopted by students who saw themselves as marginalised by dominant racist discourse and practices. This strategy was sanctioned by anti-racism at Maple Heights. As we will see, however, the empowerment was also double-edged.

Ann and I established rapport quite early in my year at Maple Heights. She was interested in questions of equity and leadership and so became very interested in my own research project. Ann was in her final year of high school and had left another school to attend Maple Heights where she felt 'more at home'. This feeling, she pointed out, was due to the presence of large numbers of black students: 'there's a lot of intimacy' Ann told me.

> I like the fact that there are a lot of black people here. I'm not saying I'm going to get along with everyone but there is more of myself here. So when I interact with them I am not only interacting with other people but also with myself.

The sense of oneness that Ann spoke of inspired the formation of the African Queens, in which she played a leading part. The move was also in keeping with her commitment to anti-racism. In my first extended conversation with Ann, however, the feeling of intimacy that she spoke of at one moment became ambivalent and problematic the next. The feeling of ambivalence towards the African Queens also became more and more apparent not long after the group's formation.

Ann lived in an area of Toronto that is well known for its concentration of Caribbean people, particularly from Jamaica. Along one of its main streets there are stalls carrying tropical fruits and barrels for shipping goods to the islands line the pavements. Restaurants and barber shops along the same street are named after places in the Caribbean. Ann's mother, whom she described as 'Jamaican but prejudiced towards Jamaicans' also lived in this area. She saw her mother as 'detached from her roots' and used this to explain her ambivalent attitude to fellow islanders. Partly because of this 'detachment' and partly because Ann was born in Canada, she described herself as having grown up 'very Canadian'. In her passion for identity, this family background can be troublesome, she explained: 'Sometimes culture can be so confusing because if I was looking for an identity, what would I be? My father was born in Jamaica but raised in Trinidad and now lives in Toronto.'

Ann's comments display the notions of displacement and hybridity which were so central to the lived experiences of many students at Maple Heights. But while Ann, like other students, defied the rigidity of identity categories in their everyday experiences, she also hankered after community and the stability and affective investments that it might entail. Such a situation, of wanting to belong while not wanting to be constrained, produces its own tension. Consequently, while living the conditions of hybridity and change, in our conversations Ann laid claim to essentialist notions of culture in the form of Afrocentrism. She told me 'we have all been detached from Africa, from our culture, so that we have adopted every culture to survive. So we are all mixed up inside about who we are.' In this these remarks hybridity was acknowledged but in the next an appeal to essence was made. 'There is so much more to our entire race than we know. Sometimes I am in awe of who we really are and what our identity and our culture are.' Speaking about her disenchantment with whiteness, Ann spoke of her plans to celebrate the African-American tradition, Kwanza, the following year while noting that she had little knowledge of this festival. Despite the fluidity of the positions Ann demonstrated with respect to culture and identity, it was the discourse of Africanness that prompted her active involvement in the formation of the African Queens.

The African Queens was an organisation of ten females at Maple Heights. It set as its goal consciousness-raising around concerns with race and gender. The group's aspirations were shaped by the discourse of 'black underachievement' and it encouraged popular multicultural principals of positive role-modelling and self-esteem building as strategies for addressing these concerns. The organisation set out to be a peer support network for empowerment in the face of the disempowering effects of racism and sexism. They staged a successful dance performance at the very beginning of the academic year (the performance featured the theme of black pride) and they met during lunch breaks to review their school work and offer each other support. Peer support and group pressure, it was argued, improved academic results. In addition they wrote poetry reflecting black pride and organised open lunch-time discussions for the rest of the school to attend. One notable discussion was on the subject of inter-racial dating. The forum was notable for the ways that discourses of woman conflated with race to engender race and conversely to racialise gender. Dating preferences, dating 'rules', modes of dress and attitudes were all rendered racially specific and masculine and feminine roles were fixed and sanctioned within the public space of this discussion. These public discussions were significant ways that the power/knowledge of the discourses of race and gender served to discipline 'black students' and at the same time provoke a range of contradictions, ambivalence and, in some cases, open antagonism among members of the African Queens and their fellow black students who attended the discussion.

The African Queens also set as their agenda the need to work for unity and cooperation in the face of what they saw as 'disunity' among 'their people'. Within a few weeks of the group's formation, however, cracks began to appear in their cohesion and the goal of unity began to fall apart. Several factors were behind this development. There were internal disagreements around such issues as what constituted appropriate dress; what members described as 'petty jealousy' towards each other; intolerance of each other's difference; and, as one member summed it up, 'too much attitude'. By the end of the first term, members' interest in the group seemed to have disappeared. There were instances of verbal abuse among members towards one another and the group began to disintegrate. An instance of physical abuse at the beginning of the second term signalled, sadly, the group's death.

The short history of the African Queens may not have been any shorter or less turbulent than that of other school groups. Its history, however, offers insight into the limits of the theory of power and empowerment that structured their sense of empowerment, which seemed to be contingent upon the stability of both race and gender. However, internal arguments about what constituted 'black', and about what constituted appropriate Queen-like behaviour, demonstrated that there were no guarantees of the stability of either of these two categories. Empowerment also seemed to work on the basis of suppressing difference, ambivalence and contradictory subject positions within the group. This practice may have seemed logical in light of desires to address 'disunity'. It also appeared to fulfil the multicultural and anti-racist mandate. The trope of cultural relativism that frames it, however, privileges differences between groups while closing down engagement with difference within them. Suppressing difference seemed appropriate in terms of 'strategic essentialism' for confronting the racist practices that worked against this section of the school population. However, once identity – specifically black identity – was empowered around race, what became more difficult was tolerating and working with differences within this social formation. Students' ambivalence, their contradictory actions and their shifting desires acted upon the power effects (and their disciplinary implications) invoked by the category 'African Queens', and at the same time they undermined the organisation.

I return to my conversation with Ann, who had drifted away from the African Queens before its demise. As noted, Ann embraced the racialised category black in her desire for connectedness and community. She also did so in the face of racist practices and the discourses of resentment that circulated at Maple Heights. Recall the anxieties among teachers over blacks 'now receiving disproportionate attention' and the populist discourses that collapse race, immigration and crime. In the face of the racist discourse that circulates, Ann spoke of the need to reclaim the identity category 'African' even if it meant new hyphenated categories such as 'African-Jamaican'. These are further signs of her desires for categories through which she can be empowered. But while Ann worked with the categories for empowerment of her choice she simultaneously worked against their disciplinary constraints. At a dramatic moment in our conversation about the importance of reclaiming identity categories, Ann proclaimed:

> At one stage I thought of myself as a black person but that limits me because as a black person there are things I am suppose to be. So I had to shed that. I am not just black. I am also a woman, and that limits me as well. We learn that and that is a sort of oppression because if I think that I am limited then I don't dare risk anything or try anything. So

'bust' being black and 'bust' being a woman. That is a form of oppression because you are limited in those two little notches.

Ann's pronouncement was astounding for me, particularly as it came very early in the year I spent at Maple Heights. She alerted me to the duality of discourse – living by the object that is made of oneself while working against the objectification at the same time. Her reflections on the constraining effects of the discourses of 'woman' and that of 'black' spoke volumes to the strategic deployment of identity and to Spivak's 'strategic essentialism'. Ann demonstrated her capacity to work with the categories to achieve specific projects in the face of racist practices. However she refused to be constrained by the power of the discourse that produced those categories in the first place. She refused to be made a mere object, a unitary thing, of the categories with which she worked.

## Conclusion: the question of ambivalence and power in anti-racism

What are some of the issues to be discerned from these ethnographic snapshots from Maple Heights regarding questions of power, empowerment and disempowerment? Returning to my conversations with teachers, among the many issues that seem to be at stake, two stand out. One, as already noted, concerns the relationship between what teachers imagine multiculturalism and anti-racism require them to do and how their fantasies about these policies become enmeshed in populist discourses of identity and the discourse of new racism. Throughout the conversations we see the discourse of ethnic distinctiveness being re-enacted. But by re-enacting the pluralist paradigm, of dominant culture and multicultures, a 'multicultural war' is also evoked in which there are perceptions of winners and losers. The sides in this war, however, take up sliding positions which are far from clear-cut. This is because teachers do not simply enact discourses. They also act upon them. In so doing, there is a constant sliding across positions. Power emerges through these practices not as zero–sum and hierarchically held but dispersed; not as unidirectional, as might be envisaged, but as multi-directional.

The second related issue harks back to Bauman's notion of the 'war against ambivalence'. With respect to teacher conversations, this war centres around the question of who has the right to decide which culture will enter into the curriculum. Here culture is again imagined as group attributes over which communities have a legitimate claim through inheritance. If the 'culture' of the Other is therefore centred, anxieties arise over what will happen to existing (read European/Canadian) knowledge? The ways that ambivalence structures this conundrum means that teachers must also worry over who they are becoming in these arguments. Consequently, those who are perceived as closely associated with official policies on multiculturalism and anti-racism

are caricatured by others as 'caught up in their mission' or carried away by their
'political correctness'. Again, however, lest those who level such charges are
accused of sabotaging the policies, or, worse, mistaken for being racist, they
claim that they are merely describing what they 'see'. These examples demonstrate how the power of discourse acts upon those it produces. In these 'actions
upon actions', however, ambivalence returns as a recurring theme. On the one
hand multiculturalism and anti-racist policies, like the reified notions of culture
and identity that produce them, act as though identities are stable and timeless,
rather than as opportunities to engage difference and hybridity. On the other
hand, in the conversations with both teachers and students their shifting subject
positions undermine beliefs in the stability of the categories that frame the
policies. One of the questions that these observations give rise to is: can
there be an anti-racist curriculum that accommodates ambivalence and difference? Or, can there be ambivalence in anti-racism?

The snapshots of the African Queens in this ethnography show how they
followed the anti-racist text in empowering themselves by organising around
race and gender in order to negotiate the racist and sexist structures of schooling. What seems to be crucial, however, are the terms through which those
categories are imagined. Race was reduced to celebrations of culture and identity in ways that compromised the political definitions and possibilities of this
term. This tendency is reflected in the choice of 'African Queens' as their
group name as well as in their appeals to Africanness and in the discipline
imposed around what was considered appropriate 'queen-like' behaviour.
The formation of the group was a very bold political act but the possibilities
such politics might suggest then began to give way to mimicking the cultural
content of Africanness rather than critically engaging that content. Their
name alone left little scope for a critique of the structures that sustain queens,
or kings. Empowerment began to break down as ambivalence and differences
within the group began to undermine the conformity and discipline that the
particular strategy of empowerment demanded of its members.

While students were unable to tolerate their ambivalence and differences, we
see teachers similarly unable to tolerate the same in their engagement with
multicultural and anti-racist policies. While the African Queens were
empowered by their definition of race as culture, we see teachers making
appeals to their notions of nationhood for empowerment. But while the
passions of identity produce its own contestation, even such appeals to nationhood or race were no guarantee of certainty. Recall, for example the teacher
who, like Tom Walkon in the *Toronto Star,* celebrated Canada for being
different from the United States because of Canada's multicultural policies.
What became intolerable, however, or 'bothering' as he put it, is when difference is seemingly beyond control by the dominant culture. But here again,
recall the teacher's own uncertainty and ambivalence with regard to his own
utterance. 'Maybe I'm wrong', he said. Perhaps the search for fundamentals
and certainty will constitute him either right or wrong. But what if he is

neither? The question that remains is, can anti-racism work with his ambivalence? And, with respect to the working of power in these ethnographic details, can anti-racism work with the possibility of empowerment and disempowerment occupying the same moment?

## Notes

1  My thanks to Deborah Britzman for our conversations and her comments on an earlier draft; to Lyndon Phillip for a newspaper search; and to the students and staff of Maple Heights who gave me the material upon which I reflect here.
2  This ethnography is the subject of my forthcoming book, *Elusive Culture* (forthcoming 1999). The concept 'elusive culture' tries to capture the sense by which students slide ambivalently between and among the cultural categories through which they are imagined. It attempts to engage the fluid, contradictory and sometimes ironic positions that are taken up in relations to discourses of race, culture and identity. The elusiveness of these everyday cultural practices defies the rigidities of fixed notions of identity and culture.
3  These policies were embodied in a Federal Declaration on Multiculturalism in 1917, in the Canadian Charter of Rights (1981) and the Equity Now Programme (1984). School boards were subsequently required to produce their own policy document detailing how policies on equity, multiculturalism and anti-racism were to be effected.
4  *Toronto Star* 28 October 1995.
5  Here, influenced by Giddens (1984), rather than see actions as existing outside of structures, I engage the two as a duality. Structures are enacted through and as actions and discourse.
6  While scientific racism is distinguished for its beliefs in fixed biological differences, 'new racism' (Barker 1981) is premised on beliefs in fixed cultural perceptions of groups. New racism continues to be dependent on attaching cultural assumptions to the reading of bodies. It draws upon the reconstruction of everyday practices and 'common sense' to render itself intelligible (see also Gilroy 1991).
7  These ethnographic observations highlight the limits of theories of resistance and accommodation which have framed much research in education. The binary of resistance and accommodation poses conceptual difficulties for thinking about ambivalence, contradictions and the sliding suggested in 'the double narrative movement'.

## References

Barker, M. (1981) *The New Racism: Conservatives and the Ideology of the Tribe*. London: Junction Books.

Bauman, Z. (1990) *Modernity and Ambivalence*. Cambridge: Polity Press.

Bhabha, H. (1994) *The Location of Culture*. London: Routledge.

Brant, G. (1986) *The Realization of Anti-Racist Education*. London: Falmer Press.

Fine, M. (1994) Working the Hyphens – Reinventing Self and Other in Qualitative Research. In *Handbook of Qualitative Research* (eds) N. Denzin and Y. Linclon. London: Sage (pp. 70–82).

Foucault, M. (1980) *Power/Knowledge*. Brighton: Harvester Press.

—— (1990) *History of Sexuality*. New York: Vintage Books, Random House.

Giddens, A. (1984) *The Constitution of Society*. Berkeley: University of California Press.

Gilroy, P. (1991) *There Ain't No Black in the Union Jack: The Cultural Politics of Race and Nation*. Chicago: Chicago University Press.

—— (1992) The End of Anti-Racism. In *Race, Culture and Difference* (eds) A. Rattansi and J. Donald. London: Sage Publications (pp. 49–61).

Hall, S. (1987) Minimal Selves In *Identity. The Real Me*. ICA Document. London: ICA.

Laclau, E. and Mouffe, C. (1985) *Hegemony and Socialist Strategy: Towards a Radical Democratic Politics*. London: Verso.

Rattansi, A. and Boyne, R. (eds) (1990) *Postmodernism and Society*. London: Macmillan.

Smart, B. (1983) *Foucault, Marxism and Critique*. London/Boston: Routledge and Kegan Paul.

Spivak, G. (1990) *The Post-Colonial Critic: Interviews, Strategies, Dialogue*. New York/London: Routledge.

Troyna, B. (1987) Beyond multiculturalism: towards the enactment of anti-racist education in policy, provision and pedagogy. *Oxford Review of Education* 13, 3: 307–20

Tyler, S. (1986) Postmodern ethnography: from document of the occult to occult document In *Writing Culture* (eds) J. Clifford and G. Marcus. London/Berkeley: University of California Press (pp. 122–40).

Yon, D. (1995) Identity and difference in the Caribbean diaspora. In *The Reordering of Culture* (eds) A. Ruprecht and C. Taiana. Ottawa: Carlton University Press.

—— (forthcoming 1999) *Elusive Culture*. Albany, NY: SUNY Press.

Chapter 4

# 'Father did not answer that question'

## Power, gender and globalisation in Europe

*Sigridur Duna Kristmundsdottir*

> What is really important is to know how the cultural traditions of one country combine with elements which reach it from another. What is interesting is to know how globality behaves when it dissolves into a specific particularity.
>
> (Esteva-Fabregat 1995: 9)

In his rejection of the levelling influence of the global village, Esteva-Fabregat points to the fact that although we live in a world that seems to be shrinking due to a process called globalisation, this same world continues to recreate its cultural diversity. Not only do human beings continue to separate themselves into diverse cultural traditions, they seem to use globalisation itself in the process. How they do that and how that affects power relations between women and men in European societies is the subject of this chapter.

As with most concepts of the same order, anthropologists have attempted to define the limits, uncertainties and even dangers of the concept of globalisation. Some have argued, for example, that the concept suggests 'a totality which always gives anthropologists a *frisson* of delight', attracting 'total solutions' to 'total problems', simplifying the complexities of social and cultural processes (Hobart 1995: 50). Long (1996: 36–9) warns anthropologists that 'we should not be seduced into believing that globalization has uniform impact everywhere', quite the contrary: 'globalization has generated a whole new diversified pattern of responses at national, regional and local levels'. If we do not acknowledge this we run the risk of formulating a universal or grand theory that seeks to identify 'laws' of change, which, besides being decidedly un-postmodern, is according to Parkin (1995: 143) not our *forte*.

While the language of this criticism, that of delight and seduction to be valiantly resisted, is itself an interesting subject, I shall do no more than acknowledge it as a legitimate postmodern hangover from too much grand theory. The warnings sounded by this criticism are well kept in mind, but I do not accept that it is futile, wrong, or anthropologically untrue to attempt to discern similarities in patterns of change or in social and cultural processes generally for a larger entity than that encompassed by an anthropologist's fieldwork or a society. To abandon the broad view is an unnecessary limitation to the anthropological endeavour and to the anthropologist as a concerned member of human society. What has to be remembered is that the broad view is just that, and not something else, and that it is bound to be an estimation or a thesis rather than a detailed analysis of a localised cultural phenomenon. It has also to be kept in mind that 'broadness' or universality only applies to certain categories. Thus gender is universally found as a cultural construct, while there is no such thing as a universal womanhood or a universal manhood. In adopting the broad view this chapter is concerned with the former and does not attempt to detail the different cultural expressions of gender in the societies it deals with.

I begin by defining what I mean by 'globalisation' and discuss its ambivalent effects. I then move on to gender boundaries as one form of cultural boundary and to a discussion of how European societies are reacting to globalisation in this respect. Finally I explore how cultural values are used towards specific ends and how resilient they are in the face of social change. My perspective is supra-local, i.e. I attempt to draw an elementary picture of how globalisation is affecting the position of European women in this last decade of the twentieth century. On these grounds, I draw the conclusion that globalisation can empower women in European societies, but fails to do so when it creates a resurgence of traditional gender values. In so doing, globalisation can in certain respects be seen to disempower women in European societies.

## Globalisation

By globalisation I refer to what people perceive of as a shrinking of their world due to such things as new technology in mass communication, the pervasiveness of international business interests, the toppling of old regimes and a weakening of long-established borders between countries. In Europe, the supra-political and economic unification process of the European Union is an added impetus towards the perceived process of globalisation. Anthropologists have observed that people tend to react to globalisation by emphasising the opposite, that is by emphasising what is local in each culture as opposed to what is global. Others have maintained that emphasis on the local is not a reaction to globalisation but an inherent part of it (Robertson 1995). When the big world out there seems to be taking over, people turn to what makes them culturally different from others, not what they have in common with others. Or, as Sharon Macdonald puts it, 'Notions of "us" and "them" become stronger still' (Macdonald 1993: 1).

This process is by no means simple or unified. It is culturally contextual, utilising different cultural elements such as ethnic identity, regional identity, religion, kinship values, gender, political structures, etc. Yet its outcome is often relatively uniform, that of strengthening or reinventing cultural boundaries between differently defined and sometimes in other respects overlapping social groups. Lai (1995) in his review of studies of social and cultural change in rural societies of Mediterranean Europe finds that the prevalent hypothesis in these studies is that globalisation has led to a 'strident' reproduction of cultural and political differences.

> In this sense a problem that is becoming more and more serious from the viewpoint of culture or politics than from that of science, arises from the increasing ferocity of ethnic and religious conflicts . . . and from funda-mentalist movements as a reaction against social and cultural transforma-tions that have come about too quickly.
>
> (Lai 1995: 196)

Similarly Shore in his study of the ECs attempts to forge a supranational 'European identity' finds that:

> the idea of a 'European identity' appears as yet another ideological device designed as much for the exclusion of Europe's 'Other' as a mechanism for achieving European political and social integration . . . celebrat[ing] power at the center . . . tend[ing] to provoke anxiety and vulnerability at the peri-pheries, which is then translated into local chauvinism and xenophobia.
>
> (1993: 795)

In other words, by attempting to unify Europe politically and socially, the EC strengthens local cultural boundaries and the resulting culturally constructed ideologies.

In spite of the EC's attempts at unification, the concept of cultures as bounded wholes and the idea of cultural preservation are very much alive in its institutional workings and approved strategies. Maryon Mcdonald finds that the EC slogan '"unity in diversity" . . . has now moved from optimistic ideal to virtual self-irony . . . for some of those employed in EC institutions' (1996: 47). This is so because, in spite of its proclaimed goal of European unity, EC institutions utilise the concept of national cultures in their strategies and public discourse, continually tripping over the idea of European unity in the process. Indeed, the idea of cultural unification presupposes the idea of cultural diversity and is therefore capable of emphasising cultural boundaries.

Furthermore, as Lai (1995: 197) points out, 'cultural and productive specifi-city is no longer an obstacle to modernisation, but is a resource to be used in the present'. The marketing of Italian local food outside Italy, for example, is facilitated by the fact that the food is culturally specific and that that specificity is perceived as desirable by the buyer. Hence globalisation has itself generated a situation where cultural specificity is highly rated as commodity on the common market, creating an economic as well as social impetus towards the enhancing of local cultural elements in Europe.

The strengthening of cultural boundaries brought about by globalisation is the opposite of the levelling influence globalisation is often perceived to have. Yet as Robertson (1995: 26) has pointed out, 'the contemporary assertion of ethnicity and/or nationalism is made within the global terms of identity and particularity'. Therefore the cultural diversification brought about by globalisation is, on another plane, levelling in the sense that cultural diversification is everywhere brought about on the same global terms. Hence there is a certain ambivalence attached to globalisation, it simultaneously both creates and evens out difference. Put another way, globalisation is both homogenising and heterogenising and these tendencies are mutually implicative. But, as Robertson (1995: 28) points out, 'Nevertheless, we appear to live in a world in which the expectation of uniqueness has become increasingly institutionalised and globally widespread'.

## Diverse voices

The voices calling for the reinforcement of cultural boundaries in Europe are indeed diverse. Two examples will serve to illustrate the point. In May 1996, Pope John Paul II, addressing an assembly of artists and academics in Slovenia, deplored the present state of upheaval in Europe and voiced the opinion that cultural identities were in danger of being lost forever. Now was Europe's moment of truth, said the Pope, the walls are down, but they have left an empty space which can only be filled by traditional and Christian values.

> Only a vigorous and living national culture can protect you from chaos and from disappearing in a world that is threatened by grey uniformity. A strong national culture will also help you to enter a new Europe and be there the equals of others.
>
> (*Morgunbladid* 21 May 1996, my translation)

The message of the Pope is unequivocal; in the face of globalisation revive your cultural values and strengthen your cultural boundaries.

In the *European Journal of Women's Studies*, May 1996, there is a report on the feminist conference 'Women in the northern light', held in August 1995 in Oulu, the European far north. The conference concluded:

> The masculine idea of progress and emphasis on economic growth and competition cause the structural marginality of the Northern areas and women . . . . If we are turning the centre-centered perspective to the perspective of the periphery, we can make visible the cultural strength of the Northern areas . . . . The Conference and the action of women showed the power of Northern women. They are living in the Northern light of knowledge.
>
> (Anttonen 1996: 179–80)

Here the message is that in spite of structural marginality brought about by global ideas on economics, the European far north, and especially its women, possess cultural capital that in itself represents power. Cultural specificity with its inherent cultural boundaries is therefore something to be valued in a changing world.

European feminism has always been multivocal but there is no record of a specifically papal variant. Nor can Pope John Paul II easily be defined as a feminist. Yet on the subject of the importance of traditional culture and how to react to globalisation, the voices of the northern feminists and that of the Pope are not divergent. These examples also illustrate the homogenising influence of globalisation. These otherwise culturally and ideologically divergent voices are sounding the same ideas, advocating cultural diversification on the same terms.

## 'Father did not answer that question'

Gender as a cultural construct can create one form of a cultural boundary. Other cultural boundaries or discourses may at times override those of gender (see e.g. Howell 1996), but gender remains one of the fundamental building blocks of cultural diversification and distinction.

If, as is maintained above, globalisation can have the effect of strengthening cultural boundaries generally, we might expect that this can also apply to gender boundaries. It means that where we find that people perceive that their society is changing due to outside influence or globalisation, we might expect to find increasing emphasis on women and men as different cultural beings. This has been repeatedly observed for the fundamentalist Muslim world, where, in the face of 'Western influence', religion and traditional cultural values have been used to strengthen cultural boundaries, the one between men and women being clearly emphasised with, among other things, women's seclusion (see e.g. Ahmed 1992; Brooks 1995). When globalisation can be observed to have this effect, women, not men, seem to be especially targeted as the preservers and symbols of what is local as opposed to what is global in a culture. Mernissi (1994) writing of her childhood in a Moroccan harem during the 1940s and 1950s, a period of strong French influence on Moroccan society, gives a vivid account of this divide between women and men:

> Indeed we children found the thought of switching codes and languages (i.e. French and Moroccan) to be as spellbinding as the sliding open of magic doors. The women loved it too, but the men did not. They thought it was dangerous, and Father especially did not like Mrs. Bennis, because he said she made trespassing seem natural. She stepped too easily out of one culture and into another, without any regard for the *hudud*, the sacred boundary. 'And what's so wrong with that?' asked Chama. Father replied that the frontier protected cultural identity, and that if

Arab women started imitating European ones by dressing provocatively, smoking cigarettes and running around with their hair uncovered, there would be only one culture left. Ours would be dead. 'If that is so,' argued Chama, 'then why can my male cousins run around dressed like so many imitations of Rudolph Valentinos and cut their hair like French soldiers, with no one screaming at them that our culture is about to disappear?' Father did not answer that question.

(1994: 180–1)

As is clearly spelt out in this passage, at a time of social and cultural change women and not men were expected to embody in their behaviour and dress the traditional cultural values that seemed to be threatened by outside influence. It points to the fact that not only does such outside influence, or globalisation, strengthen the cultural boundaries between women and men. It does so by placing the burden of tradition on women to a greater degree than on men.

## Europe

As most Europeanists have found, it is by no means a simple task to define Europe as some sort of a unit. We can easily delineate Europe as a geographical area, but any definition in terms of culture or society is bound to be problematic and complex, if not impossible (Goddard et al. 1994).

The salient characteristic of European cultures which is most relevant for the subject of this chapter is that they are traditionally patriarchal cultures. They are cultures where men are the ones who are traditionally visible in the public sphere of society, in politics, in academia and in the arts, in business and finance, etc. – and where women are half-hidden in society's private sphere, the home. They are cultures where men are generally paid higher salaries than women on the labour market, and where women do most of the unpaid work of home-making and bringing up children. They are cultures where women are more often than not looked upon as appended to men, be it their fathers or their husbands, or their sons when women grow old. They are cultures where men control the public discourse which then shapes the lives of everybody, men and women. The concept 'patriarchal' is after all a European one and an apt one for describing this European cultural element.

Feminism as an organised social phenomenon is also a European cultural element, providing the opposite to patriarchy in the traditionally dualistic and gendered European cultural construction. During this century women's rights activities have been instrumental in securing European women the same or comparable civil rights to men (Bolt 1993). In Europe women are rarely prohibited by law to undertake the same tasks as men be it in politics, academia, business or whatever. Formal discrimination can still be found, e.g. women cannot inherit titles in the British aristocracy, but generally such discrimination has been on the wane. In short this century has seen a drastic change in the civil position of women in European societies. This change has been global in the sense that ideas on the rights women should be entitled to have spread from one society to another, making 'the status of women . . . a gauge of the relative modernisation and progress of individual societies and cultures' (Goddard 1994: 59).

## West . . .

Nordic societies are often seen as progressive examples of the egalitarian incorporation of women in civil society. Iceland, a relatively stable welfare society, is a case in point. In 1980 Icelanders were the first in the world to democratically elect a woman as head of state. Since then a number of women have been elected to publicly visible positions in Iceland, such as speaker of parliament, mayor of Reykjavik, etc. Since 1983 there has been a successful women's party in Iceland, having women elected into parliament and municipal governments.

However, with few exceptions, most of the publicly visible women in Iceland occupy symbolic positions, not positions of real political or financial power. The fact that there is a women's party, dedicated to changing the position of women in Icelandic society, indicates that something is wrong with the position of women in Iceland. A closer look at the reality of Icelandic women reveals that 80 per cent of married Icelandic women are on the labour market. Those women also bear the brunt of housework and childrearing. On the labour market women, married and unmarried, have on the average 68 per cent of men's salaries. Education does not raise women's wages to the same degree as men's; a young woman can expect to raise her earning power by 42 per cent by becoming university-educated whereas her fellow student who is male can expect to raise his earning power by 104 per cent (*Launamyndun og kynbundinn launamunur* 1995). This is so in spite of the fact that women in Iceland have long had all the same formal rights as men have, and that since 1976 discrimination against women on the labour market has been prohibited by law (*Lög um jafnrétti kvenna og karla* 1976).

The discrepancy between women's formal rights and their actual situation can be explained by examining cultural ideas on family and gender in Iceland. As I have argued elsewhere (Kristmundsdottir 1997a), in Icelandic culture women are first and foremost viewed as mothers and housewives. Whatever else they do outside their homes is considered secondary and not defining for women as social persons. Because women's work on the labour market is defined as secondary to their traditional role, women's salaries continue to lag behind those of men. Women are neither seen to need such high salaries as men nor are they according to traditional gender values culturally suited to having men's salaries. This has, for instance, been brought forward when women have entered previously male-dominated professions like the teaching profession that saw a great increase in women practitioners in the 1960s and

1970s. The teaching profession quickly became feminized, it was associated with women's role of bringing up children and teaching salaries dropped accordingly. There is a vicious circle in this; because women have lower salaries than men it is more difficult for women to obtain financial independence, which in turn restricts the social space women have to change their situation, including their primary definition as mothers and housewives and their resulting low salaries.

I have found (Kristmundsdottir 1997b) that the dominant political discourse in Iceland strengthens these traditional cultural ideas about women, and that in this respect there is not much difference between women and men as politicians. Basically, politicians reflect the culture of their society, and female politicians, no less than male politicians, are informed by their society's culture and strive to keep their vote by saying what people understand, i.e. by reflecting basic cultural values.

Public discourse in Iceland on whether the country should become a member of the EU is to an extent characterised by the fear that Icelanders would lose their cultural specificity, their language and way of life. This discourse also emphasises traditional ideas about women, that women are the mothers who tend the nation's children and, therefore, the nation's heritage. They are the keepers of the hearth, the keepers of Icelandic culture and the wearers of national costumes. This was forcibly brought forward during the Second World War when foreign armies occupied Iceland. Women who associated with the soldiers were castigated as national traitors and polluters of Icelandic cultural heritage (Bjornsdottir 1989).

As in the Moroccan harem in which Mernissi grew up, it is women in Iceland who bear the burden of preserving cultural traditions in a changing world. This is not a phenomenon confined to Morocco and Iceland: O'Brien (1994), for instance, has reported the same for women in Catalonia. The cultural traditions women are expected to preserve incorporate at the same time ideas on family and gender that effectively prohibit women from obtaining equality with men. Accelerating globalisation, e.g. in the form of greater emphasis on European unity, might, by increasing the importance of traditional gender values as a resistance to that globalisation, therefore make it harder still for West European women to obtain the equality with men that the law presently grants them.

### . . . and East

That brings me to the eastern and central part of Europe where social change has in recent years been most rapid and unsettling. Anthropological research in these societies is still scanty, but from the UNESCO publication, *Gains and Losses: Women and Transition in Eastern and Central Europe* (UNESCO 1994) it can be gleaned that women in central and eastern European societies are dealing with much the same cultural forces as I have outlined for women in Iceland. Adamik, writing about women in Hungary during the political transition, observes:

> . . . the declining economy is pricing many of the social services from which women benefited under communism out of existence, and a reactionary male backlash is interfering with the rights of women to choice in matters of birth control and abortion. Women run the risk of finding themselves powerless, overworked, and resocialized in the new democracy as much as they were during the period of communism.
>
> (Adamik 1994: 1)

Izhevska, writing about Ukrainian women during the transition period notes:

> The independence of Ukraine having opened up new career possibilities in many lines of work, the prospects of women should improve; however, the same prejudices towards the achievements of women remain, and moreover, the severe economic crisis which has resulted from political and economic transition is multiplying the effects of this prejudice.
>
> (Izhevska 1994: 8)

And Gjipali and Ruci writing about women in Albania state:

> Today women are suffering both as the result of the general economic and political crisis which continues to grip Albania and because of a resurgence of traditional male attitudes.
>
> (Gjipali and Ruci 1994: 32)

Social change, economic instability and the perceived effect of globalisation is much greater in these countries than it is in the western part of Europe. Its effect on the position of women in these societies is described in strong words. Adamik speaks of a 'reactionary male backlash', Izhevska of 'multiplying the effects of . . . prejudice', and Gjipali and Ruci of 'a resurgence of traditional male attitudes'. What seems to be happening is that traditional cultural ideas about gender and family are being emphasised in reaction to the globalising change taking place in these societies.

Although the former communist states in Europe may be the clearest examples of this process, we can also find it in the western part of the continent. Garcia (1994) finds that the restructuring of the Spanish labour market, which among other things has brought about higher unemployment of women, re-creates the old gender inequalities traditional to Spanish society, as well as generating new ones. Here we find a resurgence of traditional gender values and the gender inequalities adherent to them. And we also find that renewed emphasis on traditional gender values and gender cultural boundaries disempowers women in these societies.

## How to use a cultural value

In January 1996 president Jacques Chirac of France addressed an assembly of women he had invited to the Elysée palace. In his address he extolled the virtues of motherhood and emphasised how important it was for the well-being of France that women should bear more children. A growing population, he said, was a prerequisite for economic growth and hence for the disappearance of unemployment (*Morgunbladid* 23 January 1996). As Irigaray (1977, quoted in Goddard 1994) has pointed out:

> 'Motherhood' provides the focus for a definition of 'woman' which runs through the entire Western philosophical tradition. Whereas 'man' is recognised as separate and separable from 'father', there is no space within (male-centered) discourse for 'woman' disassociated from 'mother'.
>
> (Goddard 1994: 74)

From this point of view the president was only affirming that motherhood is a central family and gender value in European cultures, defining the human beings assembled to listen to him. He was also using that cultural value towards specific political ends. As has emerged in the examples already cited, motherhood is important among the values emphasised when attempts are made to strengthen or reinvent gender boundaries. It should, however, not be assumed that it is only men that uphold this value. Women are often the most fierce defenders of motherhood, placing supreme value on their role as mother. In patriarchal public discourse women are in a double bind concerning motherhood. They are constantly told that motherhood is their most important role, and because it is their most important role they are without the means to change the primary definition of themselves as mothers.

An example of how motherhood can be used to strengthen the cultural boundaries between women and men, disempowering women in the process, comes from studies of the Latin American *marianismo*. *Marianismo* is the association of women with the figure of the Virgin, entailing that like the Virgin women as mothers are spiritually superior to men. This phenomenon came about as a reaction to the legal emancipation of Latin American women, which in turn was largely due to the globalising of ideas on women's rights during this century.

> [T]he main thrust of *marianismo* in male patriarchal practices is to assert the need to confine women to the domestic sphere and to reinforce sexual control over women, particularly those who do go out to work . . . . The principle of women's equality was undermined by the principle that women were spiritually 'different' from men.
>
> (Gledhill 1994: 198–9)

The key element here is 'difference'. In order to deal with change, or the globalising of ideas on women's civil rights, women and men needed to be culturally re-differentiated in respects that did not touch on the equalising brought about by equal civil rights. The cultural value of motherhood in combination with religion is used to reinforce the cultural boundary between women and men. By instituting this difference, the differences among women are at the same time minimised or denied, giving women as a gender group a homogeneous appearance, which further facilitates the management of culturally defined gender boundaries.

## Resilience of cultural values

As pointed out above, globalisation has ambivalent or contradictory effects. For Latin American women, for instance, it is both levelling and differentiating, empowering and disempowering at the same time. Globalisation of women's rights and the consequent empowering of women had a levelling effect on the traditional gender boundary in Latin American societies. The reaction to this, or, as Robertson (1995) would have it, part of that globalisation, was to re-differentiate men and women or reinvent the gender boundary with *marianismo*, turning the clock back for women.

The same process can be found in Europe. While the reaction to European unification can disempower women, as I have argued above, widespread acceptance or globalisation of EU agreements – e.g. on women's rights, the labour market, family law, etc. – might at the same time empower women resident in the EC region. Such agreements provide a kind of a standard women can refer to when they wish to actualise their rights in one way or another. Again, this empowerment of women may be part of what brings about an emphasis on traditional gender values and the reinvention of gender boundaries in Europe which in turn disempowers women. From this perspective globalisation seems to bring about a reactionary circle or spiral, or to be such a spiral if we consider the reaction as part of globalisation, in which case Robertson's (1995) term 'glocalisation' would be a more apt one.

It remains to be considered whether the ambivalent effects of globalisation apply equally to all women or whether certain groups of women are more susceptible to enjoy or suffer one or the other. Although gender can be viewed as a universal category, women are differentiated by a large number of other social and cultural characteristics such as economic power, race, religion, education, age, family, etc., and it may therefore be surmised that the effects of globalisation do not necessarily apply equally to all women.

Rerrich (1996), in her study of the division of labour between women in West Germany, found that women's increasing labour market participation has led not to greater equality between women and men, but to greater inequality between women. On the one hand there are working mothers who have benefited from the globalisation of women's rights during this century, enabling them to obtain an education and use it on the labour market. On the other hand, there are the women who mind the children of the working mothers while they are working, clean their houses, etc. These women are likely to have less education, lower social status and/or to be ethnically different from the Germans. If we add to this that 'traditional family values . . . tend to be strongest (at least in theory) at the poorer end of the labour market' (*The Economist* 1996: 23), we might conclude that at least for these two groups of women, the latter is likely to suffer more from the disempowering effect globalisation can have for women.

But is that necessarily so? As *The Economist* (1996: 29) points out:

> Despite a huge social change during the past 30 years, traditional sexual attitudes retain a stubborn hold. A survey for the EU found that more than two-thirds of Europeans (ranging from 85% in Germany to 60% in Denmark) thought it better for the mother of a young child to stay at home than the father. Mothers, said this survey, should take care of nappies, clothes and food; fathers are for money, sport and punishment.

This indicates that a large majority of women in the EU holds, and is surrounded by people (women and men) who hold traditional, gender-defined family values, which, as has been argued above, can be used to disempower women. This suggests that most women, regardless of social and cultural denominators other than gender, have in one way or another to deal with the disempowering effects renewed emphasis on these values can have for them. Doubtless there are differences in the degree and in the way in which women find they have to deal with the effects emphasis on these values have on their lives. There are also doubtless differences in how women value these effects: some would welcome them while others would not. But the fact remains that most if not all women have to deal with them one way or another.

And these gender-defined values appear to be extremely resistant to change. They do not seem to be altered by the fact that many blue-collar European males are losing their jobs because of structural economic changes and therefore cannot fulfil their breadwinning role. Nor do the facts that women in increasing numbers are able to meet those changes, turn them to their advantage and earn the bread seem to have much impact. These values remain strong, to such an extent that unemployed men will not take over the reproductive work in their homes while their wives are working outside the home, nor enter feminised jobs on the labour market (*The Economist* 1996).

Rerrich (1996: 31) maintains that, in Germany, 'women's participation in the labour force and involvement in the public arena are tolerated and encouraged to the extent that women mobilise paid or unpaid female support in the home (or elsewhere), as their own private affair'. Whichever way we look at it, in the face of globalisation, in the face of a perception of a pervasive change that threatens to wipe out difference, Europeans cling to their gender-defined values which culturally differentiate women and men. Although women's range of social participation has expanded enormously this century, reproductive work continues to be women's work, clearly defining the boundary between European women and men in this respect.

In this regard women and men are different cultural beings and, even if they have the same formal rights, this difference is crucial. As the data from Iceland demonstrate, formal rights such as those embodied in the Icelandic 1976 equality legislation, do not suffice to bring about a situation of equality between women and men on the labour market. Neither does the fact that Latin American women have the same formal rights as men prevent the creation and employment of *marianismo*. Cultural values seem to be stronger than formal rights in this respect, and therefore the empowering force of formal rights is accordingly limited.

## Power and globalisation

In this chapter I have argued that at least one way that 'globality . . . behaves when it dissolves into particularity', as Esteva-Fabregat had it, is to reinforce traditional cultural values and hence strengthen cultural boundaries. I do not exclude the possibility that globality may also behave in different ways. Still, the evidence related in this chapter clearly points to an overriding emphasis on the present reinvention of cultural boundaries in Europe. I have outlined how a cultural value can be used in the construction of cultural boundaries and pointed out that when globality produces emphasis on cultural exclusiveness, the gender boundary between women and men is one that can be reinforced in the process. I have argued that when that happens, women bear the burden of maintaining tradition to a greater degree than men. Furthermore, I have argued that the very tradition women are expected to preserve often involves ideas and values that make it more difficult for women to obtain equality with men. In this way globalisation can disempower women. Finally, I have demonstrated the resilience of cultural values and pointed out that, in the face of this resilience, formal rights have limited empowering force.

The concept of disempowerment is not a straightforward one. I use it here in the sense of the withdrawal of publicly defined authority, the hushing down of women's public voices and the reinforcement of the cultural obstacles women have to face when using their formal civil rights. In this sense I argue that globalisation can disempower women. This does not mean that globalisation always has this effect. As has been pointed out, globalisation was instrumental in bringing about women's civil emancipation during this century. Only because originally nineteenth-century European liberal ideas on women's rights became globalised, were women in diverse societies given rights that empowered them as civilians. Globalization is therefore not necessarily disempowering for women, it can have the opposite effect. What I do argue here is that when globalisation behaves in a vicious spiral and brings about the reinforcement of traditional gender values, women's disempowerment in the public sphere may become more than a possibility. That, I argue, is presently the case of European women.

## References

Adamik, M. (1994) Women in Hungary during the political transition. In *Gains and Losses: Women and Transition in Eastern and Central Europe*. Bucharest: CEPES (pp. 1–8).

Ahmed, L. (1992) *Women and Gender in Islam*. New Haven, CT: Yale University Press.

Anttonen, S. (1996) Women in the northern light. *The European Journal of Women's Studies* 3, 2: 179–81.

Bjornsdottir, I. D. (1989) Public view and private voices. In *The Anthropology of Iceland* (eds) P. Durrenberger and G. Palsson. Iowa: Iowa University Press (pp. 98–121).

Bolt, C. (1993) *The Women's Movements*. New York: Harvester.

Brooks, G. (1995) *Nine Parts of Desire: The Hidden World of Islamic Women*. London: Hamish Hamilton.

Esteva-Fabregat, C. (1995) Interview with the *Doyen* of Catalan anthropology: Claudio Esteva-Fabregat. *European Association of Social Anthropologists Newsletter* 16: 6-9.

Garcia, S. (1994) The Spanish experience and its implications for a citizen's Europe. In *The Anthropology of Europe: Identities and Boundaries in Conflict* (eds) V. Goddard, J. Llobera and C. Shore. Oxford: Berg (pp. 255–75).

Gjipali, S. and Ruci, L. (1994) The Albanian woman: hesitation and perspectives. In *Gains and Losses: Women and Transition in Eastern and Central Europe*. Bucharest: CEPES (pp. 32–42).

Gledhill, J. (1994) *Power and its Disguises: Anthropological Perspectives on Politics*. London: Pluto Press.

Goddard, V. (1994) From the Mediterranean to Europe: honor, kinship and gender. In *The Anthropology of Europe: Identities and Boundaries in Conflict* (eds) V. Goddard, J. Llobera and C. Shore. Oxford: Berg (pp. 57–93).

Goddard, V. A., Llobera, J. and Shore, C. (1994) Introduction: the anthropology of Europe. In *The Anthropology of Europe: Identities and Boundaries in Conflict* (eds) V. Goddard, J. Llobera and C. Shore. Oxford: Berg (pp. 1–41).

Hobart, M. (1995) As I lay laughing: encountering global knowledge in Bali. In *Counterworks* (ed.) R. Fardon. London: Routledge (pp. 49–73).

Howell, S. (1996) Many contexts, many meanings? Gendered values among the northern Lio of Flores, Indonesia. *Journal of the Royal Anthropological Institute* 2, 2: 253–71.

Izhevska, T. (1994) Ukranian women during the transitional period: basic trends. In *Gains and Losses: Women and Transition in Eastern and Central Europe*. Bucharest: CEPES (pp. 8–15).

Kristmundsdottir, Sigridu Duna (1997a) *Doing and Becoming: Women's Movements and Women's Personhood in Iceland 1870–1990*. Reykjavik: University of Iceland Press.

Kristmundsdottir, Sigridur Duna (1997b) Fjölskylda, frelsi og réttlæti, *Íslensk félagsrit* 7–8: 71–87.

Lai, F. (1995) Social and Cultural Change in Rural Societies of Mediterranean Europe: A Brief Review of Studies. *Europæa*: 185–93.

*Launamyndun og kynbundinn launamunur* (1995) Reykjavik: Skrifstofa jafnréttismála.

Long, N. (1996) Globalization and localization: new challenges to rural research. In *The Future of Anthropological Knowledge* (ed.) H. L. Moore. London: Routledge (pp. 16–37).

Lög um jafnrétti kvenna og karla (1976) *Lagasafn*, Reykjavik, Dómsmálaráðuneytið: 612–13.

Macdonald, S. (1993) Identity complexes in Western Europe: social anthropological perspectives. In *Inside European Identities* (ed.) S. Macdonald. Oxford: Berg (pp. 1–27).

Mcdonald, M. (1996) Unity in diversities: some tensions in the construction of Europe. *Social Anthropology* 4, 1: 47–61.

Mernissi, F. (1994) *Dreams of Trespass: Tales of a Harem Girlhood*. Reading: Addison-Wesley.

*Morgunbaldid* 23 January 1996, Reykjavik.

*Morgunbladid* 21 May 1996, Reykjavik.

O'Brien, O. (1994) Ethnic identity: gender and life cycle in north Catalonia. In *The Anthropology of Europe: Identities and Boundaries in Conflict* (eds) V. Goddard, J. Llobera and C. Shore. Oxford: Berg (pp. 191–209).

Parkin, David (1995) Latticed knowledge: eradication and dispersal of the unpalatable in Islam, medicine and anthropological theory. In *Counterworks* (ed.) R. Fardon. London: Routledge (pp. 143–64).

Rerrich, M.S. (1996) Modernizing the patriarchal family in West Germany: some findings on the redistribution of family work between women. *The European Journal of Women's Studies* 3, 1: 27–39.

Robertson, R. (1995) Globalization: time–space and homogeneity–heterogeneity. In *Global Modernities* (eds) M. Featherstone, S. Lash and R. Robertson. London: Sage (pp. 25–45).

Shore, C. (1993) Inventing the 'people's' Europe: critical approaches to European Community cultural policy. *Man* 28, 4: 779–801.

*The Economist* (1996) The trouble with men. 28 September: 17–18, 23–4, 29, 32.

UNESCO (1994) *Gains and Losses: Women and Transition in Eastern and Central Europe*. Bucharest: CEPES.

# Chapter 5

# The reach of the postcolonial state

## Development, empowerment/ disempowerment and technocracy

*Richard Werbner*

Glossy state-of-play reports by public service bodies are notorious for their aim of easy readability on the run. Perhaps for that very reason, powerful simplicity, currently acceptable as conventional wisdom or safe policy, is often not far from their inviting surface. An example is useful for opening the way to a discussion of the current critique of development, the changing discourse of empowerment and disempowerment, and resistance to postcolonial technocracy.

In a recent overview, *ODA Economic and Social Research – Achievements, 1992–1995; Strategy, 1995–1998,* the British Overseas Development Administration (now the Department for International Development) reported its aim to promote 'good government' elsewhere (1996: 25).[1] In line with that aim for 'developing or poorer countries', the ODA [DfID] has funded research showing participatory perceptions,

> Perceptions of the appropriate role of government in the development process has [sic] changed radically in the last decade. There has been a move away from the view that the state should be the mechanism for achieving developmental goals. This was matched by increasing expectations in the market and the private sector providing such a mechanism. At the same time there was an increasing interest in the role of civil society in challenging undemocratic regimes.
>
> (1996: 26)

The immediate emphasis is on neo-liberal ideas for privatisation of once public services, the implication being that non-governmental organisations should now do what the state was once expected to develop into doing. Where the state is weak, the non-governmental organisations can and should be strong. Little is said about the funding of these non-governmental organisations, and nothing at all about the importance for new or old power structures of the patronage flowing in and through them. The understood background is a vast recent increase in foreign funding, often government aid from countries in the North; it has been shifted to the non-governmental organisations to match and stimulate their recent phenomenal growth (Gardner and Lewis 1996: 107–8).

What the ODA [DfID] did propose for the coming year was to commission a major research programme on Good Government, Human Rights and Civil Society, but its use of empowerment rhetoric was remarkably limited, at least in its overview of achievements and strategy. Only in reporting ODA [DfID] funded research on credit and loan schemes for the poor was the mention of empowerment explicit, and there it was significant for being sceptical: 'Some over–optimistic claims about the effectiveness of the schemes should be dampened. For example, there is little evidence about . . . the poor being politically empowered, or that the majority of the poor can benefit' (1996: 17; for a more specific evaluation of credit in rural Zimbabwe, based on a working paper of the Overseas Development Institute, see Muir 1995: 279).

Here the poor have become one of what development-speak now calls 'target groups', those who are subject to the current development 'objective of including people who have been "left out" of the development process' (Gardner and Lewis 1996: 106). Labelled in the emerging development cate-gory of the disempowered and disadvantaged, through participatory develop-ment they ought to become both empowered and beneficiaries. But the expressed doubt is that they are becoming neither, although the possibility of contradictions between the two is not raised. A policy aimed at a move from disempowerment to empowerment and yet sceptical in recognition of public doubt about practice, about the actual fulfilment of the avowed aim, and per-haps about the very technology of power itself – we seem to be in a world of official rhetoric at once Foucauldian and post-Foucauldian.

This example from development discourse under British crown copyright leads me to a series of basic questions, which I want to ask for postcolonial Africa and most particularly for Zimbabwe (on contradictions of development in Zimbabwe see Mandaza 1986; Sylvester 1991). Is there a distinctive moment emerging in the stream of Western-derived projects in modernity or moderni-sation? If so, how is that linked to the problematic reach of the postcolonial state? And if the most challenging breakthrough in recent critique has come from Foucauldian analysis of development constructs, how are this moment's apparently post-Foucauldian aspects to be understood?

In itself, critique of 'Third World development' is not at all novel (Escobar 1988, 1991; Apffel Marglin and Marglin 1990; Ramphele 1991; Sachs 1992; Hobart 1993). It is at least as old as the invention of 'the Third World' and 'development' (Escobar 1988). There has long been scepticism about social engineering, critical doubt about planned socio–economic change, and much visible discontent with their own practice among development experts them-selves, including 'applied anthropologists' (Bennett and Bowen 1989; Porter *et al.* 1991; Pankhurst 1991; Worby n.d.). In the immense literature on development as failure, the consultancy report on why this or that project did not succeed has become virtually a dominant genre, and one with countless, fleeting examples (Ferguson 1990). The report on satisfaction, reaching intended consequences of improvement, has remained the great rarity, of course – a fact that is all the more surprising given the power struggles over creating the *appearance* of satisfaction through the management of official ignorance, no less than official knowledge (Quarles van Ufford 1993).

Yet much of this, it might be argued, falls squarely within the Foucauldian analysis of power and knowledge in development discourse. Such analysis, perhaps most importantly in Ferguson's path-breaking critique of the basic political effects of a 'failed' state intervention in livestock and range management, has illuminated a now familiar technology of power (Ferguson 1990). In it, the greater reach of the national state, accompanying bureaucratic expansion and increased surveillance, is made out to be something apart from politics, as if it were justified on objective, scientific grounds, merely a matter of technical practice, perhaps for the sake of better marketing or more efficient distribution of welfare benefits. Ferguson's Foucauldian analysis also disclosed the limits and closure of certain development constructs, images and rhetoric by taking a World Bank text as representative for an international development agency. But there is a fresh challenge to Foucauldian analysis where the central state, if not the local state, is on the retreat or already virtually absent.

Of course, neutralisation is at work as a process by which radical ideas and agents perhaps once potentially subversive are assimilated or coopted, leaving an existing discourse still dominant and without radical change to entrenched power structures (Gardner and Lewis 1996: 113). Nevertheless, the fresh challenge for analysis arises where the development images and rhetoric are deployed in post-Foucauldian ways which appeal to 'empowerment', 'community participation', 'self-determination' and 'own goals'. The people themselves are supposed to be active agents responsible for taking their own aims and objectives in hand. Beyond that, this new participatory-cum-empowerment development-speak thrives in the secondary elaborations of belief, to use Evans-Pritchard's phrase for witchcraft discourse (1937), which are its own scepticism about 'disempowerment', scepticism even by the very aid donors themselves who are still the major drivers of development.

Here Zimbabwe presents a distinctive challenge within the broader problematic of power, empowerment and disempowerment in postcolonial Africa. If the state is now on the retreat from welfare services, it is very much the heir to the centralising legacies of the authoritarian colonial state and still in many respects a strong state compared to others in postcolonial Africa. Winning independence at the barrel of a gun did not mean the collapse of the central state or its powerful bureaucracies. The contrary is more the case, and the postcolonial regime has heavily invested in efforts to assert its central dominance against tendencies of the local state towards decentralisation. Drawing on detailed evidence from one district, Alexander puts the argument more generally:

The government quickly undermined the autonomy of the local political party by coopting key groups, maintaining central control over development resources, and, in Matabeleland, by military and political repression. People in Zimbabwe's rural areas were largely unable to influence policy-making processes; instead, patronage, squatting and opposition by traditional leaders dominated rural politics. Far from empowering the disadvantaged through democratic bodies, policies reinforced patriarchal authority within communities, thus helping to marginalise women, the young and the poor.

(1996: 180)

The best attempt to draw on case studies from Zimbabwe in order to represent non-governmental organisations and the current contradictions of the emerging postcolonial moment is, to my knowledge, Anne Muir's contribution to *Non-Governmental Organizations and Rural Poverty Alleviation* (1995). I quote from her argument at length because she shows further how the practice of empowerment stops short of the rhetoric:

NGOs in Zimbabwe have tended not to enter the stage of national public policy advocacy, to lobby for either improvement in group interests or changes in national or indeed provincial policies which might lead to a greater allocation of resources to the poor or a strengthening of their power to act for themselves. Even in the sphere of communal area development, in which they have been most heavily involved, very few NGOs have been active individually or in groups attempting to influence the formulation of or alterations to agricultural and rural development policies.

(1995: 244)

Having made this point about the non-governmental organisations' apparently apolitical practice, Muir goes on to wonder how that meshes with the rhetorical stress on empowerment:

This is doubly strange because of the stress laid by so many NGOs working among the rural poor in the resettlement and communal areas on the concept of empowerment and the benefits obtained from group action. Group work has been dominated by trying to maximize the gains that groups could obtain within the wider context, rather than in trying to alter that environment or engage in debate to initiate change.

(1995: 244)

One is tempted to say that avoidance of policy formulation is itself a strategy in competition for maximising gains within parts of an environment which are perceived to be beyond the subject's control or even knowledge. There is a great dearth of research in any depth about the political learning in and through

Zimbabwe's non-governmental organisations, and I have in mind not merely learning about the current direction of spoils in patron–client networks, of politics as competition over who gets what from whom, but even more, political discovery about what it is to be a subject of the postcolonial state in the presence of other internationally backed agencies. How does such discovery constitute fresh contradictions in central state–local state relations? At present, we can only speculate. But a familiar point still bears rehearsal: in rural Zimbabwe, apart from the non-governmental institutions, there is and long has been considerable locally effective resistance to technocracy, its top-down development plans, and its purposive rationality, and by resistance I mean the whole gamut from everyday non-confrontational tactics to openly active opposition.

This point is demonstrated by recent responses to efforts by technocrat modernisers to reintroduce rural centralisation projects under a Communal Area Reorganization Policy. As Drinkwater (1989) pointed out, the purposive rationality of contemporary bureaucrats reflected a continuity from the colonial to the postcolonial period in which the state has been a dominant institution. Centralisation now suits the purposive rationality of certain contemporary state officials as technocrats, just as it did that of their colonial predecessors. In Zimbabwe, there has been, as Alexander argued, an 'uneasy relationship between the government's technocratic and authoritarian development policies and its need to make compromises and concessions in order to maintain support and implement policies in rural areas' (n.d.). The relationship is all the more uneasy in western Zimbabwe, because of the impact of the civil war in Matebeleland which followed Zimbabwe's war of liberation and in which the Fifth Brigade of the national army, unleashed as a violently punitive force of occupation, left a legacy of hostility and mistrust towards the state and its officials (Werbner 1991, 1995, 1998; Robins 1996: 74).

The Communal Area Reorganization Policy represented a retreat in government policy harking back to the colonial Land Husbandry Act of 1951. The emphasis was no longer on the redistribution of land to meet land hunger – the policy promised after the liberation war – but on more technically modernised control and more productive management of the land the people already had. Once again, as in the colonial period, heavy hidden costs, such as arise from moving house or from the loss of productive fields, were to be shifted on to the people themselves; and although compensation was promised, this was not readily forthcoming. The Reorganization Policy called for heavy expenditure in measures for control, information gathering and surveillance, such as in mapping and pegging fields' limits.

Although the government had announced plans and actually begun to buy commercial farmland for resettlement on a large scale, these plans were intended for people regarded as 'productive farmers', having considerable access to capital and technical expertise. The government's purchases were mainly in marginal areas; the most productive ones were hardly touched by the new policy. Its formulation called for local farmers themselves to manage development projects. However, against that official rhetoric stood, as it were in revived strength, the trend towards top-down planning of land-use projects by the centre for the periphery in the countryside (Alexander n.d., 1991; on planning for more decentralisation and 'rural democracy', see Reynolds 1991). At the same time, in some parts of Matabeleland, for technical reasons of efficient use of pasture, the scale of state recognised 'community' was increased, but without the social relations needed to sustain that scale (Robins 1994). As one 'community', members had to share the allocation of resources, such as grazing in rotation in a ranch. As a consequence, conflict intensified between local communities locked in competition with each other for scarce land and yet brought together within a project as one 'community'.

In many other parts of southern Africa besides Zimbabwe, the intensification of conflict within and between communities is a tendency that centralisation of rural settlement often fosters, whatever its intended benefits in welfare or modernisation might be. In turn, and also as a general tendency, the intensification of conflict within and between communities drives forward resistance to state intervention in the form of centralisation. Throughout much of southern Africa, it is remarkable, given the rhetoric of progress surrounding these centralisation projects that in many instances so much about them, their techniques of spatial rationalisation, their underlying logic, core ideas and basic assumptions, virtually an official episteme in itself, in Foucauldian terms, has so widely and for so long been relatively static.

The subjects or clients of development projects are often said to resist change, but what is too easily missed is the conservative or reactionary guidance of entrenched ideas influencing the developers themselves (Leach and Mearns 1996; Scoones 1996). It is not that the specific projects have been unchanging over time, or without opposition and criticism by officials and developers themselves, no less than by clients. After all, each project generates its own micro-politics over personnel, benefits, techniques and objectives, and often over the very existence of the project (Moore 1996: 132–3).

Government bureaucracies, divided into rival ministries competing for influence in line with specialist expertise, pursue contradictory objectives even within the same development project (on such conflict and the deployment of disparate models for the rationalisation of space during recent agrarian reform in Zimbabwe, see Alexander n.d.; and on colonial precedents, Werbner 1991, Drinkwater 1989: 303). If the clients are sometimes victims of mismanagement and pseudo-scientific expertise, they are rarely passive victims. On the contrary, their power is to find ways to subvert, to counter-attack, and to renegotiate state interventions they do not like.

It is, of course, not my view that the clients necessarily, or even readily, form a unitary bloc acting in unison against the bureaucrats. Bureaucrats have no monopoly on rivalry. Often enough, members of rival government bureaucracies and non-governmental agencies do find their own client allies who give them political support selectively, for certain officials or for certain policies, and not always in return for obvious patronage.

Here what needs to be stressed is simply this. Development, whether by the state or by non-governmental organisations, is ever and always a political battle-ground, never a mere technical exercise or a foregone conclusion. That is a very general suggestion which has to be appreciated along with the Foucauldian reality still found in many parts of southern Africa: there is an episteme for the rationalisation of space that has been reproduced time and again, at least in the plans and rhetoric of developers; relocated from place to place, it has often been re-embodied in variable yet recognisably similar forms of practice.

In land-use projects in Zimbabwe, and elsewhere in southern Africa, the pur-posive rationality of bureaucrats as developers has often turned the actor ration-ality of the developers' clients, once regarded as 'the objects of development', into something problematic. Official rhetoric readily makes the bureaucratic out to be technical, scientific, apolitical, by contrast to the client rationality which, in the people's opposition and resistance, is denigrated as irrational, traditional or simply tribalistic (see also Ferguson 1990). It would be a mistake, however, to miss the argument in which the rhetoric belongs. Some developers argue as if the technical can be separated from the political; others insist that their clients have technical problems calling for technical solutions; still others now contend that the very definition of 'the problem' is a matter of politics in which the people must be empowered, rather than turned into clients.

The argument extends to the technical ideas and categories upon which plan-ning depends. The validity of these ideas has been called into question, and the expertise of developers is actually less certain than it has appeared in the presen-tations to clients (Pankhurst 1991; on absurdities in expert land-use planning, contrary to local management of soil fertility, see Scoones 1997). In Zimbabwe, for example, land-use planning for centralisation has long relied upon assess-ments of 'carrying capacity', the number of livestock an area can sustain, with-out degradation. It has been associated, both in colonial and postcolonial state intervention, with control measures, rotational grazing and paddocks perma-nently fenced with barbed wire. Although very drastic destocking and extensive demarcation of land has been rationalised in terms of 'carrying capacity', the notion has been shown to be dubious (Pankhurst 1991; Behnke and Scoones 1989). It does not take into account the drought cycle and micro-climatic fluc-tuations from year to year. Similarly, paddocks have been found to be too inflexible to allow for variable or opportunistic access to the patchy distribution of grazing and such temporary water resources as *vleis* or open pans (Werbner 1982). However, much of this critical argument remains in papers and reports that circulate apart from the general public or the clients themselves (Sandford 1982; for an important review of entrenched technocrat ideas and rangeland policy, see Scoones 1996). When people in the countryside defend themselves against the unwonted impact of development, they rarely have access to the technical objections currently raised against what has otherwise publicly passed for scientific rationality among the developers. The possibility of somewhat more inclusive access is only now emerging in those rural parts of southern Africa to which ex-civil servants and former developers come home in retirement at the end of their careers (Werbner 1992). More commonly, the clients draw primarily on cultural knowledge that is practical, that recognises how their everyday activities make the spaces in which they live (Bourdieu 1977). It is informed by memories of colonial encounters with state intervention and past defences of local autonomy. The erection of fences for paddocks in the postcolonial state brings back memories of colonial destocking and fencing. Such practical knowledge is holistic; it brings together what the purposive rationality of bureaucrats compartmentalises, for example into planning for housing and for production; it usually has the strength and the weakness of being more finely, if not exclusively, localised than the developers' knowledge. The clients also rely on strategic perceptions of the social relations they need to implement that practical knowledge.

It is revealing that technocrat policies for rural centralisation were actually labelled 'development' even at first in the colonial period from 1929 onwards. Only much later did 'development' become a common-or-garden label for planned change, state intervention, modernisation, directed schemes for public betterment, projects of 'instrumental rationality' and much else. Rural centralisation is thus especially salient for the analysis of existing technocracy and the emergence of 'development', as we now know it (on the forging of a distinctly modern discourse of colonial development, see Worby 1994: 386–8). This is so, not merely because official history later renewed that label in retrospective legitimation: 'the rising tide for development' (Chief Native Commissioner, Annual Report 1961, cited in Drinkwater 1989: 293). Even more important is the prefiguring of 'development' under the postcolonial state of the present and the fact that colonial state interventions, redirecting the use and management of tribal land, continue to precondition the popular perceptions many Zimbabweans have of current development. What remains a strong force are their much rehearsed memories that earlier measures announced and rationalised as being for improvement were actually a means of oppression by the colonial state, and this is recalled in popular rejection of measures perceived to be similar despite their postcolonial dress in technical development policies and in the rhetoric of empowerment and participation (on social memory of linear resettlement and postcolonial struggles over resources and the definition of community, see Moore 1998).

Centralisation schemes, which eventually involved forced resettlement, were introduced in many reserves by the Southern Rhodesian government from 1929 onwards. Part of the official justification was that the reserves were, as a Chief Native Commissioner put it, already 'overcrowded with human beings and cattle' (cited in Phimister 1986: 270). But the drive to implement land management and conservation policies was also openly tied to colonisation and land appropriation, to promoting the interests of white settlers at the expense of legalised dislocation of Africans from areas kept for white settlement under the Land Apportionment Act.

The 'overcrowded' reserves were to be planned to contain bigger popula-tions. Despite the mounting dislocation, as more and more people were expelled from farmland occupied by white settlers, adequate land to meet the pressure was not provided. Instead, the open range was controlled by fencing; and all the resettled land was divided, according to function, into arable, residential and grazing areas (Scoones 1997: 621–3). Contour ridges were built, often badly and causing more soil erosion. Villages were consolidated in 'lines', along roads, in between the arable and grazing blocks. The emphasis was on defined, well-demarcated spaces, controlled by appointed authorities of the state (for a recent account recognising the Foucauldian resonance, see Worby 1994: 387).

This rationalisation of space was ostensibly for the sake of soil conservation and more efficient land use by more viable farming units. Economically, the consequences were largely counter-productive; many of the resettled people were left worse off than before. But the functional and tripartite rationalisation of space took on an extended life of its own in projects of developers in neigh-bouring countries, starting in the Ciskei (de Wet 1989; Kruger 1991) and later in Botswana and elsewhere (Werbner 1982), no less than in Zimbabwe itself (for an overview and related case studies, see the special issue of the *Journal of Southern African Studies* on 'The Politics of Conservation in Southern Africa', Beinart 1989).

## A case of abandoned centralisation

I observed an abortive attempt to centralise, according to a tripartite scheme, in colonial Zimbabwe among Eastern Kalanga of Bango chiefdom and its neigh-bours within Matabeleland (see also Werbner 1991). The successful local resistance to centralisation – at Bango, it never got beyond a preliminary phase – was part of the increasing confrontation across much of the country. It was an advance in the nationalist struggle, which forced the colonial state to abandon centralisation and other authoritarian policies of agrarian change.

During the couple of decades before the abortive centralisation, many Eastern Kalanga, dispossessed by the encroachment of settler ranching, had managed to recreate their communities in areas of marginal lowlands remote from their original highland homes. Within what was known as Sanzukwe Special Native Area, Bango Chiefdom occupied the land along one river; along the next came its competitor, Tshitshi Chiefdom; and the interior of their valley became a buffer zone between them, a potential prize in their competition for land, but somewhat inaccessible for settlement at first, due to the distance from available water. There state intervention was initially kept to a minimum; *laissez-faire* was the ruling policy, for purposes of resettlement.

It was a process of reconstruction reliant upon personal links to create chains of immigrants, rather than simply being the relocation of clusters of hamlets or administrative divisions; and it was also a process that called upon considerable social knowledge of how to reactivate trust, loyalty, authority and interdependence between kin and neighbours in the face of much wider social mobility, including the increasing circulation of migrant workers between town and country.

None of the fruits of this process of reconstruction were taken into account in the colonial developers' attempt to rationalise land use. The centralisation plans dismissed and thus devalued Kalanga social knowledge of zones of interpersonal interaction, zones of neighbours and neighbourliness, along with their practical knowledge of preferred land use.

Kalanga opposition to centralisation was a defence of the value of their own highly specific and locally grounded knowledge, no less than a resistance to alien domination or a defence of community and local autonomy against outside manipulation. Refusing to be 'penned up like donkeys', they did not allow the developers to go unchallenged in the public claim to rationality. They gave explicit reasons, sometimes in direct debate with developers, which reflected their perception that the development plans were socially and economically flawed. They anticipated the damaging consequences of losing control of the location of their everyday activities, of being limited to herds of a certain size and standard plots, without regard to the needs of interdependent kin.

Kalanga also recognised, and pursued, strategic interests which divided them among themselves. A pipeline, built in support of centralisation, primarily for watering livestock, opened out the interior of the valley between the chiefdoms of Bango and Tshitshi, a valley for which they advanced conflicting claims to land. As Chief Bango explained it to me, a tactical campaign had to be waged, and it had to be won, to secure the permanence of his chiefdom against threats coming to the land from outside. His intent was to get his people placed to the best advantage in the struggle over the land. The analogy he drew was a comparison to a battle. 'In a battle you go to the place of the fewest soldiers', he said. In addition, to cope with the technical reasoning of the planning officials, he had argued with them that on a high ridge in the interior the soils were best for an arable block around homesteads. Having that location would give the further benefit of a domestic water supply, if taps were added to the pipeline.

One outcome of the strategic expansion by competing land-hungry chiefdoms was a heightened ambiguity in the definition of political community. Neither chiefdom emerged as a political community in the sense taken for granted in development planning. Neither became territorially discrete, having its people distinct on its own land. Not only did the chiefdoms have conflicting claims to land, but they also came to overlap in the actual interspersion of their people. Against that, for the sake of clear responsibility for land use, including the maintenance of contour ridges and fences, the planning was predicated on territorial discreteness, and at all levels from the chiefdom down to the 'administrative village' or division under a headman. Instead of the existing ambiguity or zones of frontage, clear boundaries were required. But where were they to be drawn? And on what basis? Was it to be by reference to history, or to immediate frontage? Or was it to be in disregard of tangled claims, by reference to an arbitrary landmark, such as the straight lie of a pipe-line or a fence? The officials' preference for the straight lie was seen by themselves to be a technical matter, for permanence and administrative convenience. For the chiefs and their subjects, however, it was a political decision: it favoured the interests of some at the expense of others and was problematic in the face of the continued interspersion of members of the different chiefdoms.

Although the colonial officials planning and directing the centralisation were also divided among themselves about the wisdom of specific measures, they shared a conviction that they were above the rivalry between African chiefs. It was as if they had convinced themselves that they alone were not in any battle; that being disinterested, they were the true judges of what was in the best interests of all the Africans in different chiefdoms. Such conviction legiti-mising a lack of accountability was, of course, a great advantage in the assertion of authority by alien officials.

Among themselves, the officials acknowledged that they had miscalculated the amount of land available and that more was needed than they had realised. They knew that their area of allocation was not enough to provide for viable economic units, according to their own planning criteria. They shifted from one plan to another, attempting to fix future responsibility for what they called 'overpopulation' within each political community. Interests in soil con-servation and administrative control became paramount, although a desired objective was to get the people mainly to become beef producers for the market, even at the expense of their arable agriculture.

The technocrat wisdom was that it was a part of the country best suited for beef production, preferably on a large scale within vast paddocks, as on com-mercial ranches. Arable agriculture was regarded as something of a necessary evil, needed for mere subsistence but not a positive factor in development. On this view, since the arable agriculture was not as extensive as livestock rear-ing, it was useful for cramming more people within less land, but it was not the most profitable or beneficial use of the land. The plans were not explicitly designed to protect the food security of the people working the land. There were, thus, contradictions in the colonial developers' situation which they attempted to manage *unofficially* through *ad hoc* decisions, but which they obscured *officially*, in public, by their formulation of a whole blueprint for development.

Such formulation was not taken at face value by the people promised the fruits of development. Instead, much of the popular response assumed that the officials had a hidden agenda, about which they had to be challenged and confronted. What was put in official terms of economic improvement, such as greater profit from beef production or labour saving from grazing of cattle in paddocks without herders, was popularly perceived to be part of a continuing campaign of dispossession and dominance. The officials were said to be motivated by their interests in imposing on others what was 'the way of their own home', ranching. A widely held suspicion was that fencing the land would attract encroachment by Europeans ready to take over the 'ranches'. The regulation of fields was recognised to be an attack on the people's control over flexibility in their use of land; it was seen to be a means of penning the people themselves in, stopping them from making needed moves to and from fallow land.

At one phase during the attempted centralisation, there was a semblance of consultation in which popular opposition was voiced in public debate. It was not long, however, before the resistance became more militant, with threats or actual cases of direct action, including the cutting of fences of nearby ranches in order to drive cattle to graze on them. This was part of the much wider civil disobedience across the country, which forced the colonial government to abandon its centralisation projects and agrarian development measures.

## Power, rationality and the long-term perspective

In conclusion, I want to argue first in defence of a Foucauldian approach because of the need, particularly in the postcolonial states of southern Africa, for a long-term perspective on state-planned development in which there is a rationalisation of space through rural centralisation. Foucault made us understand the technology of power which disciplines through commanding the distribution of individuals in space (1977). It is a technology of power that is called upon as the rationalisation of space in development for the pursuit of the objectives of modernity. Following Foucault and writing on colonial Egyptian villages, Mitchell conceptualised a colonially invented method of order and discipline which he called 'enframing':

> Enframing is a method of dividing up and containing, as in the construction of barracks or the rebuilding of villages, which operates by conjuring up a neutral surface or volume called 'space'.
>
> (1988: 45)

As Foucault originally argued, the method uses plans to demarcate standardised spaces; it breaks down social life into discrete functions, each with its own location; and it creates frames or containers within which items can be set apart, kept and counted (1977: 141–9). The techniques of enframing are useful for a state in extending its dominance over its own countryside, no less than for a colonising power. Indeed, for a postcolonial state like Zimbabwe, reconsidering the land rights of individuals and communities (on the debate around the 1993–4 Commission of Enquiry into Appropriate Agricultural Land Tenure Systems, see Potts 1996) and making a major retreat from the provision of welfare services, such as in free schooling and free clinics, the usefulness of enframing techniques may be all the greater. The gains sought include greater knowledge and surveillance of the subjects within communities owing their definition to the central authorities of the state, more efficient control of the subjects' public consumption of all that the state provides, and the means of making them coordinate their efforts in order to increase their productivity as a unit.

My own argument is based primarily on my observations of projects of centralisation in Botswana and Zimbabwe, during both colonial and post-colonial periods, although within present limits I have concentrated mainly on Zimbabwe (see also Werbner 1977, 1981, 1991). The long-term perspective reveals what has become entrenched and is cumulative, from the colonial to the postcolonial periods. Perhaps most importantly, against the background of entrenched 'problems' and 'solutions', can be seen tendencies towards endemic contradictions in spatial rationalisation as a process of development.

This perspective also highlights the importance of what I would call 'formu-lation' and 'historicity', and the distinction relates to the public representation of and resistance to planned change. At one extreme, formulation is used by developers to present a scheme as an innovatory blueprint for space. The appeal is atemporal or oriented primarily to the future, for example, in the promise of improvement and progress, and the justifications are grounded in general principles, such as the market or conservation or, most recently, rural democracy, empowerment and 'participation from the bottom up'. At another extreme is historicity as the mode of counter-representation that clients use to recontextualise within social memory what has been formulated apart from it. Clients bring to bear their accounts of pre-established claims, debts and interests which may be tied to moral and religious commitments, no less than to political and economic priorities. The remembered accounts eventually register, also, past 'failures' or confrontations with development. I have put this initially in terms of extremes, but of course in actual practice and over time, the process is a mediation of the extremes. This engages developers in historicity and clients in formulation and it produces hybrids of practice, involving a tension between the modes.

In southern Africa, the rationalisation of space by the central state, often represented as resettlement for improvement and progress and now implemen-ted with appeals to participation and empowerment, is a process involving the entrenched ideas of technocrats (on basic policy assumptions, see Scoones 1996). It is also a process that is intensely politicised, under conditions of land hunger. What the centre plans, the different coalitions at the periphery subvert or re-work in local practice (on elite and subaltern coalition building in the face of externally planned change in rural Zimbabwe, see Moore 1996, 1998). What must be stressed is the highly local nature of the develop-ment process that swings between popular appropriation and resistance: it arises in the seemingly parochial politics of elites and subalterns within local communities, in their specific conflicts of interest, in their perceptions of strategic value at a micro-scale, in their historic understanding of how and where actual benefits and resources may come from development, in their political learning from practical assertions of power as against top-down 'empowerment'. The locally proved realities of alliances within, between and beyond communities at the periphery drive forward the renegotiating of state planned rationalisations of space and condition the actual reach of the post-colonial state technocracy.

## Note

1 Since this article was originally written, the new British government under New Labour has refocused its aid priorities in a White Paper on 'Eliminating World Poverty' (Secretary of State for International Development, CM 3789), and following the Comprehensive Spending Review of July 1998, there is to be a major increase in British aid targeted on the poor.

## References

Alexander, J. (n.d.) Tradition, modernization and control. Unpublished manuscript. Cited with the author's permission.

—— (1991) The unsettled land: the politics of land distribution in Matabeleland 1980–1990. *Journal of Southern African Studies* 17: 581–610.

—— (1996) Things fall apart, the centre can hold: processes of post-war political change in Zimbabwe's rural areas. In *Society in Zimbabwe's Liberation War* (eds) N. Bhebe and T. Ranger. Oxford: James Currey.

Apffel Marglin, F. and Marglin, S. (1990) *Dominating Knowledge – Development, Culture and Resistance*. Oxford: Clarendon Press.

Behnke, R. and Scoones, I. (1993) Rethinking range ecology: implications for rangeland management in East Africa. In *Range Ecology at Disequilibrium* (eds) R. Behnke, I. Scoones and C. Kerven. London: Overseas Development Institute.

Beinart, W. (ed.) (1989) The politics of conservation in southern Africa. *Journal of Southern African Studies* 15, 2: 143–62.

Bennett, J. W. and Bowen, J. (1989) *Production and Autonomy – Anthropological Studies and Critiques of Development*. Monograph in Economic Anthropology 5. Lanham, MD: University Press of America.

Bourdieu, P. (1977) *Outline of a Theory of Practice*. Cambridge: Cambridge University Press.

Drinkwater, M. (1989) Technical development and peasant impoverishment: land use policy in Zimbabwe's Midlands Province. *Journal of Southern African Studies* 15: 287–305.

Escobar, A. (1988) Power and visibility: the invention and management of development in the Third World. *Cultural Anthropology* 3: 428–42.

—— (1991) Anthropology and the development encounter. *American Ethnologist* 18, 4: 658–83.

Evans-Pritchard, E. (1937) *Witchcraft, Oracles and Magic among the Azande*. Oxford: Clarendon Press.

Ferguson, J. (1990) *The Anti-Politics Machine*. Cambridge: Cambridge University Press.

Foucault, M. (1977) [1979] *Discipline and Punish*. Harmondsworth: Penguin Books.

Gardner, K. and Lewis, D. (1996) *Anthropology, Development and the Post-Modern Challenge*. London: Pluto Press.

Hobart, M. (ed.) (1993) *An Anthropological Critique of Development*. London: Routledge.

Kruger, F. (1991) The legacy of 'homeland' policy. In *Restoring the Land* (ed.) M. Ramphele. London: Panos.

Leach, M. and Mearns, R. (eds) (1996) *The Lie of the Land: Challenging Received Wisdom on the African Environment*. Oxford: James Currey.

Mandaza, I. (ed.) (1986) *Zimbabwe: The Political Economy of Transition 1980–86*. Dakar: Codesria.

Mitchell, T. (1988) *Colonising Egypt*. Cambridge: Cambridge University Press.

Moore, D. (1996) Marxism, culture and political ecology. In *Liberation Ecologies* (eds) R. Peet and M. Watts. London and New York: Routledge (pp. 125–47).

—— (1998) Clear waters and muddied histories. *Journal of Southern African Studies* 28, 2: 377–404.

Muir, A. (1995) Zimbabwe. In *Non-Governmental Organizations and Rural Poverty Alleviation* (co-authored by) R. C. Riddell and M. Robinson. London: Oxford University Press.

Overseas Development Administration (1996) *ODA Economic and Social Research Achievements, 1992–1995; Strategy, 1995–1998*. London: ODA.

Pankhurst, D. (1991) An undeclared war for sustainable development. Paper presented to the Development Studies Association Conference, Swansea.

Phimister, I. (1986) Discourse and the discipline of historical context: conservationism and ideas about development in Southern Rhodesia 1930–1950. *Journal of Southern African Studies* 12: 263–75.

Porter, D., Allen, B. and Thompson, G. (1991) *Development in Practice – Paved with Good Intentions*. London: Routledge

Potts, D. (1996) Migrants must keep their land. *The Zimbabwe Review* October: 6–8.

Quarles van Ufford, P. (1993) Knowledge and ignorance and the practices of development policy. In *An Anthropological Critique of Development* (ed.) M. Hobart. London: Routledge.

Ramphele, M. (ed.) (1991) *Restoring the Land*. London: Panos.

Reynolds, N. (1991) Rural democracy revisited. In *Restoring the Land* (ed.) M. Ramphele. London: Panos.

Robins, S. (1994) Contesting the social geometry of state power: case study of land-use planning in Matabeleland, Zimbabwe. *Social Dynamics* 20, 2: 91–118.

—— (1996) Heroes, heretics and historians of the Zimbabwe revolution: a review article of Norma Kriger's *Peasant Voices* (1992). *Zambezia* 22, 1: 73–92.

Sachs, W. (1992) *The Development Dictionary: A Guide to Knowledge as Power*. London: Zed Books

Sandford, S. (1982) *Livestock in the Communal Areas of Zimbabwe*. London: Overseas Development Institute.

Scoones, I. (1996) Range management science and policy: politics, polemics and pasture in southern Africa. In *The Lie of the Land: Challenging Received Wisdom on the African Environment* (eds) M. Leach and R. Mearns. London: James Currey.

Scoones, I. (1997) Landscapes, fields and soils: understanding the history of soil and fertility management in southern Zimbabwe. *Journal of Southern African Studies* 23, 4: 615–34.

Secretary of State for International Development (1997) *Eliminating World Poverty: A Challenge for the 21st Century: White Paper on International Development*, CM3789. London: HMSO.

Sylvester, C. (1991) *Zimbabwe: The Terrain of Contradictory Development*. Boulder: Westview Press.

Werbner, R. (1977) Small man politics and the rule of law: centre-periphery relations in East-Central Botswana. *Journal of African Law* 21: 24–39.

—— (1981) The quasi-judicial and the experience of the absurd: remaking land law in north-eastern Botswana. In *Land Reform in the Making* (ed.) R. Werbner. London: Collins.

—— (1991) *Tears of the Dead*. Edinburgh: Edinburgh University Press; Washington: Smithsonian Institution Press.

—— (1992) Elites and the geo-politics of land in Botswana, in *African Agrarian Systems* (eds) Thomas Bassett and Donald Crummey. Madison: Wisconsin University Press.

—— (1995) Human rights and moral knowledge: arguments of accountability in Zimbabwe. In *Shifting Contexts* (ed.) Marilyn Strathern. London: Routledge

—— (1998) Smoke from the barrel of a gun: postwars of the dead, memory and re-inscription in Zimbabwe. In *Memory and the Postcolony* (ed.) R. Werbner. London: Zed Books.

de Wet, C. (1989) Betterment planning in a rural village in Keiskammahoek, Ciskei. *Journal of Southern African Studies* 15, 2: 326–45.

Worby, E. (1994) Maps, names and ethnic games: the epistemology and iconography of colonial power in northwestern Zimbabwe. *Journal of Southern African Studies* 20, 3: 371–92.

—— n.d. *The (Un)Corrupted Anthropologist? On Morality, Reciprocity and Accountability in Development-Related Fieldwork* (unpublished manuscript). Yale University.

# Chapter 6

# The guardians of power

## Biodiversity and multiculturality in Colombia[1]

*Peter Wade*

In some circles, native American indians are often talked about as guardians of the environment. Here I examine the notions of power, control, empowerment and disempowerment involved in such a perception. In Colombia, not only indians are involved, since some rural black communities are also being construed in this way. At the same time, multiculturality has been instituted as an official reality in the nation such that the politics of cultural and biotic difference are intersecting in interesting ways. The tapping of powers of nature and culture takes place within a hall of mirrors where images of nature are reflected in culture and vice versa. The discourse of native guardianship or stewardship has very different meanings and political implications depending on who is using it and for what ends.

## Indians as guardians

Hornborg notes that 'throughout the world, environmental movements and indigenous movements have been developing in a kind of conceptual symbiosis' (1994: 246), but the idea of indians as guardians is perhaps most elaborated in a certain romantic primitivism. Harries-Jones notes that some First Nation people in Canada clash with environmental NGOs run by middle-class whites who, in the eyes of indigenous leaders, hijack First Nations' concerns with the protection of land and wildlife into a spiritual New Ageism and anti-industrialism that takes indian shamanism as an iconic symbol of oneness with nature (Harries-Jones 1993: 49).

In a recent volume produced by the IUCN on *Indigenous Peoples and Sustainability*, this kind of discourse extends into international development discourse.[2] It is stated that, 'Indigenous communities possess an *"environmental ethic"* developed from living in particular ecosystems' (IUCN 1997: 37). This ethic derives from features of their societies such as cooperation, family bonding and cross-generational communication and concern for the well-being of future generations, as well as self-sufficiency and restraint in natural resource exploitation. It is hard to see how the first set of features does not apply to virtually every human society, while the notion of 'restraint' presupposes an active process of self-denial which smacks of a puritanical ethnocentrism. It seems likely that indigenous people do not 'restrain' themselves, but rather live in culturally appropriate ways which usually cause little environmental damage. The IUCN volume, however, argues that 'the concept of sustainability is embodied in indigenous agricultural systems' (IUCN 1997: 36) through a whole range of practices. First, indigenous people conserve and foster diversity, by planting a wide variety of species. Second, they have a spiritual relation with the environment in which the earth is seen as a living being intimately related to people. Often there are rules about resource use, generally based on this spiritual relationship. Third, such people have a very detailed and intricate knowledge of local flora and fauna. In addition, landscapes that appear at first sight to be 'natural' may turn out to be have been 'managed' by indigenous people. The so-called 'forest islands' (*apete*) of the Kayapo, created in the forest by selective planting of certain types of trees, are cited as an example. Even apparently destructive practices, such as the common indigenous Amazonian practice of chopping down a whole tree to reach a beehive or certain fruits, can be re-read as the creation of forest space then filled with diverse plantings (IUCN 1997: chs. 3, 4). It is for these reasons that the Rio Declaration of the United Nations Conference on the Environment and Development states that, 'Indigenous people and their communities, and other local communities, have a vital role in environmental management and development because of their knowledge and traditional practices' (Principle 22, cited in IUCN 1997: 42).

All this may be true, but to assume that indigenous people (apparently constituting a homogeneous category) adhere to an 'environmental *ethic*' is taking the argument too far. Ellen takes apart the 'myth' of the ecological wisdom of native peoples, arguing that it assumes that such peoples are geographically isolated and that they are part of nature in a supposedly animal-like way; these societies may not degrade their environments (although they may do so as well), but this is because they are small and their impacts on the local ecology are diverse (Ellen 1986). The attitude of the Nuaulu of the Central Moluccas towards their environment, however, is one of 'hard-headed pragmatism' not conservationism; on the contrary, the idea that local timber and rainforest could become scarce is 'barely conceivable' to them (Ellen 1993: 141).

Bebbington is also critical of approaches that glorify 'indigenous technical knowledge'. The frequent failure of Green Revolution technologies has generated 'persuasive and powerful proposals [which] argue that viable agricultural development strategies must be based on indigenous peoples' technical knowledge' (1996: 89). Bebbington argues that this view, while it can be useful, tends to see indigenous knowledge as homogeneous and static, removing it from the context of the political economy in which indigenous people operate. Problems of ecological degradation and indigenous poverty are assumed to have essentially technical solutions. In the Ecuadorian Andes, indigenous federations happily adopted the use of certain 'modern' technologies (chemical fertilisers, high-yield crops, etc.) to combat the threat of falling incomes, out-migration and the collapse of indigenous society. The central question for Bebbington is that of local control over technologies, markets and land rather than shielding indigenous peoples from the 'modernisation' that capitalism was once thought not to be delivering and is now thought to be its main threat.

Bebbington notes that the commitment to native traditional techniques found among some development activists is 'often missing in indigenous peoples' organizations' (1996: 87), but this is by no means always the case. The Indigenous People's Earth Charter states that, 'Recognizing indigenous peoples' harmonious relationship with Nature, Indigenous sustainable development strategies and cultural values must be respected as distinct and vital sources of knowledge' (cited in IUCN 1997: 35). Similarly, Fisher observes that the Kayapo of the Brazilian Amazon purvey an image of themselves as resisting the threat of environmental degradation because it is in their 'nature' to do so. Fisher argues, however, that this is the essentialism of strategic engagement with the state, not 'environmental consciousness' as such (1994: 229–30). He traces Kayapo engagement with various elements of Brazilian society as they have impacted on Kayapo territory since 1945. Despite their relatively powerless position, the Kayapo manipulated extractive industry managers, government indigenous affairs agencies and now the federal government itself in order to promote their interests. Conserving land and forest is vital to these interests, but the point is not so much to preserve them *per se,* as to maintain the continuity of Kayapo society (Fisher 1994). However, when Kayapo pragmatism is re-read as an ethic of ecological consciousness by crusading environmentalists, the Kayapo are happy to feed back such images (more or less self-consciously) to an eager public. Or people simply remain unaware of the distance between the different discursive contexts which change the meaning of Kayapo behaviour from pragmatism to greenness.

In Colombia, the same patterns can be seen. Many indigenous organisations make much of the organic and mutually nurturing relationship between indians and the land. Meanwhile, the state has put 22 per cent of the nation's land surface under indian control (on paper, at least), including some of the most biotically diverse areas in the country and indeed in the world.

## The noble savage

The root of these ideas lies in the concept of the noble savage who, in the Rousseauesque version, represents the unsullied moral integrity that modern progress undermines. More generally, what is at issue here is a fundamental ambivalence about modernity. Whereas the civilising project of European countries has generally been seen as a positive step forward, the history of this process is also marked with doubtful and often backward glances which seek out an image of goodness in the very savagery against which civilisation is defined. This is one element in the long-running debates about the status

of the native Americans after their 'discovery' by Europeans. Were they inno-
cent Edenites or savage barbarians? Such questions betrayed a much greater preoccupation with 'civilisation' than with 'primitives': Rousseau's 'natural man'
was a construct for reflecting on the law and government of contemporary
Europe. The same ambivalence about modernity was present in the Romantic
movement with its search – begun not surprisingly during the Enlightenment –
for an expressive inner life and an unsullied nature, seen as threatened by the
excesses of reason, science and technology. Against these forces of progress,
the movement deployed the sublimities of wild nature, the quixotic romance
of the medieval past, the supernatural, the emotive imagination – and the
American indian. The power of the ambivalence about modernity is shown
by the striking fact that Romanticism was harnessed to such ideologies of
modernity as nationalism and abolitionism.

More recently, the same ambivalence is evident in the Primitivist movements
of early twentieth-century art and literature. Jean Franco argues that the
European avant-garde's attention to savagery, to its supposed emotive and sen-
sual force, spurred the development of *indigenismo* and *negrismo* movements in
Latin American intellectual circles, glorifying American indians and, to a
much lesser extent, Latin American blacks (Franco 1967; see also Torgovnick
1990). Such literary interests interwove political nationalism with challenges
to Euro-American definitions of the racial purity needed for a modern
nation-state. Interestingly, alongside indians and blacks, the third focus of
these literary movements was, according to Franco, land itself, a repository of
integrity, rootedness, identity, wholesomeness and value.

To see indians as guardians of the environment today fits into a long-standing
tradition of challenging the 'dark side' of modernity and of looking to realms
considered to be before or beyond modernity to sustain those doubts.

## The power of the Other

I want to take this further by focusing on power. It is not enough to observe
that modernity has always had its counter-current nor that current and
counter-current have always been in a relation of ambivalence, opposed yet
merging, imitating while deriding each other. It is also necessary to observe
that each taps the other for the powers it is held or claims to have: they feed
off each other, empowering and disempowering in unpredictable ways. This
is perhaps most evident in a colonial relationship, where the relation between
modernity and its alter is most clearly that between modernity and primitivism
(Bhabha 1994; Young 1995).

Taussig explores this ambivalent interdependence, taking up ideas about the
'wild powers' of indians and blacks and their relation to 'civilisation'. In
Colombia, indians are a tiny minority, yet 'the enormity of the magic attributed
to those Indians is striking' (1987: 171). The more 'savage' and remote the
indians, the more powerful they are said to be – even among the indians them-

selves. The power they are said to control is coveted for its influence in the resolution of life's classic problems – *amor, salud y dinero* (love, health and money). Indian curers can be found in frontier towns and in the major cities. The hallucinogenic drink, *yagé*, used in ritual curing, comes from the Amazon region, but is also on sale in Bogotá. Taussig argues that this attribution of magical power is 'a cunningly wrought colonial *objet d'art*': it stems from ideas about 'wild men' – savage yet powerful – that existed before the conquest of the Americas and were transferred on to indians; it is also, however, 'third world modernism, a neocolonial reworking of primitivism' (1987: 172) since with the spread of capitalism people feel more distant from the source of 'primitive' strength, making indians seem yet more powerful and magical.

In a more recent work, Taussig develops the idea of the interdependence of modernity and primitivism. Like many other commentators, Taussig contends that civilisation needs primitivism to establish difference and hierarchy (1993: 79). More than this, however, civilisation uses primitivism to routinise and naturalise its achievements. Taussig uses the example of the dog logo of His Master's Voice, an original painting purchased for use as a logo by the Victor Talking Machine Company. The dog, here representing the primitive, the animal senses, attests to the naturalness of the sound produced with its naturally acute sense of hearing and auditory discrimination – yet it is fooled or at least confused (hence its quizzical expression) because it is paying attention to a talk-ing machine. The dog brings out the naturalness of the machine, but also the wizardry of the technology – Edison said he was never so taken aback in his life when he heard himself singing 'Mary Had a Little Lamb' (Taussig 1993: 211). This wizardry, however, becomes 'second nature' to later generations. This is the crucial point: as second nature it is routinised and naturalised.

Taussig also observes that the Kuna indian women of Panama's San Blas islands are well known for their use of emblems from popular Western culture in their *molas* or appliquéd designs stitched on to blouses. One popular mola design is the HMV logo. Taussig notes that westerners are fascinated by the indians' apparent fascination with western technology and commodities: when Westerners see the HMV mola they laugh with pleasure. He argues that this is because the indians seem to portray Western technology in ways that 'bring out' its magical power (1993: 231). Thus, for example, the phono-graph was an important tool in many 'first contact' situations – explorers, anthropologists and other scientists were captivated by the ability of the phono-graph to captivate the natives. In addition, however, this captivation was often recorded, on camera, to demonstrate the magical effect of Western technology as attested to by 'magicians' themselves. Thus in Robert Flaherty's film, Nanook of the North is shown amazed by the phonograph and then testing the record with his teeth. As with the logic of the master's dog, his 'naturally' acute senses testify to the authenticity of the recording, but he is fooled in some way by the wizardry (1993: ch. 14).

Underlying all this is mimesis. This is in one sense a human faculty – 'the nature that culture uses to create second nature' (1993: xiii) – the symbolic or representational faculty if you will; but it also has a (colonial) history. Mimesis involves copying, but also contact – similarity and contagion in Frazerian terms. The copy carries within it something of the sensuousness and concreteness of the original; it involves copying but also becoming, immersion in, the Other; hence the power of the symbol (1993: 21). In the history of mimesis, this sensuousness has often been linked to the primitive: for Hegel, sensuous immediacy was an original state of consciousness; for Horkheimer and Adorno, spontaneous mimesis had been taken over by controlled mimesis; for many explorers and scientists, it was 'the natives' who seemed to have uncanny powers of mimicry (Taussig 1993: chs. 4, 6). The primitive has been attributed the power to do and thus to validate mimesis. Primitivism is thus 'implicit in technology's wildest dreams' (1993: 208), because it makes technology second nature and yet also mysterious.

Thus there is an intimate connection between civilisation and primitivism, modernity and tradition, indians (and blacks) and the modernising nation-state. How does this relate to the question of indians (and possibly blacks) as guardians of the environment and to the state-directed development of bio-diversity? My argument is that, in Colombia, the state is beginning to use indians (and to a lesser extent blacks) to naturalise future technologies of synthesis and at the same time to legitimate political projects of democracy based on ideas of 'unity in diversity' (for many, the problematic of anthropology itself, but also a classic refrain of nationalism). Biodiversity and multiculturality intersect in the state's attempt to control and exploit the power of difference. This is not in itself an unprecedented development. What is interesting here is the spread of such intersecting discourses and their normalisation at different levels: the state, alternative developmentalists and indigenous peoples themselves. Yet it is vital to see the different potentials involved in such discourses and practices. First, however, I want to look in a little more detail at the primitivist notions at the heart of modernity, distinguishing between blacks and indians in the Latin American context as potential candidates for being summoned as guardians of the forest.

## Blacks and indians

From the start, native Americans had a rather different status from Africans in the Latin American social and racial order. Both categories were deemed savage, barbarian and pagan, but there were also differences. In the sixteenth century, slavery was deemed not a fit status for indians (although they continued to be enslaved illegally in some areas). They were vassals of the Crown and there was doubt as to whether they could ever be captives of a 'just war' against infidels (a legitimate cause of enslavement at the time), since they had never heard the word of God. Africans, on the other hand, were well-established as infidels under Muslim influence, enslavement of them was already practised in Europe and the legitimacy of enslavement was a distant question since relations with Africans were of trade, not colonisation and settlement.

Indian identity was relatively institutionalised compared to black identity (Wade 1993: ch. 2). Despite physical and cultural intermixture, the category of *indio* was embedded in colonial thought and practice. Indian identity was firmly established in the indian community within which lived tributary subjects of the Crown and from which could be extracted tributary labour. This community itself was largely a colonial creation, but indian identity was intimately linked to the land, to being on specific bits of land which underwrote their continuity. Blacks, in contrast, were rarely enumerated as such in colonial administration. Slaves were carefully counted, but free blacks entered into the amorphous ranks of the mixed – those who officially were neither slave, nor white, nor indian – where powerful distinctions of race and social condition existed but were rather indeterminate and less institutionalised.

After independence, the dominance of liberal thought brought a sustained attack on indian as an administrative category and on indian land: a free market in land and goods and common political citizenship were the ideals. Towards the end of the nineteenth century, however, the practical failure of attempts to abolish indianness as a social and legal reality in the new nations was complemented by the softening of the policies that aimed to achieve this. Indians continued to have a specific juridical and political status in many Latin American countries. The trend of *indigenismo* in politics and literature that spread across much of the continent in the early decades of the twentieth century reinforced this trend, glorifying antique indigenous origins. The indian community survived, based as before on landholding. It became the favourite subject of anthropological investigation.

In contrast, 'black communities' existed but they had no administrative status that was different from any other peasant community. Therefore although 'black' was a recognised social category and blacks suffered discrimination as such, they were seen as ordinary (albeit 'inferior') citizens. They were not Other in the same way as indians, they were not perceived as tied to the land in the same way, they were rarely held up as a symbol of national identity or as the object of anthropological attention (Wade 1993).

Meanwhile, indians were and still are venerated for their real or supposed healing powers, especially jungle indians (Taussig 1987). Blacks were and are also seen as healers – especially in Cuba and Brazil where the evident African-ness present in black religious culture favours such imaginings, but also in the Pacific coastal area of Colombia where a long history of social segregation, poverty and blackness combine to create a black Other that is not so different from the alterity attributed to indians in that country. Even so, jungle indians are admitted by everyone to be the most powerful sorcerers and healers. Blacks tend more often to be attributed powers as musicians, dancers and sexual athletes – powers which may be imagined as very healing for the tortured and alienated modern soul.

Indians are therefore good candidates to be labelled – and to label themselves – as guardians of the environment: tied to the land, defenders of the institutions which defined that tie, controllers of mystical forces, some of which emanate from the land. There is the imaginative possibility of a mystical participation between indian and land.

Blacks are less likely to be labelled or label themselves in this way. The Pacific coastal region of Colombia is an interesting area to examine this domain of the colonial and neo-colonial imagination. An area minimally settled by the Spanish, it was exploited with slave and indian labour for gold deposits. After abolition, blacks and indians continued to live there, with blacks doing most of the mining. Although mining was a small-scale activity, it was still more environmentally damaging than agriculture. The use of pumps, mini-dredgers and mechanical diggers speeded up such destruction. Although this degradation was presaged by multinational mining companies at work since the early decades of this century and some of the destruction is caused today by big companies and incoming capitalists, much of it is still in the hands of small-scale local black operators. Local blacks are also used as labour in the lumbering activities, controlled mainly by large timber firms, that are also destroying large areas of forest. In short, then, local blacks are less easily imagined as environmental guardians.

In his attempted reassessment, Colombian anthropologist Jaime Arocha characterises black peasants and urban migrants living in the Tumaco area of the southern Pacific coast as having a highly flexible and inventive culture that allows them to adapt to a changing ecological niche and the instability of a boom–bust economy (Arocha 1991). He argues that government biologists working in the area see the blacks as 'anti-environmentalist' because, for example, they fish with fine-weave nets that damage the diversity of marine species. He responds that, in a political economy of externally controlled natural resource exploitation, the local blacks do whatever is necessary in order to live in a context of extreme uncertainty about the future. The implication is that any environmentally unfriendly activities are not the fault, as it were, of the blacks, and also that these will be of short duration as new ways are found of making ends meet. Arocha tries to link this flexibility with what he calls *huellas de africanía* (traces, tracks or prints of Africanness), i.e., the presence of African cultural elements or cognitive orientations in Afrocolombian culture (1991: 93–6). This is, in my view, a dubious exercise in this particular case, since inventiveness and flexibility are human rather than African traits. It is interesting, however, that Arocha tries to supply deep-seated cultural roots to legitimate black attitudes to the environment, just as indians have their own traditions of ties to the land to legitimate their potential role as guardians.

In more recent work focused on the Baudó River valley of the northern Pacific coast region – a more rural area where mining is less important –

Arocha restates the idea of a 'polyphonic economy' that he described for Tumaco and explicitly sees this as preserving the biodiversity of the region. From a Batesonian perspective, he elaborates the notion of *sentipensamiento* (feeling-thought), a mode of being integrating rational thought and emotions, which is opposed to the destructive efficiencies of capitalism. He states that many people consider indians to have this mode of being, but suggests that black groups also have a high degree of environmental *sentipensamiento*.[3]

Like Arocha, Restrepo sees the black peasants' exploitation of the forest (mostly through timber-cutting) of the Satinga River region, just north of Tumaco, as driven by the priorities of an externally controlled economic system. However, while he recognises that, for these blacks, there is no sharp break between person and environment, he denies that these people have any relation of 'profound harmony' with their environment, or that they seek to conserve it. For them the forest is exploited by means of destruction – and this is not dangerous because, to them, the idea that the forest might 'run out' is absurd; nor can its reproduction be promoted since the forest is born spontaneously from the soil, not through the intervention of people (Restrepo 1996a: 344–6). Terms such as biodiversity, resources and nature, as employed by environmentalists and developers, do not map semantically onto the concepts of local black peasants (Restrepo 1996b: 240)

## Biodiversity and multiculturality

This re-imagining of black identity is taking place in the context of a redefinition of Colombian nationhood. In 1991, a new constitution formally recognised Colombia as a multicultural and pluri-ethnic nation, replacing the 1886 constitution which recognised no such diversity and underwrote a concept of the nation as culturally, religiously, politically and legally homogeneous. Indigenous organisations played a significant role in the drafting of the new constitution which contained articles protecting indigenous cultural, political and land rights. Black organisations were younger, less consolidated and had less national and international backing. Many Constituent Assembly delegates were opposed to seeing blacks as an 'ethnic group' with a legitimate claim to special treatment (Arocha 1992). The constitution did, however, include a provisional article which later resulted in Law 70 of 1993, which defined land rights for rural riverine Afrocolombian communities in the Pacific coastal region and outlined the defence of cultural rights for black communities in Colombia as a whole. This initiated a convergence between black identity and indian identity in the national arena of cultural politics: both identities were seen to be based on the 'traditional community', rooted in the land and defined by cultural difference (Wade 1995).

The new constitution and the re-imagining of black identity also took place in the context of the opening up of the Colombian economy to the international free market. The Pacific coastal region was seen by the state as crucial in the development of economic openness, since it is located within the Pacific basin, supposedly the future focus of the global economy. Large-scale plans were proposed for the region, mostly outlining infrastructural investment to create 'development' of a standard modernisationist kind. Even so, the name given to the latest of these plans included the words 'sustainable development' (Departamento Nacional de Planeación, *Plan Pacífico: Una Nueva Estrategia de Desarrollo Sostenible para la Costa Pacífica Colombiana*, 1992). In 1992 the government also started Proyecto BioPacífico, funded by the World Bank and the United Nations, aimed at cataloguing biodiversity and finding sustainable resource-use options (Barnes 1993; Escobar and Pedrosa 1996).

Here, then, is the confluence of three processes: multiculturalism, neo-liberal economic restructuring and environmentalism. The links between the last two are examined by Escobar (1997) for the Pacific coastal region. Following O'Connor (1993), he suggests that capital has entered an 'ecological phase' in which it has two tendencies, destructive and modernisationist on the one hand and conservationist on the other. These correspond to two successive but overlapping regimes for the production of nature: one in which nature is seen as external to capital, to be appropriated and exploited; another in which nature itself is reconstructed by science, as technology permits intervention into genetics and organisms become cyborg ensembles of organic and technological elements. 'Conservation' therefore is largely about maintaining or creating the biotic environment as a reservoir of (future) value for capital – in a word, bio-imperialism. As O'Connor argues:

> Capitalism, through purporting to take a hand in the reproduction of the conditions of production, tries to invent a new legitimation for itself – *the sustainable and rational use of the environment*. This process is aided by the co-option of individuals and social movements in the 'conservation' game.
>
> (1993: 9)

Escobar notes that local people in tropical rainforest areas may then be cast as custodians or stewards (see also O'Connor 1993: 11). Although Escobar looks at black collective political action and identity formation in the Pacific coastal region as a reaction against the 'development' taking place there, I think the intersection between multiculturality and the other two processes (restructuring and environmentalism) is worth examining in more depth.

In Colombia, I am interested in the intersection between official multiculturalism, official environmentalism and neo-liberal restructuring within an overall project of state control. Environmentalism and minority rights movements may be growing in some kind of symbiosis (Hornborg 1994), but so are state-oriented versions of these trends. The idea is widespread that 'the goal of sustainable development is inseparable from the goal of maintaining cultural diversity' (Gedicks 1996: 37), but the political potential and implications of these ideas need to be assessed very sceptically when they become part of state discourse. The link of biodiversity with cultural diversity may be seen as a positive sign, but political and symbolic co-option or subsumption is a continuous process.

Official multiculturality in Colombia is linked to a great extent with the defusing of indian and black protest. It is also a process of compensating (at least symbolically) local groups located in zones of strategic economic interest in a process of economic restructuring and integration into a free world market. In this regard, Colombia is no different from many other instances: official multiculturality is generally a way of defusing protest. When twinned with the protection of 'nature' in Latin America, the whole history of colonial and postcolonial imaginings of indian and, to a lesser extent, black powers comes into play. And, as in Taussig's argument, with the construction of indians and blacks as custodians of nature, the wizardry of (future) technology in the synthesis of chemicals and the construction of genotypes is underwritten as nature – or second nature – but is also magical. It is naturalised because it is attested to by indians (and blacks) whose nature, according to primitivism, naturally detects the natural; it is magical, because of indians' (and blacks') wonderous powers of curing and their mystical participation in nature. It is no coincidence that Kayapo leader Ropni's most publicised magic was his attempt to cure a Brazilian naturalist of cancer (Fisher 1994: 222), while one of the wonders held out by the promise of yet unanalysed biodiverse reservoirs of genes and chemicals is a synthesised cure for cancer.

Twinning multiculturality with biodiversity is also about the control of the power of difference. Cultural difference is a source of threat – the undermining of national unity, the disruption of order. But it is necessary to the establishment of hierarchy and the valorisation of civilisation; in Colombia, it is necessary in order to think the possibility of a country that draws unity from diversity. Biotic difference is likewise a threat – the uncontrollable savagery of nature which must be tamed for orderly production (Merchant 1996: ch. 2). But it is also necessary for continued invention. Capitalism works from difference and reproduces difference – the differences it works on include those of gender, race, class and ethnicity, as well as locality.

Difference, as well as sameness, is at the heart of projects of production and domination. As Asad says:

> The claim that many radical critics make that hegemonic power necessarily suppresses difference in favour of unity is quite mistaken. Just as mistaken is their claim that power always abhors ambiguity. To secure its unity – to make its own history – dominant power has worked best through differentiating and classifying practices.
>
> (1993: 17)

Difference is located everywhere and can be reproduced by many different agents; the point is that it is also reproduced by the state or, more generally, by dominant powers (cf. Bhabha 1994: 145-7). It is not new to point out that capitalism works by exploiting difference; it is commonplace to observe that capitalism exploits differences of place, race and gender in the labour force. Foucault also highlighted the importance of the abnormal and different to processes of normalisation. But recent emphases on the homogenising power of state discourses have tended to obscure how the state can work through *normal*, non-pathological differences to achieve subtle effects of co-option and domination.

Multiculturality is about controlling cultural difference, trying to give it delimited and predictable space. It legitimates projects of democratisation by reference to natural human difference. I am not talking here about attributions of genetic or, more broadly, biological difference: most state discourse does not tread such racist ground. Rather, ideas of multiculturality tend to naturalise cultural differences as deeply ingrained; they also evoke cultural difference among humans as itself a fact of human nature – humans are naturally diverse, even if the shapes taken by that diversity are plastic. Therefore it is 'only natural' to recognise such difference, which is worked into ideas of (postmodern) democratisation. Interweaving multiculturality with biodiversity thus naturalises human difference and uses that naturalisation to naturalise the technology that will eventually make biodiversity produce the wizardry that will soon become second nature.

Indian and black organisations in Colombia mobilise to contest and influence official visions of development – most of which is still 'business as normal' (not to mention overt repression) – and they have been successful in challenging specific aspects of change (e.g. in the Pacific coastal region: Atkins and Rey-Maqueira Palmer 1996). But the language of biodiversity and multiculturality that they sometimes employ is subject to resignification by official discourses in ways that undermine their objectives. This newly emerging state discourse and action in Colombia involves deeply rooted interdependencies between ideas of modernity and primitivism, built around the colonially and post-colonially elaborated images of indian and, in a different but seemingly converging way, black powers. In this process, a difficult and ambiguous line is trodden between, on the one hand, pointing out that local peoples may have modes of resource use that are sustainable and possibly helpful in thinking about social and environmental change in ways that protect those peoples' livelihoods and, on the other, invoking essentialist and romantic images of Otherness which work towards controlling and exploiting those people and their territories. As Merchant shows for the case of environmentalism and feminism – where many of the same issues arise – there are many different positions that can be taken in this respect and ecofeminism need not be essentialist in this way:

Appropriated representations [of nature as female] can be apolitical, ahistorical, acontextual and essentialist. Yet most images are reinterpreted, recontextualized and given new meaning by later societies and social movements. They can be used to show how essentialist notions, such as the conflation of women and nature, are historically constructed over time and function to keep women in their place as 'natural' caretakers or green homemakers. Yet reclaiming and recontextualizing past images does not mean people are necessarily chained to the past or advocating a romantic return to it, but instead are claiming the power to change it.

(Merchant 1996: xxi)

Yet she cautions that, in her view, the 'cultural baggage associated with images of nature as female means that gendering nature is at present too problematical to be adopted by emancipatory social movements in Western societies' (1996: xxii). Likewise, images of indians and blacks as the natural custodians of nature, while they may be useful as strategic essentialisms, are also fraught with dangers which play very easily into the strategies to control difference outlined in this chapter.

These issues are of central significance because they raise the question of the potential of social movements for real change. The question is whether *anything* that indigenous and black communities say and do in Colombia will inevitably be co-opted by the state. State politics in Colombia is a sort of enclosed, self-referential circuit which deals with antagonisms through violent repression, often masked as 'uncontrollable' paramilitary activity, and through co-option. The state is generally only interested in mediation when it can define the channels through which mediation take place. For example, in the political negotiations that led to a law giving black communities in the Pacific region legitimate claims to special land rights, the state named black organisations to represent the communities in the drafting process. Some of these organisations did not yet exist at the time of their naming and were, in a partial but never-theless real sense, created by the state (Wade 1995). However, such organisa-tions can also go beyond the hand that created them in the first place.[4] Just as the discourse of indigenous greenness can play in different ways – legitimat-ing the neo-liberal restructuring and funding strategies of the state, but also the struggle for autonomy of indigenous groups – so these organisations cannot necessarily be limited to their original remit. A struggle continues over how to shape and direct social change. It is not, of course, a new struggle, but a continuing struggle which takes new forms – now it is taking on the mantle of multiculturality and biodiversity, both terms that have different political potentials. Given the power of the state in Colombia to both bulldoze and co-opt, I do not feel sanguine about the future.

## Notes

1 I am grateful to John Hutnyk and to Dick Werbner for comments on an earlier draft of this chapter.
2 Membership of the World Conservation Union (originally the International Union for Conservation of Nature and Natural Resources) in 1996 included 72 states, 99 government agencies and 693 NGOs in 133 countries.
3 This perspective is outlined in a project proposal, 'Biodiversidad y sentipensamiento chocoanos' (Jaime Arocha, Centro de Estudios Sociales, Universidad Nacional de Colombia, Bogotá, September 1992) to which Arocha was kind enough to give me access.
4 Hardt and Negri develop the Marxist idea that capitalism creates forces that it cannot ultimately control. When the state dealt with the antagonisms involved in the exploitation of labour by cooperating with labour in the creation of a welfare-based civil society, it created forms of organisation of labour that later become 'independent of the organizational capacity of capital', and the basis of a new subjectivity that is a 'fundamental figure of resistance' (1994: 282, 283). This is despite the fact that the whole of society has become a factory and the logic of capitalist production is pervasive, leading to the emergence of the postmodern state in which civil society withers away, the institutional trade unions weaken, the state rules not so much through discipline as through control, and civil society only exists as a sort of simulacrum projected by a state that circulates images within a controlled system (1994: 257, 261).

## References

Arocha, J. (1991) La ensenada de Tumaco: invisibilidad, incertidumbre e innovación. *America Negra* 1: 87–111.
—— (1992) Afro-Colombia denied. *NACLA Report on the Americas* 25, 4: 28–31.
Asad, T. (1993) *Genealogies of Religion: Discipline and Reasons of Power in Christianity and Islam*. Baltimore, MD: Johns Hopkins University Press.
Atkins, A. and Rey-Maqueira Palmer, E. (1996) *Ethno-Development: A Proposal to Save Colombia's Pacific Coast*. London: Catholic Institute for International Relations.
Barnes, J. (1993) *The Colombian Plan Pacífico: Sustaining the Unsustainable*. London: Catholic Institute for International Relations.
Bebbington, A. (1996) Movements, modernizations and markets: indigenous organizations and agrarian strategies in Ecuador. In *Liberation Ecologies: Environment, Development, Social Movements* (eds) R. Peet and M. Watts. London: Routledge (pp. 86–109).
Bhabha, H. (1994) *The Location of Culture*. London: Routledge.
Ellen, R. (1986) What Black Elk left unsaid: on the illusory images of Green primitivism. *Anthropology Today* 2, 6: 8–13.
—— (1993) Rhetoric, practice and incentive in the face of the changing times: a case study in Nuaulu attitudes to conservation and deforestation. In *Environmentalism: The View from Anthropology* (ed.) Kay Milton. London: Routledge (pp. 126–43).
Escobar, A. (1997) Cultural politics and biological diversity: state, capital and social movements in the Pacific coast of Colombia. Paper presented at the Guggenheim Foundation Conference on Dissent and Direct Action in the Late Twentieth Century, Otavalo, Ecuador, 15–19 June 1994. Published in revised form in *Between*

*Resistance and Revolution: Cultural Politics and Social Protest* (eds) R.G. Fox and O. Starn (1998) New Brunswick, NJ: Rutgers University Press.

—— and Pedrosa, A. (eds) (1996) *Pacífico ¿Desarrollo o diversidad? Estado, capital y movimientos sociales en el Pacífico colombiano.* Bogotá: CEREC, ECOFONDO.

Fisher, W.H. (1994) Megadevelopment, environmentalism, and resistance: the institutional context of Kayapó indigenous politics in central Brazil. *Human Organization* 53, 3: 220–32.

Franco, J. (1967) *The Modern Culture of Latin America: Society and the Artist.* London: Pall Mall Press.

Gedicks, A. (1996) Native people and sustainable development. In *Green Guerrillas: Environmental Conflicts and Initiatives in Latin America and the Caribbean* (ed.) H. Collinson. London: Latin America Bureau (pp. 34–9).

Hardt, M. and Negri, A. (1994) *Labor of Dionysus: A Critique of the State-Form.* Minneapolis: University of Minnesota Press.

Harries-Jones, P. (1993) Between science and shamanism: the advocacy of environmentalism in Toronto. In *Environmentalism: The View from Anthropology* (ed.) Kay Milton. London: Routledge. (pp. 43–58.)

Hornborg, A. (1994) Environmentalism, ethnicity and sacred places: reflections on modernity, discourse and power. *Canadian Review of Sociology and Anthropology* 31, 3: 245–67.

IUCN (1997) *Indigenous Peoples and Sustainability: Cases and Actions.* Utrecht: International Books.

Merchant, C. (1996) *Earthcare: Women and the Environment.* London: Routledge.

O'Connor, M. (1993) On the misadventures of capitalist nature. *Capitalism, Nature, Socialism* 4, 4: 1–34.

Restrepo, E. (1996a) Los tuqueros del Pacífico Sur de Colombia. In *Renacientes del Guandal: 'grupos negros' de los ríos Satinga y Sanquianga* (eds) J. Ignacio del Valle and E. Restrepo. Bogotá: Proyecto Biopacífico and Universidad Nacional (pp. 243–348).

—— (1996b) Cultura y biodiversidad. In *Pacífico ¿Desarollo o diversidad? Estado, capital y movimientos sociales en el Pacífico colombiano* (eds) A. Escobar and A. Pedrosa. Bogotá: CEREC, ECOFONDO (pp. 220–41).

Taussig, M. (1987) *Shamanism, Colonialism and the Wild Man: A Study in Terror and Healing.* Chicago: Chicago University Press.

—— (1993) *Mimesis and Alterity: A Particular History of the Senses.* London: Routledge.

Torgovnick, M. (1990) *Gone Primitive: Savage Intellects, Modern Lives.* Chicago: University of Chicago Press.

Wade, P. (1993) *Blackness and Race Mixture: The Dynamics of Racial Identity in Colombia.* Baltimore, MD: Johns Hopkins University Press.

—— (1995) The cultural politics of blackness in Colombia. *American Ethnologist* 22, 2: 342–58.

Young, R. (1995) *Colonial Desire: Hybridity in Theory, Culture and Race.* London: Routledge.

# Chapter 7

# The dialectics of negation and negotiation in the anthropology of mineral resource development in Papua New Guinea

*Colin Filer*

George Marcus has recently discussed the development of a 'multi-sited' form of ethnography which moves:

> from its conventional single-site location, contextualized by macro-constructions of a larger social order, such as the capitalist world system, to multiple sites of observation and participation that cross-cut dichotomies such as the 'local' and the 'global,' the 'lifeworld' and the 'system'.
>
> (1995: 95)

This multilocal form of ethnographic inquiry is one which may, amongst other things, serve to locate a variety of communities or stakeholders in the 'social grounds that produce a discourse of policy' (ibid.: 100).

Reflecting on his own social impact assessment of a prospective mining project at Wapolu in Milne Bay Province, Papua New Guinea (PNG), Michael Young made up the following allegory to explain this particular piece of 'quick and dirty' research to the people of the impact area:

> The house of custom is full of many things, some of them robust and some of them fragile. Some things are in daily use, others lie on shelves to be taken down and admired occasionally. The Government comes and asks the Householder one day, 'Will you let this stranger come to stay for a while? He needs to find something under your house, something you cannot use yourself, but which will benefit us both if he can find it.' The Householder lets him enter. But the Company is a blind man. During his search he stumbles and fumbles under and around the house, knocking things over and sometimes breaking them. While he pays for some of his blunders, the Householder is terrified of what damage he might do next. Now the Government in its wisdom invites an Anthropologist, who is not quite as blind as the Company, to ask the Householder how the search is going, and how best he might take the blind man by the hand and guide him away from the fragile things in his house.
>
> (1987: 3)

In this chapter I shall explore the significance of this allegorical 'policy narrative' by proposing: that a multilocal, multivocal and multifocal form of ethnographic inquiry has *already* developed out of the political setting of mineral resource development in PNG; that this form of inquiry normally begins with an assessment of the perceived interests of each 'stakeholder' in this political setting *by means of dialogue with all of them*; and that *this particular setting* is one in which it *normally* does make more sense for anthropologists to act as 'honest brokers' in mediating the relationships between different stakeholders (including the multinational companies) than it does to act as the partisans or advocates of local communities in their struggle against the 'world capitalist system'.

On the other hand, there will always be *specific circumstances* in which the anthropologist is obliged by the dynamics of the public policy process to adopt a more radical position, of the kind associated with a unilocal, univocal and unifocal form of ethnography, where the goal of 'political anthropology' is to achieve a transfer of power from the 'system' to the 'community'. For this reason, it is necessary for the discipline to develop something akin to a 'code of practice', whereby the necessity or desirability of movements between the radical and the moderate position can *also* be negotiated, within particular political settings, in order to avoid a breakdown in the dialogue which constitutes the discipline itself.

A 'political setting' is defined here as something which is necessarily larger than a single 'community', which may be equivalent to a single jurisdiction (or nation-state), but which will normally also have some sectoral component – e.g. 'health', 'conservation', 'mining', etc. Further analysis reveals that this sectoral component is a bundle of policy problems. This means that a political setting can also be defined as *the intersection of an area and an issue*. In the present case, we may define the issue, or the basic policy problem, as 'the social and environmental impact of mineral resource development'. In any given political setting, there is a *policy process* in which political decisions are the outcome of stakeholder relations *and vice versa*. The political anthropologist is one type of stakeholder in this policy process – though we could perhaps say that 'radical' and 'moderate' anthropologists operating in the same setting would need to be counted as two different types of stakeholder because of the difference in their aims, perspectives and methods.

The radical version of political anthropology deserves this name because it assumes a radical and irreconcilable opposition of interest between strong and weak stakeholders in some or all political settings. In the case considered here, it assumes that such an opposition exists between a variety of multinational corporations and government agencies on the one side and a variety of 'landowning communities' or 'indigenous peoples' on the other. The radical position thus contains an essentially dualistic conception of stakeholder relations which resembles the classical Marxist conception of the 'class struggle', even though most radical anthropologists would substitute some other category for the proletariat. The role of the radical anthropologist in the process of 'empowerment' is normally understood to involve some combination of 'local and global' action, where a particular 'community' which has been the subject of intensive ethnographic study gains additional power from the advice, material assistance or mere presence of the anthropologist, while the anthropologist *also* seeks to mobilise additional opposition to the main source of this community's oppression or disadvantage by 'advocating' their cause before some kind of global jury whose paradoxical function is to pass judgement on the fundamental conflict of interest identified in a given setting (see Kirsch 1996). In the setting considered here, this third party is generally identified with a middle-class 'environmental lobby' in the 'developed countries'.

The moderate version of political anthropology deserves this name because it is the position of the moderator, the mediator, the negotiator. This moderating position assumes the existence of several stakeholders in a given setting, whose interests are not necessarily, or even normally, such as to place them in one of two opposing camps, either in reality or in their own consciousness. In other words, this position prefers a pluralistic conception of the policy process, in which the ethical constraints on anthropological practice are construed as rules regulating the flow of information between stakeholders, and where the 'business' of the anthropologist is to function as a messenger whose messages are justified primarily by the contribution which they make to various kinds of 'agreement' over the terms and conditions of the development process. In this case, the object or subject of study is not a 'community' (or even a group of them), but the *structure of the political setting or the policy process itself*. The anthropologist becomes a kind of policy analyst or political scientist whose practice can still be distinguished in terms of 'local knowledge' and 'participant observation' because of the need to engage in *real dialogue* with all the other players in the game.

Both of the approaches or positions distinguished here are forms of *political* anthropology, whose *common* assumption would be that the anthropologist has a right or duty to engage in a policy process within a particular setting. When I say that one way of doing political anthropology makes 'more sense' than another, within a particular setting, I am making a statement about the extent to which each approach can succeed *on its own terms*. The relative viability, effectiveness or justification of the two positions cannot be determined at a global level. This might be construed (by radicals) as a moderate rather than a radical argument. But what I mean to say is that the capacity of anthropologists to achieve the objectives which they set themselves in *either* of the two positions described here varies a good deal between different political settings.

## The recent history of mineral resource development

The neo-colonial phase of mineral resource development in PNG began in 1962, when a visiting United Nations mission criticised the failure of the

Australian colonial administration to make plans for the immediate economic development of the Territory (see O'Faircheallaigh 1984). As a consequence, the Australian government encouraged a new round of hard-rock mineral exploration in the hope that large-scale mining would sooner or later yield a substantial portion of the revenues needed to pay for the development of PNG's indigenous 'human resources'. In 1964 Conzinc Riotinto of Australia (CRA) identified a substantial porphyry copper and gold deposit at Panguna on the island of Bougainville. Despite the evidence of local opposition to the prospect of large-scale mining, the Australian administration agreed to the company's development plans in 1967. The mine started production in 1972, just after elections to the Territory's House of Assembly had produced a nationalist government, under the leadership of Michael Somare, whose principal demand was an early end to the colonial regime. The Somare government achieved self-government in 1973 and full independence in 1975. In the years between these two events, it re-negotiated the Bougainville Copper Agreement in order to secure what was generally regarded as a more rational and equitable distribution of mineral revenues between the company and the state (see Mikesell 1975).

By this time, a second mineral deposit, of similar size and substance, had been identified in Mount Fubilan, at the opposite end of the country, in the mountainous interior of mainland New Guinea, close to the border with the Indonesian province of Irian Jaya. However, the Somare government was unable to persuade Kennecott, the company responsible for this discovery, to develop it on terms which were similar to those contained in the renegotiated Bougainville Copper Agreement (see Jackson 1982). An agreement to develop the Ok Tedi mine (named after one of the rivers draining the slopes of Mount Fubilan) was only reached in 1981, after gold and copper prices had reached unusual heights. Ok Tedi Mining Limited (OTML), the joint venture established by this agreement, included Broken Hill Proprietary Ltd (BHP) as the operating partner, Amoco (the American oil company) and a consortium of German mining interests. The government also bought a 20 per cent stake in the joint venture, just as it had done in Bougainville Copper Ltd (BCL). The Ok Tedi mine started production in 1984.

The renegotiated Bougainville Copper Agreement was the cornerstone of a technocratic mineral policy regime designed by expatriate experts for the benefit of a national political elite whose own National Constitution appeared to commit them to a wide range of social democratic policies premised on the foresight and benevolence of central government. Although the economic components of this policy regime were sometimes presented as a set of mutually consistent propositions (see Tilton *et al.* 1986), most were manufactured from the stuff of compromise between the economic reasonings of public servants or consultants and the sort of rhetoric which held most obvious appeal to big- and small-time politicians. Despite these elements of compromise, the apparent stability of the technocratic policy regime during the first decade of national independence was partly responsible for a second mineral exploration boom which followed the rise in relevant commodity prices at the end of the 1970s and which seems to have reached its peak in 1988, thus producing several new prospects for development.

The 'postcolonial', 'postmodern', or 'anti-technocratic' phase of mineral resource development began in 1989, when a rebellion by militant landowners from BCL's lease areas and ethno-nationalist elements from other parts of North Solomons Province forced the closure of the Panguna copper mine. This sent proverbial shock waves through the mining industry, and has created an enduring crisis of governance for the state of PNG. One of the victims has been the coherence and influence of the technocratic policy regime and its supporters in the corridors of central government. On the other hand, the exploration boom which they were able to encourage during headier days has lived up to its promise of maintaining the country's economic dependency on the mining and petroleum sector, as well as providing a constant supply of fresh fuel for public debate over the distribution of the benefits. Placer Pacific secured a Special Mining Lease and Mining Development Contract for development of the Misima mine in Milne Bay Province in December 1987, and Misima Mines began production of gold and silver in June 1989. Placer also became the operating partner in the Porgera Joint Venture whose gold mine in Enga Province was granted the necessary approvals in May 1989 and started production in August 1990. The Kutubu Joint Venture received its Petroleum Development Licence in December 1990, with Chevron as its operating partner, and this project started exporting oil in June 1992. The national government has taken a minority equity stake in all these ventures, just as it did in BCL and OTML.

In 1995, PNG's mineral exports were valued at K2,435.4 million (equivalent to US$1,837.5 million), which represented 71.6 per cent of domestic exports. Crude oil exports from the Kutubu project accounted for roughly one-third, gold for another third, and copper and silver together for the remaining third of this total export value. Exports from the Ok Tedi, Porgera and Misima mines were worth about K916 million, K431 million and K172 million respectively. In 1995 the national government's Mineral Resources Stabilisation Fund collected K281.7 million from the mining and petroleum sector, most of it (91 per cent) in the form of corporate income tax. These receipts represented 18.9 per cent of the government's non-grant revenues, but a variety of other taxes levied on the mining and petroleum companies would probably have raised at least another K50 million, thus making the sector responsible for something between one quarter and one-third of all non-grant revenues.

Given the current extent of known mineral reserves, the Kutubu, Ok Tedi, Porgera and Misima projects are all destined to cease operation before the year 2010. On the other hand, a number of new mining and petroleum projects were still in the pipeline at the end of 1995. Two 'medium-scale' gold mines (Tolukuma and Wapolu) both started production in December of that year, and two or three more are likely to be developed in 1997. Of far greater significance, in both its scale and its duration, is the development of the Lihir gold mine in New Ireland Province, where production is now expected to start in May 1997, and the value of output is expected to average about K287 million a year for the first fifteen years of a 30–40 year mine life. The Gobe petroleum project, a virtual extension of the existing Kutubu project, received its development licence in 1996 and has thus extended PNG's role as an oil exporter for another few years. There has even been talk of developing a liquid natural gas project whose capital cost would be greater than the combined cost of all existing mining and petroleum operations.

## Social science and the technocratic policy regime

In the years since the Somare government first set out to modify the Bougainville Agreement, most of the books, reports and papers which have been published on the general subject of mining in PNG have been exclusively concerned with the derivation or merit of the technocratic policy regime. These concerns are also found in historical accounts of the actual process of negotiation between government and company representatives over the development of the Bougainville and Ok Tedi projects (O'Faircheallaigh 1984; Jackson 1982; Pintz 1984). But once outside the dismal intrigues of political economy, we find that other social scientists approached these projects from directions which have altered through the period in which each one was planned and executed. In the years before Independence, their view of the Bougainville project as a form of industrial development was understandably occluded by the clamourings of secessionism (see Mamak 1979). In the years after, when the introduction of the provincial government system had apparently taken the heat out of the secessionist movement, and Bougainville was no longer the flavour of the month, their interest in the Ok Tedi project (and other mining projects) was largely subsumed under the steadily unfurling banner of environmental planning and protection. Although some anthropologists were to be found on one or other of these battlefields, they never seemed to be too clear what they were doing there.

Douglas Oliver was possibly the one exception to this rule. By his own account (1991: xiv), Oliver was engaged as a consultant by BCL, from 1968 to 1978, to tell them how best to 'shield' the local population from the negative effects of their own operations. As part of this arrangement, BCL provided funding to the Pacific Islands Research Corporation at the University of Hawaii, and Oliver then distributed this money to other social scientists, so that they would be able to serve the planning needs of Bougainvillean leaders without appearing to be compromised by their corporate connections (see Wesley-Smith 1992). Despite Oliver's own professional standing (or possibly because of it), anthropologists had less to say about the social impact of the mine itself than did the other social scientists participating in the exercise. The nearest thing to an ethnographic account of this impact is to be found in Bedford and Mamak's (1977) monograph on the question of compensation, but neither of the authors was an anthropologist.

The fieldwork on which this monograph was based, like most of the other activities funded by Oliver's arrangement with BCL, had come to an end by the time that Kennecott decided to walk away from the Ok Tedi project. But this last episode was also the moment of Richard Jackson's initiation into the mysteries of the local mining industry, and receives a quasi-ethnographic treatment in his own (1982) account of technocrats as midwives in the labour of delivering this mine. Jackson's period of attachment to the Geography Department at the University of PNG, from 1975 to 1985, coincided with the life-span of his favourite government institution, the National Planning Office. He was the first social scientist to become actively involved in the planning of the Ok Tedi project, he actively coordinated its official socio-economic impact assessment, and he then tried to establish a socio-economic monitoring programme from his temporary base at the Institute of Applied Social and Economic Research. However, the experience of monitoring the mishaps of the construction phase caused a serious bout of disillusionment (see Jackson 1993), and so he turned his attention to the planning of new mining projects which might avoid some of the mistakes made at Ok Tedi – Lihir, Hidden Valley, Mount Kare and the Hides gasfield.

While I think it would be true to say that Jackson inherited Oliver's mantle as the key player in research on the social impact of the PNG mining industry, there were significant differences in both the academic character and the political context of his performance. Apart from his ill-fated attempt to organise the monitoring of the Ok Tedi project, Jackson had neither the opportunity nor inclination to take an entrepreneurial role in funding other people's research. The significance and influence of his own reflections on the mining industry (apart from their quantity and continuity) is a function of the personal and intellectual connections which he made between the practice of field research and the application of government policy under the technocratic regime. In this sense, his work is especially pertinent to the problems which the rise and decline of this policy regime poses for the practice of anthropology.

Anthropologists got more engaged in studying the social impact of the mining industry during the period from 1975 to 1989, partly because the discipline was obliged to prove its relevance to the monumental task of national development, and partly because anthropologists and other social scientists were persuaded, and often paid, to participate in the process of environmental planning for major resource projects.

There were four anthropologists who figured prominently amongst the bundle of social scientists who followed Jackson's lead and involved themselves in the planning of the Ok Tedi project. Rob Welsch was a member of Jackson's official social impact study team (Jackson et al. 1980), although the larger part of his contribution to this enterprise was rather curiously omitted from the final report (see Welsch 1987). David Hyndman was one of the scientists who contributed to the truly monumental environmental baseline study produced for OTML (Hyndman 1982), despite the fact that he later adopted an attitude of total hostility towards the mine and all its works (see Hyndman 1994). Fredrik Barth and Unni Wikan accepted an invitation from Andrew Strathern, in his capacity as Director of the Institute of PNG Studies, to produce a separate and semi-official assessment of the project's cultural impact on the landowning community (Barth and Wikan 1982).

One of the babies to emerge from the prolonged bureaucratic and academic labour which accompanied the gestation of the Ok Tedi mine was a standardised procedure for organising the social impact assessment of mining projects in PNG. The 'Socio-Economic Impact Studies' produced under this procedure were commissioned by a Steering Committee assembled by the relevant project coordinator in the Department of Minerals and Energy, which included representation from the mining company, other national government departments and the department of the province in which the project was to be developed. During the height of the last mineral exploration boom, between 1985 and 1988, such studies were commissioned for the Misima and Wapolu projects in Milne Bay Province, the Lihir project in New Ireland, the Porgera project in Enga, the Hidden Valley project in Morobe and the Lakekamu project in Gulf. This procedure was terminated in 1988, when the government decided that mining companies should bear sole responsibility for the production of social impact studies as part of their statutory obligations under the terms of the 1978 Environmental Planning Act, though this made very little difference to the terms of reference under which further studies were undertaken for the Mount Kare project in Enga, the Hides gasfield in Southern Highlands or the more substantial Kutubu petroleum project in the same province.

The results of this work are still locked in the vaults of the grey literature (unpublished agency and consultancy reports), where their influence has largely been confined to the main stakeholders in the project planning process, but some of their authors have since published academic reflections on the nature of this process (Gerritsen and Macintyre 1991; Jackson 1991; Filer 1995). Although several anthropologists were involved in this series of studies, the relative size of their contribution appears to have been inversely related to the government's estimation of the difficulties associated with the development of each project and the importance of finding appropriate technocratic solutions to these problems. While the social impact assessment of minor projects like Wapolu and Lakekamu could safely be left in the hands of anthropologists like Michael Young or myself, anthropologists were notable by their absence from the multi-disciplinary teams assembled, at much greater expense, to undertake the equivalent studies of the Porgera and Kutubu projects. The Misima and Lihir studies represent the intermediate case in which it was considered that an anthropologist should be one of the two consultants engaged to do the work.

## Anthropologists in blue helmets

It is only in the period since 1989 that anthropologists have finally come to be seen as the major ingredient in consultancy work which is concerned with the social impact of mineral resource development. Only a small part of this work can now be classified under the heading of social impact *assessment*, considered as one ingredient in the project planning process, because there has been a significant decline in mineral exploration activities and consequently in the rate at which new feasibility studies are being commissioned (see Filer 1997). So far as the mining and petroleum companies are concerned, the game now is to protect investments which have already been made and, if possible, to ride out the political storms which surround them. In this phase of turmoil and uncertainty, the companies have called in the anthropologists because they have 'landowner problems' hovering over their risk insurance and their bottom lines. The riddle posed for anthropologists who heed the call is whether the companies, their village neighbours, the national political elite and a wide variety of 'unofficial stakeholders' can find a way to coexist in an increasingly 'postmodern' political environment.

For a period of three years, from mid–1991 to mid–1994, my own relationship to this expanding market for 'ethnographic services' was mediated by my role as the Projects Manager of Unisearch PNG, the business arm of the university of PNG. This enterprise was established in 1990, largely as a result of pressure from a group of university staff who were already heavily engaged in consultancy work on the social and environmental impact of various mining projects within the country. It was somewhat fortuitous that my own involvement in the planning of the Lihir project had brought me into direct contact with the militant Panguna landowners at roughly the same time as another team of consultants were making a last-minute effort to dilute their grievances in the cold water of common sense (Applied Geology Associates 1989; Connell 1991), but having then become involved in the ensuing academic debate on the significance of the rebellion (Filer 1990, 1992), I also found myself having to realign the combination of my research and consultancy activities to take account of the growing interest of non-academic customers in the results of this debate. This in turn created the situation in which it made sense for a university to take the unusual step of appointing a social anthropologist to run its business arm.

When I resigned from Unisearch in the middle of 1994, the company and I both lost our pivotal role in the 'commercialisation' of research on the social impact of mineral resource development in PNG. However, this has not meant a decline in the numbers of anthropologists and other social scientists currently engaged as 'social impact consultants' of one kind or another, nor a diminution in the overall scale of the research effort directed to this subject, whether on a commercial or a purely academic basis. What we have seen instead is a process of specialisation and diversification in the academic division of labour, which relates both to the complexities and uncertainties of the mineral policy environment and to the consolidation of a social network of scholars and consultants with a common set of political and theoretical problems.

There is no space here for me to review the many products of this intellectual enterprise, much of which is still in the process of being reproduced for public consumption. Let me rather make some general remarks about the lessons which I have learnt from my own experience as a policy analyst, an individual consultant and a university company manager about the role of the anthro-pologist as a mediator or negotiator in the process of mineral resource develop-ment in PNG. These remarks are intended to establish the 'dialectical' quality of the relationship between the process of engagement, as a consultant, and the process of disengagement, as an academic analyst, in a policy environment which encourages and constrains the development of this relationship.

There is an obvious double jeopardy to the 'moderate' position enjoined by the act of doing business in this industry. On the one hand, the simple fact that most of this work has been commissioned by the mining and petroleum com-panies themselves exposes us to the criticism of those radical colleagues who believe that there is only one role for the anthropologist in any relationship between mining companies and 'indigenous peoples' – and that is to defend the latter against the former. On the other hand, those colleagues who prefer to conceal their political opinions in the deconstructed buildings of post-modernism must positively squirm at the idea of doing the sort of research which might actually make sense to corporate executives – let alone illiterate tribal landowners.

Our activities are certainly inconsistent with the idea that multinational capital is the root of all evil or the idea that large-scale mining represents an intolerable threat to the physical or cultural well-being of the Melanesian environment, and I would not expect to receive much sympathy from people who subscribe to such ideas. On the other hand, PNG is probably the only country in which I could have felt reasonably comfortable with the role which I played as the manager of a university consultancy company. The peculiarity of our political setting resides in the power of the customary landowner and the relative (though obviously not total) weakness of multi-national capital *and* the machinery of government. And this peculiar balance of power between the players in the 'Mining Development Agreement Game' confronts the anthropology of 'development' with an equally peculiar bundle of constraints and opportunities.

Although anthropologists may feel that they have an instinct or duty to sympathise with the underdog, we should be wary of assuming that landowning communities have collective interests which are diametrically opposed to those of the mining companies, and then defining our own intellectual position by the further assumption that the weaker party must be defended against the stronger. As Jackson (1991) has pointed out, the indigenous customary landowner in

PNG is not the downtrodden romantic hero beloved of Cultural Survivalists, but a true force to be reckoned with in the political landscape of the country-side – as mining companies well know. Far from defending the authenticity and integrity of traditional village life, this force is normally applied to the search for some form of 'development', even if the definition of this goal commands no general consensus. This force is so fractured by internal conflict that its application is endlessly problematic and unpredictable – and that is how 'developers' have discovered the value of anthropology.

Although anthropologists may also feel that they have an instinct or duty to be critical of multinational corporations, they should in this case be wary of assuming that all local or national critics of the mining companies have the clean hands and pure motives that may sometimes be detected in the rose-tinted telescopes of First World academics. One does not have to shake hands with the devil to appreciate this point. Our own role as consultants within the industry is not one that requires us to take sides with the mining companies against the other players in the game, but it is one which still requires a certain measure of professional detachment from the play itself, and a some-what sceptical regard for the aims and methods of all those who participate with too much enthusiasm.

The preponderance of the mining and petroleum companies amongst our current clientele might well provoke the observation that 'he who pays the piper calls the tune'. In practice, however, we would still be doing the same kind of work, and would still distribute the results of that work in much the same way, whatever the distribution of the cost between the interested parties. Our role as mediators remains much as it was in earlier times (see Filer 1990). The novelty since 1989 lies rather in the tendency of other stakeholders to demand that such activities be funded by the companies alone, and in the tendency of company executives to think that it is both essential and extremely difficult to grasp the true significance of certain messages which they receive from other corners of the playing field – especially from the 'grassroots'.

While it is true to say that some of our engagements with these companies are actually intended to satisfy the demands of government, it must also be said that the government's own capacity to sponsor, control or evaluate this kind of work has diminished in proportion to the growth of that public concern which has prompted the companies to pay more attention to the social impact of their operations as a matter of simple corporate self-interest. This is not the paradox that it might seem to be, since the government's own method of dealing with intractable problems is to multiply the number of possible solutions and correspondingly reduce the possibility of making any choice between them.

As manager of Unisearch, I tried to compensate for the obvious inequalities of wealth and power between different stakeholder groups by adjusting our own company's charge-out rates to the client's notional ability to pay – a famil-iar Melanesian principle – and thus offering to advise community organisations at rates that were lower than those normally charged to government agencies, and much lower than those normally charged to mining and petroleum companies. As a matter of fact, the organisations which represent landowning communities in this sector have shown themselves to be reasonably adept at securing the kind of professional advice they think they need. But we should hardly be surprised if they prefer to hire expensive lawyers as their champions than to engage much cheaper social scientists, because they may well realise that social scientists are no less useful if their fees are paid by someone else. When Lihir community representatives secured my own services as a consultant, they were much less interested in the substance of my advice than in the demonstration of their own capacity to force another stakeholder to pay for these services, and were even more amused than I by the fact that the mining company eventually had to pick up the bill because the government had run out of money (see Filer 1995).

But how can claims to genuine professional detachment be supported by consultancy activities of any kind? What political or intellectual advantage can accrue from selling anthropology to any of the parties in our field of observation? Surely we can play a better tune if no one pays us for it?

Of course it is possible for anthropologists to observe, discuss and criticise the social impact of mineral resource development without embroiling themselves in the consultancy business. And those who keep their hands clean are not necessarily forced to adopt a purely critical position, but can also seek to encompass a variety of stakeholder perspectives in their own analysis. Nevertheless, for those who still wish to engage themselves directly with the policy process or the development process, the luxury of a position on the sidelines may now involve some sacrifice of access to the field, as well as the continuing indifference of key protagonists within that arena. Foreign anthropologists wanting official permission to undertake field research in PNG have long been accustomed to perform compulsory acts of ritual obeisance at the altar of 'development', and have been equally accustomed to find that their humble offerings are consigned to an actual or metaphorical dustbin. But while these rituals continue as before, I think the public attitude to anthropology in PNG has shifted somewhat in the period since Independence. Where once we stood accused of feeding the stereotypes of colonial prejudice, or practising our own peculiar form of capitalist enterprise by selling bits of 'culture' stolen or cajoled from our more gullible informants, we have more recently encountered an indifference which grew from the belief that we are relatively harmless creatures, but that our advice, if free, must be by definition worthless.

This alone would seem to warrant our adoption of consultant's clothing, even if it did not guarantee a market for our views. But while the process of development itself has given us this market, anthropologists are finding that the study of this process now entails the risk of opposition or antagonism from some vested interests who might prefer to hide their deeds from ethnographic scrutiny and redirect the discipline towards the formerly 'irrelevant' pursuit of tribal custom. The mining and petroleum sector is one arena where this risk has recently increased. In this environment, institutions like Unisearch or the National Research Institute may be compared to armoured personnel carriers which enable us to do research around a battlefield that has too little space for unprotected academics.

There is, of course, another kind of risk arising from the strength of our financial linkage to the private sector, for even if we are allowed to tell the truth, we may still find that those who pay the piper wish to be the only ones who hear the tune. While it is certainly necessary for us to maintain a low media profile in order to develop and maintain our reputation as 'honest brokers', it is no less important to persuade our clients that the kind of information which we gather will not serve their purposes unless it is disclosed to other interested parties – including our academic colleagues. In this way we have sought to ensure that research, consultancy and advocacy are mutually compatible activities. By and large, the mining and petroleum companies have accepted our arguments on this score, despite the risk (to them) that such disclosure keeps the other interested parties from contributing towards the cost of what we do.

The constraints imposed by the sensitivities of our political environment can also be conceived as opportunities for ethnographic innovation. Our role as go-betweens or honest brokers in the negotiation of mining and petroleum projects gives unique access to a veritable Wonderland of insights into the 'articulation' of the corporate and tribal worlds which are so awkwardly combined within this economic sector. Not all of these insights are suitable for inclusion in our consultancy reports, but that does not prevent us from incorporating them within a purely ethnographic contemplation of the industry and its environment.

One final argument that I would offer in defence of our 'applied' engagement with this industry is that it represents a way for Papua New Guinean anthropologists to sidestep the nationalist burble whose indulgence suits the guilty consciences or patronising attitudes of their First World counterparts. My own experience of teaching anthropology to Papua New Guineans has led me to conclude that the discipline has little to gain if its reputation is too thoroughly entangled with the pros and cons of nationalist ideology. The local market for this form of discourse is already so abundantly supplied with cheap merchandise that there is very little room for highly paid professionals to make a decent living from it. The best alternative is to purvey a form of academic enterprise whose political and intellectual merits are more precisely linked to economic and financial values.

At the same time, we might think twice before we take too much delight in the decomposition of developmental orthodoxies and the breakdown of administrative structures that have helped to turn our discipline into a more commercial proposition. Perhaps we should compare ourselves to maggots crawling through the corpse of corporate rationality. There clearly is a sense in which our business grows at the expense of 'rational' approaches to the business of 'development', and there are no doubt many anthropologists who would obtain some sense of satisfaction from this thought. But corpses have their disadvantages as customers, protectors and facilitators of our fieldwork. Once we reach Zairean scenarios, there is no place for anthropology at all.

## References

Applied Geology Associates Pty (1989) *Environmental Socio-Economic Public Health Review: Bougainville Copper Mine, Panguna*. Wellington: AGA.

Barth, F. and Wikan, U. (1982) *Cultural Impact of the Ok Tedi Project: Final Report*. Boroko: Institute of PNG Studies.

Bedford, R.D. and Mamak, A. (1977) *Compensating for Development: The Bougainville Case*. Christchurch: University of Canterbury, Bougainville Special Publication 2.

Connell, J. (1991) Compensation and conflict: the Bougainville copper mine, Papua New Guinea. In *Mining and Indigenous Peoples in Australasia* (eds) J. Connell and R. Howitt. Sydney: Sydney University Press (pp. 55–76).

Filer, C. (1990) The Bougainville rebellion, the mining industry and the process of social disintegration in Papua New Guinea. In *The Bougainville Crisis* (eds) R. May and M. Spriggs. Bathurst, NSW: Crawford House Press (pp. 73–112).

—— (1992) The escalation of disintegration and the reinvention of authority. In *The Bougainville Crisis: 1991 Update* (eds) M. Spriggs and D. Denoon. Canberra: Australian National University, Research School of Pacific Studies, Department of Political and Social Change, Monograph 16 (pp. 112–40).

—— (1995) Participation, governance and social impact: the planning of the Lihir gold mine. In *Mining and Mineral Resource Policy Issues in Asia-Pacific: Prospects for the 21st Century* (eds) D. Denoon *et al.* Canberra: Australian National University, Research School of Pacific and Asian Studies, Division of Pacific and Asian History (pp. 67–75).

—— (1997) Resource rents: distribution and sustainability. In *Papua New Guinea: A 20/20 Vision* (ed.) I. Temu. Canberra: Australian National University, National Centre for Development Studies, Pacific Policy Paper 20 (pp. 222–60).

Gerritsen, R. and Macintyre, M. (1991) Dilemmas of distribution: the Misima gold mine, Papua New Guinea. In *Mining and Indigenous Peoples in Australasia* (eds) J. Connell and R. Howitt. Sydney: Sydney University Press (pp. 35–53).

Hyndman, D.C. (1982) Population, settlement and resource use. In *Ok Tedi Environmental Study, vol. 5: Population and Resource Use, Ethnobiology*, Working Paper 12. Melbourne: Maunsell and Partners P/L for Ok Tedi Mining Ltd (pp. 1–71).

—— (1994) *Ancestral Rainforests and the Mountain of Gold: Indigenous Peoples and Mining in New Guinea*. Boulder, CO: Westview Press.

Jackson, R.T. (1982) *Ok Tedi: The Pot of Gold*. Waigani: University of PNG Press.

—— (1991) Not without influence: villages, mining companies and government in Papua New Guinea. In *Mining and Indigenous Peoples in Australasia* (eds) J. Connell and R. Howitt. Sydney: Sydney University Press (pp. 18–34).

—— (1993) *Cracked Pot or Copper Bottomed Investment? The Development of the Ok Tedi Project 1982–1991: A Personal View*. Townsville: James Cook University, Melanesian Studies Centre.

Jackson, R.T., Emerson, C.A. and Welsch, R.L. (1980) *The Impact of the Ok Tedi Project*. Konedobu: Department of Minerals and Energy.

Kirsch, S. (1996) Anthropologists and global alliances. *Anthropology Today* 12, 4: 14–16.

Mamak, A.F. (1979) Nationalism, race–class consciousness, and action research on Bougainville Island, Papua New Guinea. In *The Politics of Anthropology: From Colonialism and Sexism toward a View from Below* (eds) G. Huizer and B. Mannheim. The Hague: Mouton (pp. 447–60).

Marcus, G. (1995) Ethnography in/of the world system: the emergence of multi-sited ethnography. *Annual Review of Anthropology* 24: 95–117.

Mikesell, R.F. (1975) *Foreign Investment in Copper Mining: Case Studies of Mines in Peru and Papua New Guinea*. Baltimore, MD: Johns Hopkins University Press.

O'Faircheallaigh, C. (1984) *Mining and Development: Foreign-Financed Mines in Australia, Ireland, Papua New Guinea and Zambia*. London: Croom Helm.

Oliver, D.L. (1991) *Black Islanders: A Personal Perspective of Bougainville 1937–1991*. Melbourne: Hyland House.

Pintz, W.S. (1984) *Ok Tedi: Evolution of a Third World Mining Project*. London: Mining Journal Books.

Tilton, J., Millett J. and Ward, R. (1986) Mineral and mining policy in Papua New Guinea. Port Moresby: Institute of National Affairs, Discussion Paper 24.

Welsch, R.L. (1987) Multinational development and customary land tenure: the Ok Tedi project of Papua New Guinea. *Journal of Anthropology* 6, 2: 109–54.

Wesley-Smith, T. (1992) Development and crisis in Bougainville: a bibliographic essay. *Contemporary Pacific* 4: 407–33.

Young, M.W. (1987) *Wapolu Gold Mining Project: A Socio-Economic Impact Study*. Canberra: Anutech Pty Ltd.

# Chapter 8

# Land and re-empowerment
'The Waikato case'[1]

*Ngapare K. Hopa*

In November 1995, the first of the historical tribal land claims against the New Zealand state was settled. It involved the Waikato-Tainui people and their *raupatu* (confiscation) land claim negotiated by their statutory tribal authority, the Tainui Maori Trust Board (TMTB).[2] The *Waikato Raupatu Claims Settlement* (New Zealand 1995) was hailed by the media[3] as a 'benchmark' for subsequent historical land claims against the state. For Waikato-Tainui, the settlement began the process of healing, through the provision of a formal apology from the New Zealand state and the British Crown.[4]

The concepts of power, disempowerment and (re-)empowerment illuminate, in New Zealand today, the struggles of *iwi* (tribes) to recover land and other resources, to gain recognition of their rights of ownership/sovereignty over assets guaranteed them under the Treaty of Waitangi[5] and to acquire just reparation for their colonial losses. Specifically, this chapter discusses the Waikato settlement in terms of power defined in 'zero-sum' terms: in order, to first, illuminate state policies on tribal claims, as their resolution has been influenced, if not determined, by an economic environment now transformed (Kelsey 1995); and second, to contribute to the development discourse on 'empowerment' as a 'central issue of our times' (Craig and Mayo 1995: 2).

## The discourse

This discourse addresses 'community participation' and 'empowerment' as alternative approaches to the deepening poverty, marginality and social exclusion that have been generated by global recession and the 'structural adjustments' of the World Bank and International Monetary Fund. Contributors (Chambers 1983; Korten and Klauss 1984; Annis and Hakim 1988; Kothari 1993; Costa and Costa 1993; Macrae and Zwi 1994; Craig and Mayo 1995; Trainer 1995) exhibit a range of perspectives and interests, including those of the World Bank, the International Monetary Fund, and national and local governments in promoting community participation to advance 'development' and/or its alternatives by 'empowering' local communities (Craig and Mayo 1995: 1). NGOs, voluntary, community, and 'people's' liberation' movements

(Clark 1991) and grassroots organisations (Chambers 1983) have all recognised the contribution community participation and empowerment can make to promoting 'sustainable, people-centred development, equal opportunity and social justice' (Craig and Mayo 1995: 1). But as James (this volume) indicates, such 'development-speak', especially when refracted in the new 'management-speak', may not only conceal existing human reality, but may also affect 'the structural political realities of tomorrow'.

Among these divergent institutions and organisations, conceptualisations of 'community participation' and 'empowerment' also differ, are even contradictory, according to differences in socio-political and local circumstances, countervailing political pressures, internally competing perspectives, agendas and objectives of the organisations involved.

The World Bank is interested in community participation with 'empowerment' as a major objective for ensuring that its 'Third World development projects reach the poorest in the most efficient and cost-effective ways, sharing costs and benefits through the promotion of self-help' (Craig and Mayo 1995: 2). The UNDP adopted a similar view while defining empowerment as people having 'constant access to decision-making and power' (UNDP 1993: 3). Some grassroots organisations focus on 'participatory research' to assist the disadvantaged to investigate their own living conditions and environments and improve their lives (Chambers 1983, 1992; Actionaid 1993; Dunn 1991; Trainer 1995).

These differences in perspective make it very difficult, as James (this volume) notes, to discern the differences 'between advocacy and analysis or even to see clearly what is being advocated'. Whether community participation involves rural programmes in the Third World, or urban renewal, social services or community care in the North, it has been associated with a wider strategy to promote savings and shift the resources burden away from the public sector (Craig 1993; Mayo 1994). In the North, economic restructuring has resulted in growing numbers of people being 'excluded', many in long-term unemployment or low-paid jobs (Conroy 1995). In the Third World, economic recession and restructuring have been damaging on an even wider and deeper scale (Costa and Costa 1993; Macrae and Zwi 1994; Kothari 1993). Even the World Bank has recognised that free-market/neo-liberal strategies for promoting more market-oriented economies while 'rolling back the state' have failed to benefit the poor (Lipton 1991). Yet it, together with the International Monetary Fund (Mishra 1990; Glennerster and Midgely 1991), endorses all strategies aimed at reducing state spending on social welfare and promoting alternative solutions based on the private sector, NGOs and self-help.

This emphasis on reducing public spending is a recurring theme in debates about the shifting boundaries of the 'mixed economy of welfare' in the UK (Taylor 1995), Australia (Meekosha and Mowbray 1995) and New Zealand where the 1984 Labour government reforms, continued under successor governments, have revolutionised the economy and people's lives (Easton 1989, 1994; Kelsey 1995). Within a decade major state assets were privatised and the welfare state dismantled, forcing many to rely on a shrinking welfare safety net and/or private charity (Kelsey 1995: 348–9).

Neo-Keynesian alternatives and other options were debated, including Maori economic development alternatives promoted by *iwi* (tribes), based on the fundamental Treaty right to *tino rangatiratanga* or self-determination. These goals underpinned the 1990 'decade of Maori development', with its focus on the return of resources stolen by confiscation and 'legislative theft' to re-empower Maori people. The political struggles waged over 150 years, and particularly over the past three decades, have been dedicated to re-securing tribal control to promote community or tribal empowerment.

This tribal emphasis raises questions posed elsewhere (Craig and Mayo 1995) about the meaning of empowerment, especially as it is used in development discourse. Does 'empowerment' as used by the World Bank differ from its sense when employed by progressive NGOs; or its use (O'Gorman 1995) by popular movements for liberation and transformation in Brazil, Nicaragua or Bangladesh; its use in contemporary management theory (James, this volume); or its use among the promoters of *iwi* development as exemplified by Waikato-Tainui? In New Zealand, *hapu* (lineages), not *iwi* (tribes), owned resources and signed the 1840 Treaty of Waitangi, yet tribes have been empowered, on an increasingly corporate basis, by the settler colonial state now compromising Maori claims.

## The conceptualisation of power

In their seminal anthology on community empowerment, Craig and Mayo (1995: 5–6) discuss the various ways in which power has been conceptualised. They note that Marxist perspectives assume that political power is inseparable from economic power associated with the vested interests of capitalist transnationals operating across a now-seamless globe. Empowering the relatively powerless may have limited scope in such an environment. In New Zealand this constraint is reflected in the state's desire to settle tribal claims as quickly and cheaply as possible to remove barriers to overseas investment.

Such perspectives also use the concept of hegemony (Gramsci 1971) to explain how existing systems of economic and political power are legitimated and made non-contestable in capitalist society. In New Zealand, challenging settler and state hegemony has been central to Maori tribal development, inspired to some degree by Freirean concepts (Walker 1990, 1996). Tribal development, seen as 'collective' development, is based on rebuilding 'tribal estates' to address the needs of a welfare-dependent people.

Weber (1946: 180) defined power as the ability of individuals or groups to realise their will, even where others resist, through the use of force or the threat of it, or where the powerless conform because they have accepted the legitimacy of the powerful. Accordingly, 'empowerment' gains must be achieved from the powerful (although such gains could of course be negotiated as part of a wider strategy for social reform), as illustrated in the Waikato settlement.

In contrast, Parsons (1971) conceptualised power in a society as a variable sum, not fixed but present in all members of a society and augmentable as society pursues collective goals, including economic objectives. In this perspective, the powerless may be 'empowered' within the existing social order, without significantly diminishing the power of the powerful. Thus the powerless could be empowered to share the fruits of development. and, once empowered, become agents of their own development using the tools of self-reliance.

However, if power is conceptualised in zero–sum terms, as constituting a 'fixed amount' in society, then 'empowerment' may cause problems by increasing the power of one at the expense of other groups. This perspective is especially relevant to the *Waikato Raupatu Claims Settlement Act*, which empowered an *iwi* using resources originally owned by *hapu*.[6] 'Waikato-Tainui' were defined for the purpose of the *raupatu* claim as the descendants of the founding Tainui canoe, being 33 *hapu* statutorily recognised in the Maori Trust Boards Regulations (1985/258: 1311–12) and later listed in the settlement act. There were two major problems with this definition: it ignored the state's own identification, in 1900,[7] of 88 *hapu* in the Waikato *raupatu* claim area which had suffered confiscation; and it collectivised *hapu* assets, without seeking their consent, under TMTB control.

## Maori claims and their settlement

The Waitangi Tribunal, established in 1975, has before it over 400 backlogged claims awaiting adjudication. Initially regarded with considerable scepticism, as the claim process developed it became more lengthy and complicated, generating both dissatisfaction and new ideas, about a global framework for the settlement of Treaty claims; a 'land bank' of reserved land to meet *iwi* needs, which might be used for trading (e.g. to acquire other lands); and a settlement fund. Following the controversial pan-Maori Sealords negotiations which settled the fishing claim[8] (Walker 1996: 19), tribes realised that negotiating directly with the state might achieve results more swiftly than going through the Tribunal.

In 1993, the national government declared, as part of its election manifesto, that it would settle all major claims by the year 2000 (Walker 1996: 116–19). Through the Treaty of Waitangi Policy Unit created by the previous Labour government, the state developed a global framework to settle tribal claims within a 'fiscal cap' later revealed to be NZ\$1 billion, reflecting its desire to avoid ongoing litigation and piecemeal settlements in its financial obligations to the majority *pakeha* (European) public.

These settlement proposals were taken to a number of consultative meetings on tribal *marae* (meeting grounds), and roundly rejected at Hirangi *marae* by a major gathering of Maori tribes convened by Sir Hepi Te Heuheu, paramount chief of Ngati Tuwharetoa, at the request of *iwi* around the country. Thereafter, consultation and protest progressed together, to the Maori conclusion that the envelope should be *Return[ed] to Sender* (Gardiner 1996). Problems included the state's failure to consult; its exclusion of Treaty principles from the settlement principles; its refusal to recognise Maori ownership of natural resources even while their usufructuary and value interests were acknowledged; the non-negotiability of the NZ$1 billion fund created on the basis of its affordability and acceptability to the majority New Zealand public; the assumption that NZ$1 billion was sufficient to redress claimants' sense of grievance; the lack of transparency of the method used in calculating the sum and deciding its viability.[9]

## The Waikato Raupatu Claims Settlement 1995

On 22 May 1995, the first day in the annual week-long celebrations of the 1858 founding of the King Movement[10] or *Kingitanga*, a Deed of Settlement (DOS) was signed between the New Zealand state and the Waikato-Tainui people of the upper central North Island, to resolve their claim. The DOS confirmed the Heads of Agreement (HOA) signed on 21 December 1994 and subsequently ratified by a postal referendum among the Waikato-Tainui people (Postal Referendum, March 1995). It passed through Parliament on 13 October 1995 as the *Waikato Raupatu Claims Settlement Act* (New Zealand 1995). The settlement included an apology from the state and Crown, covering the unjust invasion of the Waikato by Imperial forces, the unfair labelling of Waikato as 'rebels', and the subsequent confiscation of their lands under the New Zealand Settlement Act 1863. The apology was sealed by Queen Elizabeth's signature while she was attending the 1995 Commonwealth Heads of Government Conference in Auckland. The settlement 'finally' con-cluded Waikato's 132-year saga of attempted redress, with the return of some more lands and cash compensation and mechanisms to acquire more assets with which to re-establish tribal control and re-empower tribal members (Kelsey 1995: 365; Mahuta 1995: 2). But the *Waikato-Maniapoto Claim Settlement Act* of 1946, and its return of resources, was in its day also thought to be 'final'.

For its part, the government secured a major victory: a precedent which others among the 70+ Maori tribes might later follow, including Whakatohea and Ngai Tahu.[11] Yet, like the earlier Sealords settlement, the Waikato settle-ment was not uncontentious. Many Maori perceived Waikato to have sold out Maoridom, although at the Hirangi meeting on 29 January 1995, *iwi* genea-logically related to Waikato-Tainui acknowledged its right to make its own decisions. The TMTB's defence was that their entirely separate negotiations, begun in 1989, had progressed significantly by the time the proposals were released.[12] The 'fiscal envelope' was therefore irrelevant. Waikato-Tainui had 'never concurred with the concept of the settlement envelope or its quantum'.[13]

However, the negotiators do appear not only to have accepted a number of the Crown's proposals, but also to have settled within the framework of the 'fiscal envelope' of NZ$1 billion, because the WRCSA includes an automatic escalation clause. A 'relativity clause' apparently ensures that:

> the Waikato Settlement will always be the largest Maori settlement for the next 50 years. If another tribe receives a settlement which exceeds in value the Waikato settlement, the Crown will provide additional value . . . that ensures that the Waikato settlement . . . maintain[s] its 17% value of any monies set aside by the Crown for Maori claims.
>
> (TMTB *Annual Report* 1995: 12–13)[14]

The Waikato Deed of Settlement[15] estimated the *raupatu* value at a minimum of 'approximately NZ$12 billion' and recognised that 'Waikato, by agreeing to the Settlement, is foregoing a substantial part of the redress sought . . . as a contribution to the development of New Zealand'. The state did not fully accept this figure but apparently included it in the Deed at the insistence of the chief negotiator.[16] Having earlier prevented the state from privatising Coalcorp, Waikato-Tainui relinquished its claim to coal in exchange for access rights and the returns these would earn; and accepted that nearly 40 per cent of the land earmarked for return would remain as part of the state's 'conservation estate'.[17] Thus by the time the DOS was signed, less than 4 per cent of the land originally confiscated would be returned (DOS 1995: 25), though 20 per cent had been returned decades previously.

Waikato-Tainui's chief negotiator maintained that the uproar surrounding the state's fiscal envelope proposals had hampered their own negotiations and, in response to criticism for having 'opened' the envelope to the disadvantage of other *iwi*, published detailed explanations.[18] For Waikato-Tainui, he argued, land – valued by the state – was being returned in fulfilment of the traditional principles which had underpinned the negotiations: *I riro whenua atu me hoki whenua mai, Ko te moni hei utu mo te hara* (as land was taken so should land be returned, the money is payment for the Crown's crime) (HOA 1994: 2; DOS 1995: 4). Further, in the end people needed to consider what value might realistically better the state's offer. Two questions were posed: was the offer sufficient to settle its grievance and provide the *iwi* with the means to reverse its appalling statistical profile of ill-health, premature death, under-education[19] and unemployment? And could Waikato-Tainui afford to risk settlement negotiations under the pending new political environment of proportional representation? In the TMTB's view, the postal referendum conducted in March 1995 furnished sufficient support to indicate that Waikato-Tainui could not take this risk. So the settlement was signed on 22 May 1995.

Despite its efforts to persuade other *iwi* that this settlement was not intended to prejudice other claims, in settling its 'benchmark' claim, Waikato-Tainui clearly increased its economic power at the expense of those *iwi* with unsettled claims. If 17 per cent reflects the extent of Waikato-Tainui's loss (rather than how much they were able to gain by being first into the zero-sum fiscal envelope), then its postulated loss ought to be related to the losses of other Maori. Waikato-Tainui received NZ$170 million from a claimed loss of NZ$12 billion, so if NZ$12 billion represents approximately 17 per cent, the total loss must be some NZ$70 billion.[20]

## Post-settlement: re-empowering *iwi*, *hapu* or *Kingitanga*?

The settlement is now history and in the view of its negotiators the re-empowering process has moved 'beyond grievance' into post-settlement development (TMTB 1996). The TMTB as 're-empowering agent of the people' has been constituted as (interim) Land Holding Trustee (LHT) for the settlement assets. However, the TMTB was established by the state in 1946, allegedly to 'hold the *mana* of the *Kingitanga* until Tainui is established as a tribe',[21] although there is no such statement or even implication in the legislation. There is thus some question as to whether the TMTB's primary responsibility is to the *Kingitanga* and the royal family or to its own 35,000 commoner beneficiaries.

The *raupatu* claim was made in the name of the TMTB's thirty-three constituent *hapu*. None have had restored to them, or registered in their names, any of the assets returned. The chief negotiator of the settlement has described *hapu* (whose chiefs were the original signatories of the Treaty of Waitangi) as existing 'only in concept, only in the head', as a 'myth with no formal structure'.[22] The state has argued that, since by the time of settlement it held only a fraction of the land originally confiscated, which could not be evenly distributed among the thirty-three *hapu*, the restitution provided for in the settlement must benefit all Waikato-Tainui collectively, and the TMTB has organised for this to occur under 'the mana of the *Kingitanga*'. Activist protest about the collusive transactions between state and TMTB which extinguished *hapu* rights and identity has been ignored. The settlement legislation prohibits any further inquiry into the *raupatu* claim, the validity of the settlement or adequacy of the benefits provided (New Zealand 1995: 19). Thus all smaller *hapu* and *whanau* (sub-lineage) claims to resources in the *raupatu* claim area have effectively been extinguished (New Zealand 1995: 17–18) and their interests subordinated to those of the tribe or *iwi*. 'Re-empowering' Waikato-Tainui as (state-driven) *iwi* has thus redefined its *hapu* constituency, as the *Listener*[23] has noted.

This potential conflict of interest was reflected in the Crown's 1993 advance return (before the *raupatu* settlement) of two military bases, Te Rapa and Hopuhopu, sited on the ancestral lands of a number of *hapu* listed among the thirty-three which had suffered confiscation. These lands were vested in the Potatau Te Wherowhero title, despite a challenge in the Maori Appellate

Court by descendants of the original owners.[24] This 'deposit' return prompted the TMTB to restructure its operations and management, in anticipation of a final settlement. It started by systematically updating its beneficiary roll to redefine the social landscape of its constituency, before improving the efficiency and effectiveness of its core activities, defined as those involved with negotiations, by restructuring along corporate lines.

In 1994, the TMTB had submitted evidence to a review (Mason *et al.* 1994: 1) of the structures imposed by the 1955 Maori Trust Boards Act, noting their inadequacy for handling existing assets and those to be returned.[25] Thus by the time of the settlement in 1995, legislation had already envisaged new controlling structures to replace the old TMTB. A Grand Council of Waikato-Tainui (*Te Runanga o Waikato-Tainui*) was proposed to represent all 60-odd beneficiary *marae* as physical localities designated as dividend-receiving centres, and the TMTB began a training programme for *marae* committee members in fund and project management. Whether this scheme could be regarded as 'empowering' *marae* or leading participants to 'feel empowered' (James, this volume), will require investigation. For the moment, though, the distribution of dividends from the TMTB does not appear to be accompanied by any relinquishing of central control over resources. *Marae* must meet bureaucratic criteria; and can only challenge the TMTB in court regarding their benefit amount, since the TMTB decides[26] how much each *marae* will receive.

The proposed Council, moreover, like a mini-parliament, will be concerned only with 'governance', not management, and control of *marae* funds is meanwhile vested in the outgoing TMTB. Consultation among Waikato-Tainui for the TMTB replacement has already begun and could, according to its CEO, take three years.[27] Although not yet complete, the emerging post-settlement structures suggest a top-heavy, top-down structure, overturning an earlier emphasis on 'bottom-up' development potentially allowing greater empowerment of the people (Mahuta 1987). At present, questions are being raised over accountability, particularly as the new structures effectively 'corporatise' the new 'tribal estate' or 'tribal commons', and how the TMTB/LHT can be made to address these issues.

All assets transferred to Waikato-Tainui are to be held communally in two trusts, with an unknown proportion of the land registered in the name of Potatau Te Wherowhero, the deceased first Maori King (New Zealand 1995: 11). This title was originally created in 1975 to register the *Kingitanga's* royal graveyard on Taupiri mountain. Its use was expanded to receive *raupatu* assets, starting with Te Rapa and Hopuhopu. The outgoing TMTB as interim LHT has enormous power over properties registered in this title: 'all the rights, duties, and powers of the registered proprietor of that land or interest' to 'exercise and perform every such right, duty and power in its own name and not in the name of Potatau Te Wherowhero' (New Zealand 1995: 28), even for those lands vested in his name. *Inter alia*, the Waikato *Raupatu* Lands Trust deed provides that no land registered in the name of Potatau shall be sold or mortgaged to, or be capable of being vested in or transferred out of the name of Potatau, without the consent of the 'custodians of the Te Wherowhero Title'. The three custodians are: Dame Te Atairangikahu, as current Head of the *Kingitanga's Kahui Ariki* (royal lineage); her adoptive brother Robert Mahuta, the TMTB's chief negotiator; and her uncle Tumate Mahuta (and on the deaths or incapacity of the second and third custodians, replacement members of Waikato-Tainui elected by the TMTB's voting beneficiaries).[28] Ostensibly engineered to prevent any further transfers of ownership of this land, not only can the custodians 'recommoditise' such land, but Potatau Te Wherowhero is also reaffirmed as central to the *kawenata* (covenants) of those who continue to support the *Kingitanga*.

## Waikato *Raupatu* Lands Trust (WRLT)

The WRLT is headed by the Land Holding Trustee (LHT) and will receive over 15,500 hectares (DOS 1995: 7). The TMTB, as (interim) LHT (DOS 1995: 26.2: 33), therefore controls the settlement properties until the final management structure is approved and in place. The WRLT Deed permits the LHT to establish advisory committees which may be constituted as companies. This provision has led the TMTB/LHT to create two wholly owned subsidiaries.

The Tainui Corporation Ltd (TCL) manages commercial property assets to maximise cash returns. It will be allocated commercial property valued at approximately NZ$45 million, plus NZ$50 million in cash. With debt included in its capital structure, its funds total some NZ$140 million (TCL Profile 1996). Its property portfolio already includes the land leased to Waikato University, the Waikato Polytechnic, Health Waikato and Government Property Services, with Railcorp, Justice-Corrections, Justice-Courts, NZ Post and the Energy Corporation of NZ still to follow. TCL has also been appointed overall project manager of the Tainui Auckland Endowed College, an international residential facility for postgraduate students from all disciplines and cultures.

Tainui Development Ltd (TDL) is the second 'advisory committee', with a brief to double the properties returned within the next twenty-five years. In the meantime it manages the five existing TMTB farms as well as returned assets.

The WRLT is a 'charitable' entity to promote the educational, social, economic, spiritual and cultural advancement of its beneficiaries. The income generated (whether from one or both of its company components is unclear) will be used to meet the TMTB's social objectives, including building or rebuilding *marae*, education, and the generation of employment. In 1996, the TMTB/LHT put NZ$500,000 into 300 tertiary scholarships (for undergraduate or postgraduate degrees) and intends to increase this figure to NZ$2 million annually. It has actively promoted the new School of Maori and Pacific

Development at the University of Waikato and endowed its Professorship in Maori Development with NZ$500,000. A second Endowed College is planned near Waikato University, with an intake of one-third Waikato-Tainui, one-third other New Zealanders, and one-third international students.

## Waikato Land Acquisition Trust (WLAT)

The trustees of the WLAT have been appointed by Waikato-Tainui in consultation with the state. WLAT will, over a five-year period, receive most of the *raupatu* settlement capital of NZ$170 million, less NZ$4 million for the military bases transferred in 1993 and the value of the 19,000 ha included in the settlement. This capital has been or will be used to establish the Endowed Colleges, to provide educational grants and scholarships, to purchase farms and more land for residential and forestry development, to invest in hotels, casino shares and a corporate box at a sports stadium.[29]

Concerning post-settlement 'sovereignty', the TMTB/LHT has sought to re-establish economic sovereignty for its people.

> What the future brings to this tribe is increased numbers in higher education, increased investment in health, education and employment under its own direction and guidance, not apart from but alongside and with the general institutions. . . . More people, more institutions. Different and new institutions – especially in cities where the future of most Maori lies. The future will not be on the land or in the land, but in people development.
>
> (Ritchie 1995: 1)

## Conclusions

The state hoped that, by persuading high-profile Waikato-Tainui/*Kingitanga* to accept its offer, other *iwi* would follow down this directly negotiated settlement path, in preference to the cumbersome procedures of the Waitangi Tribunal. When the Minister of Justice and of Treaty Negotiations recently visited the operational centre of the TMTB, he recommended Waikato-Tainui assist other *iwi* to come to terms with settlement issues.[30] From the state's perspective, the backlog of Tribunal claims may impede its overall economic strategy to attract overseas investment and remove the nuisance factor of tribal claims as cheaply as possible. The path to rights and reconciliation through 'direct negotiations' had also long been the TMTB's preferred option, to avoid litigation and facilitate settlement. Perhaps the Waikato-Tainui case supports Clark's (1991) argument in favour of a closer relationship between NGOs and the state, and Korten's (1990: 186) claim that government resourcing is critical to the evolution of NGOs towards third- and fourth-generation strategies 'aimed at redefining policies, transforming institutions and helping people to define, internalise and actualise a people-centred vision'. Such contributions stress the need to link local, regional and sectional interests and programmes into wider and more strategic approaches to development which engage the state and political processes at different levels, without which local or tribal community actions run the risk of being marginalised. How to think globally and act locally, captures this view (Miller *et al.* 1995: 112). Ritchie,[31] who has long been associated with Waikato-Tainui, its claim and development plans, notes that 'this is a tribe which does think globally and act locally. That isn't trite; it is the shape of the future.'

Yet the appropriation of Maori resources and Maori exclusion from the apparatus of state under the 'amalgamation' policies of successive colonial governments have created a disempowered, marginalised, dispossessed and dependent minority struggling to correct their unequal position in the social structure of Aotearoa/New Zealand. Properly resourced *iwi* can drive their own development as well as contribute to the 'national good'. This is certainly the vision for the beneficiaries of the Waikato-Tainui Settlement. In the words of their chief negotiator, 'They will not have to ask the government for a hand-out, or rely on the welfare system'[32] – such as it now is! But this goal is linked to the larger business arena, in which the TMTB/LHT is already dealing in the share market, property, fishing and forestry.[33] The TMTB/LHT has also begun to invest in property abroad. The 'contract culture' opens yet other doors into the service industry. In these investments, TMTB/LHT confirms its twin commitment not only to tribal community development and to increasing the wealth of the *iwi*, but also to the nation's strategic development.

In the end, however, the TMTB/LHT pursues the twin *Kingitanga* goals of yesteryear: the re-creation, under the mana and autonomy of the *Kingitanga*, of an economy based on returned resources, to re-empower those of the community who are loyal registered beneficiaries, committed to the *Kingitanga kaupapa* (ideology).[34] The closely entwined histories of the TMTB and the *Kingitanga* are reflected in the structure and operations evolving within the Waikato region in local bodies (regional councils, environmental groups, energy boards, conservation boards) and the University of Waikato, among others. Here the TMTB/*Kingitanga* have representation and thus opportunities to create cooperative and empowering enterprises. The present leader of the *Kingitanga* is patron of a number of organisations at home, has an extensive network abroad, and frequently hosts national and international, including state, visitors. Especially over the past three decades, state and *Kingitanga* have been moving closer together, in forms of mutual empowerment which have yet to show that they will as adequately benefit the needy at the flaxroots as the small tribal elite controlling both the TMTB/LHT and *Kingitanga*.

## Notes

1 This title derives from papers delivered by TMTB chief negotiator Sir Robert Mahuta on *raupatu*.

2 The Tainui Maori Trust Board is one of 19 Maori Trust Boards, 13 of which were created between 1922 and 1981 to receive compensation to settle tribal grievances against the State. The TMTB was established under the Waikato-Maniapoto Maori Claims Settlement Act 1946 to administer compensation funds for what was then regarded as full and final settlement of *raupatu* involving 1.2 million acres. There is an intimate link between the history of the TMTB and of the *Kingitanga* effort to seek redress for colonial injustice (King 1977).

3 *Waikato Times* 21 October 1995.

4 *New Zealand Herald* 19 October 1995.

5 The 1840 Treaty of Waitangi secured *kawanatanga* (governance) for the Crown, guaranteed Maori *tino rangatiratanga* (autonomy/sovereignty) in their 'full exclusive and undisturbed possesssion of the Lands, Estates, Fisheries and other properties' and citizenship for all. Considerable debate has ensued over whether Maori understood the significance of government by the Queen of England as conveyed in the neologism *kawanatanga* (*Te Roroa Report* 1992: 29–30).

6 New Zealand (1995 No. 58: 16).

7 Appendix to the *Journals of the House of Representatives* 1900, vol. 2, G-1: 1–14 'Landless Maori in the Waikato, Thames Valley and Tauranga districts'.

8 Sealords was a pan-Maori solution to the Maori claim over fish by purchasing shares in the Sealords industrial fishing company. The state and four prominent Maori negotiators agreed to purchase half the Sealords shares for NZ$150 million, in a joint venture with Brierley Investments. Sealords held 26 per cent of the total allowable catch, so Maori would ultimately end up with one-third of the fisheries. No new jobs were created, but many problems emerged in the wake of the Sealords deal, including the failure of the Crown to consult and the resulting exclusion of thirteen *iwi*, the execution of the deed signatures, the validity of the mandates of the signatories and the limited time given *iwi* representatives to consider the economic and political implications of the deal (Walker 1996: 102). There is still dispute over whether this deal should have restricted control over fishing assets to coastal tribes, or – as it attempted to – spread the benefits among all Maori; and over the mechanisms to distribute such benefits.

9 New Zealand economist Brian Easton presented evidence to the 1991 Muri-whenua Waitangi Tribunal hearings which estimated that some NZ$90 billion at 1991 prices would be required to raise Maori income and living levels to equal those of settlers.

10 In 1858, the man who had for some decades led a loose confederation of Waikato and related *hapu*, Potatau Te Wherowhero was elected first Maori monarch as the 'land league' (Ward 1995) was transformed into the King Movement or *Kingitanga*.

11 The ratification (*New Zealand Herald* 1 October 1996) of the Whakatohea Deed of Settlement has not occurred because the *hapu* involved considered that it compromised, for NZ$40 million, their 130-year-old grievance over the confiscation of 70,000 ha by the Crown. They are attempting to re-negotiate. Ngai Tahu and the state settled on 5 October 1996 for NZ$170 million (*Star* 6 October 1996: A3).

12 *Kia Hiwa Ra, Nga Karere-Wharangi* (newsletter) 1995.

13 DOS 25.

14 See also DOS Attachment 9.

15 DOS s.2.3:5; s.2.4.

16 See note 12.

17 Referendum clause 7.10.
18 *Kia Hiwa Ra* (newsletter) (1995: 3–5); *Maori Law Review* Dec. 1994–Jan. 1995.
19 The 1991 census showed only half of the Waikato-Tainui people hold a school certificate or better education (*Kia Hiwa Ra* (newsletter) Sept. 1995). Part of the TMTB mission is to 'develop a well-educated tribe which carries its wealth between its ears and travels the world with that wealth' (R. Mahuta, *NZ Herald* 24 April 1996).
20 Cf. Easton's related estimate in footnote 9.
21 Transcript of the Maori Land Court Special Sitting at Taurangawaewae *Marae*, Ngaruawahia, 17 March 1993, p. 25 (evidence given by Shane Solomon).
22 *Listener* (24 June 1995: 22).
23 *Listener* (24 June 1995: 18).
24 In 1992 the Maori Land Court, on Crown application (73 Waikato 174–175), vested the two military bases in the Potatau Te Wherowhero Land Holding Trust. In March 1993, at a special hearing of the Maori Land Court held at Turangwaewae *marae*, in the first indication to those assembled that such a trust existed, it was announced that the present Head of the *Kingitanga*, Dame Te Atairangikahu, her adopted brother Robert Mahuta and uncle Tumate Mahuta had been made custodian trustees and the TMTB managing trustee of this Trust. The descendants of the original occupants of the land had not been consulted, and thirty-seven of them appealed this vesting (J. Grant, Summary of Submissions in the Maori Appellate Court of New Zealand, Waikato-Maniapoto Land District, appeal no. 1993/2), but lost to the Court's and TMTB's claim that the lands were returned to 'Waikato and not to any one individual' (TMTB *Annual Report* 1993). The die was thus cast for the extinction of *hapu* rights under the collective TMTB/ *Kingitanga* title of Potatau Te Wherowhero.
25 From distributing £6,000 annually to beneficiaries, the TMTB became a multi-million dollar operation (TMTB *Annual Report* 1993).
26 WRCSA s. 28.
27 At the first consultative *hui* at Mangatautari, 12 September 1996.
28 Deed Creating Waikato *Raupatu* Lands Trust (1995: 2).
29 The *raupatu* settlement was apparently concluded in this box: *NZ Herald* 27 April 1996.
30 *Waikato Times* 14 September 1996.
31 J. Ritchie (1995) Lecture to 'Environmental Planning and Law' course, University of Waikato, Department of Geography: circulated notes.
32 *Huntly Community News* 21 June 1996.
33 *New Zealand Herald* 27 April 1996.
34 Individuals may be of Waikato-Tainui descent, but if they are not registered with the TMTB they can expect no benefits. This also applies to those marae which did not endorse the settlement if they have not signed the *Kingitanga kawenata* (covenant).

# References

Actionaid (1993) *Actionaid Report*. Islamabad, Pakistan: Actionaid.
Annis, S. and Hankim, P. (1993) *Direct to the Poor*. Boulder, CO: Lynne Reinner Publishers.
Chambers, R. (1983) *Rural Development: Putting the Last First*. London: Longman.
—— (1992) Rural Appraisal: Rapid, Relaxed and Participatory, *Discussion Paper 311*. Institute of Development Studies, University of Sussex, Brighton.

Clark, J. (1991) *Democratising Development: The Role of Voluntary Organisations*. London: Earthscan.

Conroy, P. (1995) The voluntary sector challenge to Fortress Europe. In *Community Empowerment* (eds) G. Craig and M. Mayo. London: Zed Books.

Costa, M. and Costa, G. (1993) *Paying the Price*. London: Zed Books.

Craig, G. (1993) *The Community Care Reforms and Local Government Change*. Hull: University of Humberside.

Craig, G. and Mayo, M. (eds) (1995) *Community Empowerment*. London: Zed Books.

Dunn, T. (1991) Family farming and extension. In *Family Farming in Australia and New Zealand*. Waggawagga, Australia: Charles Sturt University, Centre for Rural Social Research, Key Papers No. 2.

Easton, B. (1989) The commercialisation of the New Zealand economy. In *The Making of Rogernomics* (ed.) B. Easton. Auckland: Auckland University Press.

—— (1994) How did the health reforms blitzkrieg fail? *Political Science* 46, 2.

Gardiner, W. (1996) *Return to Sender*. Auckland: Reed.

Glennerster, H. and Midgely, J. (eds) (1991) *The Radical Right and the Welfare State*. Brighton: Harvester/Wheatsheaf.

Gramsci, A. (1971) *Selections from the Prison Notebooks*. London: Lawrence and Wishhart.

Kelsey, J. (1995) The New Zealand experiment – a world model for structural adjustment? Wellington: Bridget Williams Books/Auckland: Auckland University Press.

King, M. (1977) *Te Puea*. New York: Hodder and Stoughton.

Korten, D. (1990) *Getting to the 21st Century*. West Hartford, CT: Kumarian Press.

Korten, D.C. and Klauss, R. (1984) *People-Centred Development*. West Hartford, CT: Kumarian Press.

Kothari, R. (1993) *Poverty – Human Consciousness and the Amnesia of Development*. London: Zed Books

Lipton, M. (1991) *The Poor and the Poorest*. Washington DC: IBRD Discussion Paper.

Macrae, J. and Zwi, A. (eds) (1994) *War and Hunger: Rethinking International Responses to Complex Emergencies*. London: Zed Books.

Mahuta, R. (1987) Maori economic development – top down or bottom up? Paper presented to Symposium on New Zealand and the Pacific, 'Structural Change and Societal Responses', University of Waikato/Social Science Research Fund, 19 June. Hamilton: University of Waikato, Centre for Maori Studies and Research.

Mahuta, R. (1995) Principal negotiator's report. In *Annual Report*, Tainui Maori Trust Board. Hamilton, NZ: Walmsley Design Assoc. Ltd.

Maori Trust Boards Regulations (1985/258). Wellington, NZ: Government Printer.

Mason, K., Jackson, J. and Ashton, S. (1994) *Report of the Mason Committee on Maori Trust Boards*. Wellington: Te Puni Kokiri/Ministry of Maori Development.

Mayo, M. (1994) *Communities and Caring: The Mixed Economy of Welfare*. London: Macmillan.

Meekosha, H. and Mowbray, M. (1995) Activism, service provision and the state's intellectuals: community work in Australia. In *Community Empowerment* (eds) G. Craig and M. Mayo. London: Zed Books.

Miller, S., Rein, M. and Levitt, P. (1995) Community action in the USA. In *Community Empowerment* (eds) G. Craig and M. Mayo. London: Zed Books.

Mishra, R. (1990) *The Welfare State in Capitalist Society*. Brighton: Harvester Wheatsheaf.

New Zealand (1994) *Crown Proposals for the Settlement of Treaty of Waitangi Claims*. Wellington: Department of Justice.

New Zealand (1995) *The Waikato Raupatu Claims Settlement Act* No 58. Wellington: Government Printer.

O'Gorman, F. (1995) Brazilian community development. In *Community Empowerment* (eds) G. Craig and M. Mayo. London: Zed Books.

Parsons, T. (1971) *The System of Modern Societies*. Englewood Cliffs, NJ: Prentice-Hall.

Solomon, S. (1995) *The Waikato Raupatu Claims Settlement Act: A Draft User's Guide to the Act*. Hamilton: University of Waikato, Centre for Maori Studies and Research.

Tainui Maori Trust Board (TMTB) (1993, 1995, 1996) *Annual Reports*. Hamilton: Walmsley Design Assoc. ltd.

Taylor, M. (1995) Community work and the state. In *Community Empowerment* (eds) G. Craig and M. Mayo. London: Zed Books.

TCL Profile (1996) Tainui Maori Trust Board Annual Report. Tainui Maori Trust Board.

Trainer, T. (1995) *The Conserver Society*. London: Zed Books.

UNDP (1993) *Human Development Report*. Oxford: Oxford University Press.

Walker, R. (1990) *Ka Whawhai Tonu Matou: Struggle Without End*. Auckland: Penguin.

—— (1996) *Nga Pepa a Rangi – The Walker Papers*. Auckland: Penguin.

Ward, A. (1995) *A Show of Justice: Racial Amalgamation in the Nineteenth Century*. Auckland, NA. Auckland University Press.

Weber, M. (1946) *From Max Weber: Essays in Sociology* (eds and trans) H. Gerth and C.W. Mills. New York: Free Press.

## Waitangi Tribunal and other reports

1987 *Orakei Report* (Wai 8) Wellington: Brookers.

1992 *Te Roroa Report* (Wai 38) Wellington: Brookers.

1995 *Hirangi Report* Turangi: Tuwharetoa Maori Trust Board.

## Deeds

Heads of Agreement (HOA) Between the Crown and Waikato in Respect of the Waikato *Raupatu* Lands Claim. 21 Dec. 1994. Department of Justice Wellington.

Deed of Settlement (DOS) – Parties Her Majesty the Queen in the Right of New Zealand and Waikato. 22 May 1995.

Deed Establishing the Waikato Land Acquisition Trust. Rudd Watts and Stone, Solicitors, Wellington.

Deed Creating the Waikato *Raupatu* Lands Trust. Rudd Watts and Stone, Solicitors, Wellington.

Chapter 9

# Indigenisation as empowerment?

## Gender and race in the empowerment discourse in Zimbabwe

*Rudo Gaidzanwa*

Outside of peasant agriculture, which in itself hardly received much support, not many opportunities were available to black Zimbabweans to engage in gainful activity as entrepreneurs prior to independence. Post 1980 . . . government policy and programmes did not accord much attention or resources to the generation and support of black business ownership. . . . The Affirmative Action Group was born out of the need for support and guidance faced by many of its founder members in their attempts to survive in this hostile environment.[1]

The group clearly recognised that public economic and social policy needed to be systematically sensitised to the special requirements of historically disadvantaged groups, so that they could both defend the little they had, and meaningfully expand their stake in the economy . . .[2]

Hazvidadisi kuona munhu mutema achishandiswa nebhangi rokunze kuti rigoita mari nevatema vazhinji vemuZimbabwe. Ko ingawani takawana kuzvitonga? Hatingawani kuzvitonga hama dzedu dzichifa nenzara, vauyi vachiguta.

(It is embarrassing to see black people in Zimbabwe being used by a foreign bank to make money. Haven't we gained our independence? We cannot be independent when our relatives are dying of hunger and settlers are living well.)[3]

## Introduction

Since Zimbabwe gained its independence in 1980, the economy has been seriously weakened by successive government policies. Most Zimbabweans continue to participate in the economy as unskilled, casual, seasonal, contract and unpaid domestic and agricultural labour. The Economic Structural Adjustment Programme (ESAP) introduced in 1991 has negatively affected lifestyles particularly of the black working classes, and fuelled the anger and despair of black people. The articulation of these economic problems, as curable by 'indigenisation' and 'the empowerment of blacks', has been dominated by the black, male, self-employed business lobby, although the sagas of 'Willowgate', the Land Tenancy Scheme, the War Victims' Compensation Fund, cellular telephones and Harare's proposed new airport, have, over time, convinced the bulk of the black population that a small fraction of black politicians and top bureaucrats are primarily interested in empowering themselves through unfair access to public funds.

Since the 1980 Presidential Directive on Africanisation of the Zimbabwean civil service, which ran for three years, there has been no significant state action on black empowerment. But as a result of that directive, parastatals, the public sector and most pension, mutual and provident funds are today managed by indigenous Zimbabweans. However, the presence of some blacks as managers, workers, policy-holders and contributors of money to the public sector and money markets, has not resulted in the economic empowerment of Zimbabweans generally. Indeed, to date indigenisation of the parastatals has been disastrous, having rewarded the political and ethnic cronies of powerful public officials rather than appointing skilled and experienced black managers. Therefore, to equate the presence of black bodies in management with black economic empowerment misses the point entirely.

The debate on indigenization in Zimbabwe has gathered momentum as the end of the millennium approaches. Some of the arguments have produced disquiet in many quarters. This chapter will analyse the discourses from the points of view of the different actors involved in them in order to understand their interests and the ways in which they seek to advance such interests.

## The Indigenous Business Development Council (IBDC)

Among the black business lobbies, the IBDC in 1992 started the first of many explicit and structured publicity campaigns to empower black people economically. Among its founders were men and women who had worked in the private and public corporate sectors and then branched out into personal businesses in the late 1980s and early 1990s. They had some insights into the ways in which black people could manipulate the economy and the political set-up in order to enhance their business interests. They also understood how the structures of disadvantage worked by race and class. Predominantly, the IBDC's membership was black and male both in orientation and in its definition and understanding of the issues. It articulated the aspirations of its members and pressured government to recognise the need to create an enabling environment for black business people to enter the mainstream of the economy and to break the 'monopoly' of whites in Zimbabwean business.

The birth of the IBDC sent signals to the white business community that black businessmen were no longer satisfied with the white business community's domination of the economy. The emphasis on the term 'indigenous' started debate on who was actually indigenous and who was not. There were different interpretations of the term: some black people considered only the black people of Zimbabwe as indigenous, while many white people who were born and raised in Zimbabwe commented, with a great deal of indignation, that they too were indigenous to Zimbabwe. There was a great deal of debate over race as a dimension in defining 'indigenous'. A few Coloured business persons were quite affronted when they were excluded from joining the IBDC on the grounds that they were not indigenous, presumably because they were bi-racial, whereas the black women's business organisations seem not to have had any problems with bi-racial women who define themselves as 'indigenous'. Over time, the term 'indigenous' came to be accepted as a reference to black people who had occupied the lowest ranks in the hierarchy of privilege in colonial Zimbabwe. The IBDC was quite willing to cooperate with white people and with the government, partly because the luminaries in it had political backgrounds and strong connections to both the ZAPU and ZANU wings of the government of national unity. In 1994, after two years of existence, leadership wrangles perhaps temporarily displaced the IBDC from centre stage. Its place was taken, until in 1998 it too was beset by leadership disputes, by the Affirmative Action Group.

## The Affirmative Action Group (AAG)

The AAG had many groups affiliated to it, including the War Veterans' Association, the Indigenous Businesswomen's Organisation (IBWO) and the Youth Employment Empowerment Council. It was more confrontational than the IBDC with both whites and the government, calling on multinationals to accommodate blacks in the economy through selling shares and other equity in their firms and targeting white-dominated bodies such as the Tobacco Association and local white firms, castigating them for not having 'socially responsible' programmes and not meeting the aspirations of the black workforce and population. The AAG did not quibble about terminology and quickly made it clear that it purported to speak for all the blacks of Zimbabwe. Its relatively young, predominantly male black leadership quickly aligned itself to the ruling party, supporting its fund-raising efforts for the Solar Summit amongst other initiatives, endorsing the candidature of Robert Mugabe in the 1996 Presidential elections and the ZANU (PF) candidate in the mayoral elections in many towns, and generally linked its fortunes to those of ZANU (PF). It took out large advertisements in the daily press to denounce the economic exploitation of the black majority by the white minority and called for government to put in place affirmative action measures to allow blacks to participate more fully in the economy. Later, identifying itself with the ruling party, the AAG leadership involved itself in fund-raising for the party. It is unclear whether the AAG saw any potential conflict between the political interests of the ruling party and the aspirations of black business people, but it acted as if it did not.

In this connection, the AAG's advertisements were telling, because many of its founder members perceived the government as useful in defending what these business people had and therefore desisted from examining government practices, even those practices that were unpopular with the impoverished masses, such as hosting the Solar Summit while poverty increased amongst the working people, and awarding tenders for the cellular phone network and the new airport building to politically connected consortia. In 1996 the involvement of the AAG and the Small-Scale Miners' Association in the cellular telephone consortium generated rifts within the memberships of both organisations.

The most glaring contradiction in the AAG was its support for the government and its inclusion of the War Veterans' Association in its structure of affiliation: its ensuing silence about the revolt of the war veterans against the elite in the ruling party over the plundering of the War Victims' Compensation Fund by top officials of the government, among others, materially affected its credibility. In July 1997, war veterans barricaded streets, demonstrated, and locked elite members of the ruling party into various locations, denouncing them as greedy, corrupt and unfit to lead the country.[4] The AAG has stated that its objectives included

> constantly [to] render active support to any member of society who is subjected to the threat of loss or disadvantaged as a result of unfair application of standards in business or at work [and] to actively and deliberately foster a culture of questioning the status quo, as a mechanism for promoting adherence to democratic principles and practices in the governance of society, particularly as regards to issues of the national management and distribution of economic assets and development.[5]

The war veterans, the disadvantaged indigenous entrepreneur who lost out in his bid for the cellular telephone contract and other Zimbabweans have noted the discrepancies between this and similar statements published and reiterated since 1994, while the AAG leadership insinuated itself into the ruling party and remained silent about the injustices visited on the populace and on black entrepreneurs by the dominant elements in the ruling party.

The AAG's leadership, like the ruling party, was tarnished by its conspicuous consumption of clothes, cars and lifestyles. The AAG President and Vice-President appeared in a chat show on television where they spoke about their millions and how quickly they had amassed their wealth. The independent press[6] commented not only on the AAG leadership's lavish spending, but also its attempted politicisation of the funeral of a banker's father in a rural area in Zimbabwe. These reports were used by members of the public to question the legitimacy of such a leadership in claiming to represent entrepreneurial and poor Zimbabweans. The alignment of the AAG with the ruling party and its contestation of party positions (e.g. the Harare Province Chairmanship) in the face of the criticisms that the poor people of Zimbabwe have for some years levelled at the ruling party, did not improve the AAG's image. While many people, particularly the working poor, could identify with the AAG's message, its involvement with the ruling party and the behaviour of some of its leaders generated scepticism about the fate of the movement for black economic empowerment in the hands of such a leadership. The AAG subsequently experienced acrimonious leadership change, with its founder-president being accused of exploiting the black empowerment movement for his personal benefit. Certainly the AAG leadership was conspicuously silent regarding the problems that one prominent black businessman and founder member of the IBDC experienced in trying to set up a cellular phone network.

Strive Masiyiwa, an engineer, tried to provide to telephone users an alternative service to the monopoly exercised by the parastatal Posts and Telecommunications Corporation (PTC), which provides a poor and unreliable service to its many subscribers who continue to lose business as a result of its inefficiencies. Notwithstanding proposals to commercialise and privatise the PTC's unsatisfactory service, the state has tenaciously defended its communications monopoly. Masiyiwa took both parastatal and state to court on numerous occasions and each time won his case, including one against a presidential decision and another, in 1997, awarding the cellular contract to a firm purportedly linked to the minister then controlling this parastatal, her husband (a former army commander) and their close business associate. Although for years Strive Masiyiwa lost out in tender procedures that have recurrently been criticised,[7] ultimately his challenge was successfully upheld by the courts and by 1998 his company was in the process of establishing cellular services in both Zimbabwe and Botswana.

The black business lobbies were conspicuous by their silence over the Masiyiwa case, where not only was government patently unwilling to 'empower' a qualified and enterprising black businessman wanting to branch into a high technology field and capable independently of mobilising massive international resources to do so, but also apparently reserved such profitable opportunities for its own inner circle of political clients. The only real 'empowerment' Strive Masiyiwa needed was fair access in bidding for business, where that access, despite ESAP, was and still is controlled by the state.

The Masiyiwa case clearly illustrates the practical limits of empowerment rhetoric in the dependence of black business people on the patronage of the ruling party and, by default, the government. Any entrepreneur who thinks he or she can dispense with party patronage is likely to be brought sharply to heel by both party and government. Given the economic trouble that the government is in, black entrepreneurs are an increasingly important alternative source of income and power to politicians, since they can offer directorships, shares, stakes and other perks to powerful officials in exchange for their influence over the allocation of state-controlled assets. New and politically independent black entrepreneurs threaten to become a countervailing power in the economy and, by gaining prestige and status, to compete with and possibly displace politicians who have built up their individual economic empires by wielding political influence in the context – even following structural adjustment – of an economy tightly regulated by the state. Perhaps the majority of (not only black) Zimbabwean entrepreneurs have had to accept that political patronage is a necessary adjunct to the conduct of business in Zimbabwe. Certainly the white farming-business community also fell into the patronage line in 1996 by giving the State President and his new bride sixteen pedigree cattle,[8] in spite of the constant denunciation by the white business lobbies of the ruling party and of the government's lavish and incontinent spending of public funds.

However, while they have both subscribed to the racialisation of the 'indigenous empowerment' discourse, the IBDC has been much less happy than the AAG with the politics of patronage, in whichever direction these may run. Siziba (1996: 3), a past President of the IBDC, would like to see the Zimbabwean polity democratised to ensure a stable transfer of political power. The dominant strand of IBDC thinking has decried the politicisation of the indigenisation and empowerment issues, as reflected in the AAG's (and IBWO's) endorsement of the politics and politicians of the ruling party. The IBDC seemed uncomfortable linking indigenisation to the control and manipulation of the Zimbabwean economy by politicians responsible for its past poor performance. The AAG (and IBWO), apparently willingly overlooking the poor record in economic management of the successive Mugabe governments, called on the government to pressure white business organisations and firms to empower blacks economically.

## The white business community

The AAG soon provoked reaction from the white business and other communities, consisting of the commercial farmers and owners of capital in manufacturing, commerce, industry and other areas where largely black unskilled and semi-skilled workers are employed. The white business community has been continuously engaged in trying to work out a mode of peaceful coexistence with the present government, the ruling party and the movers and shakers in the influential civic groups in Zimbabwe, including the Zimbabwe Congress of Trade Unions (ZCTU). Hence in 1995–6, most white business people were uncomfortable with the debate on racism in Zimbabwe and wary about making public pronouncements about the racial and class politics of the country. This discomfort and reticence partly account for why they took so long publicly to articulate their 'Team Zimbabwe' programme, in late 1997, to redress the obvious disempowerment of black people and women in the economy of Zimbabwe: periodic upheavals have rocked the white business community whenever it has been strongly criticised by the President, the ruling party and other bodies. The passing of land-related legislation has long been a source of anxiety for individual white farmers, multinational landowners and other actors in the established white community. Government plans to 'designate' land were taken to indicate the fate of all propertied whites – and perhaps also landless blacks – in Zimbabwe. The emergence of the AAG was particularly disquieting for the white business community because the AAG never took a diplomatic or conciliatory tone in the debate on black economic empowerment, as did the IBDC. Hence the responses of white business to the advocates of indigenous empowerment were until recently limited to publicising 'facts'. For example,

> The staff and board of the Tobacco Research Board is made up of 87.5% indigenous Zimbabweans. 50% of the Senior Scientists are indigenous. Recipients of the ZTA Growers' Levy are currently the Tobacco Marketing Board, Research Stations, Tobacco Training Institutes and the Farmers' Development Trust.[9]

Most contributions from the white business lobby tended to focus on the need for government to effect market-related reforms that would liberalise the economy and release it from the control of the state, without addressing the prior question of whether such liberalisation would in itself empower blacks economically.

A number of previously white-dominated organisations, such as the Zimbabwe National Chamber of Commerce (ZNCC) dominated by traders and retailers, the Confederation of Zimbabwean Industries (CZI) dominated by industrialists, and the Employers' Confederation of Zimbabwe (EMCOZ) have included blacks in their leaderships and administrations. However, the ZNCC is currently facing financial embarrassment as a result of the deficit that is hindering its own operations as well as its proposed merger with the CZI. The CZI has also suffered embarrassment through the withdrawal of white (male) activists from the organisation. The press[10] has speculated that this withdrawal might be due to the fact that the organisation now has a black chief executive. It also has a white female president who is perceived to be friendly to blacks particularly in the ruling party. At the 1997 CZI annual conference, the white presence was noticeable by its reduction from customary levels.

This failure of the white business community to deal explicitly with the issue of racism and black economic disempowerment created the conditions that made the AAG's criticisms of the white business community credible and legitimate to the majority of black Zimbabweans, notwithstanding the quality of the AAG's leadership. In 1995, a white business initiative, Partners for Growth,[11] was formed, said to be led by some thirty white chief executives in the multinational sector. The press report, reflecting the 'line' taken by that particular newspaper (which first popularised the racial debate), alleged that the partnership was able to recruit only eight black members because the other black chief executives refused to be associated with a white-led initiative which they perceived to have been initiated to counter the black empowerment movement, rather than to deal squarely with the history of black economic exploitation in colonial Zimbabwe.

In sum, the white business community does not appear to want to discuss or debate the origins and history of white economic and political power in Zimbabwe. Rather, it has recurrently tried to harness the goodwill of those blacks who have done well out of the present system, namely the politicians and the black middle-class small businessmen, whose priorities appear to be to catch up with the whites on the business front rather than to empower the black majority. Recently the government has alleged that white capital has also entered into an alliance with organised black labour, while the AAG has attacked the white business community for its exclusionary and unresponsive stance towards black economic aspirations. However, while race has been addressed, the gender issue has not featured very prominently in either the government's or the AAG's own discourses on black economic empowerment in Zimbabwe. In 1994, this near-omission spurred black businesswomen to form their own organisation.

## The Indigenous Business Women's Organisation (IBWO)

IBWO was formed by black women after they realised that they had been marginalised within existing business organisations as well as lobbies such as the IBDC and AAG. In terms of accessing funds and other capital for starting and running businesses, black women found themselves shunted to the sidelines, for example in the disbursement of a Z$400 million loan facility that had been earmarked in 1994–5 for distribution to black small business people. Even among those who accessed this first loan facility, unfairness was perceived to have pervaded the whole process since only a small core of business-people (said not to be the neediest) received such loans. IBWO's mission is '[t]o create wealth for all indigenous women through economic empowerment and the removal of financial, social, economic, cultural and political impediments',[12] and it has now mobilised thousands of women in all Zimbabwe's provinces to support each other and enable black women to access business support and inputs.

As already observed elsewhere (Gaidzanwa 1993; Cheater and Gaidzanwa 1996), the treatment of black women by the government and the public has been less than fair especially when black women have ventured into business activities requiring physical mobility. While IBWO explicitly espouses an agenda for the economic empowerment of black women, it has also aligned itself with the politics of the ruling party. It endorsed the candidacy of Robert Mugabe in the 1996 Presidential elections and relies on the ruling party for patronage. As such, it has not made a significant break from the patronage politics espoused by cognate organisations. But since women tend to be more involved in micro- and small rather than medium or large businesses, IBWO has managed to reach to the poorer female constituencies in ways that the AAG and the IBDC have not. Its class politics tend to be sharper; whereas the IBDC and the AAG, their official rhetoric notwithstanding, have not really addressed the needs of the labouring black Zimbabweans who cannot hope to be employers of black labour to any significant extent.

## Racial and gender dimensions of the black empowerment discourse

Race has featured prominently in the debate on black empowerment, but in the whole discourse gender and other internal differentiations among blacks have been underplayed. The AAG has attacked whites directly, alleging that there is no white unemployment in Zimbabwe whereas black employment currently runs at over 50 per cent of the potential working population; that there is job reservation by whites for other whites in white-run or white-controlled firms, in which merit is not a criterion used to hire blacks; that white capitalists exploit black, cheap labour and exhibit very little social responsibility; that there is a need for government to pressure capitalists explicitly to address the issue of black economic empowerment through public policy on the indigenisation of the economy. The AAG strategy in particular seems to have focused on getting a share of existing white-owned assets.

In contrast, the IBDC has stressed the importance of black entrepreneurship in the project of black economic advancement. A founder member of the IBDC, Siziba (1996) has argued that not every individual can be a business entrepreneur, therefore the need is to invest in individuals who are likely to succeed, rather than just any person who happens to be black and/or disadvantaged. While recognising that such choices will probably breed social resentment by those not deemed sufficiently entrepreneurial, he has not really dealt with how to integrate the non-entrepreneurial into the economy in ways that will not breed conflict and resentment. 'But there is no choice' (Siziba 1996: 3), indicates that social resentment is something which must be accepted as the inevitable outcome of funding unequally distributed entrepreneurial abilities.

Neither the IBDC nor the AAG has explicitly addressed gender issues in their respective strategies for black empowerment. The fact that indigenisation and black economic empowerment are profoundly gendered processes has not been taken on board by either organisation, despite – or maybe because of – the colonial and postcolonial history of black women's disempowerment throughout Zimbabwe. Although the black business organisations have allied in a broad front based on their common experiences as disempowered black people, their points of divergence and/or myopia on gender issues are notable. Given the history of gender-differentiated access to land, education, finance and other resources, maintaining these broad coalitions among black organisations will not be easy if they do not deal explicitly with these questions. As it is, the alliances between IBWO, AAG and the ruling party have the potential to transfer these differences from the political into the economic domain, thus weakening their credibility.

## The government and black empowerment

According to recent government policy papers on the indigenisation of the economy (Zimbabwe 1996a, b), indigenisation is equated with economic empowerment, a position with which Siziba (1996) would presumably agree, given his argument that skilled and experienced black managers can use their positions to empower blacks in the same ways that white managers empowered whites in colonial Rhodesia and independent Zimbabwe. Both focus on race as a factor in the economic disempowerment of black Zimbabweans, but ignore gender and other issues within processes of black empowerment and indigenisation. Regional disparities are mentioned, but not linked to the obvious ethnic issues integral to the regional differentiation of the population. Class issues are likewise ignored.

In analysing the ownership of investment in the economy, the policy papers focus on race, ignoring the fact that in the public sector, workers are segmented by gender. Most of the skilled and managerial posts are held by black males while the small proportion of skilled women is concentrated in health and education. In glossing over the gender segmentation of public sector employment, the policy papers fail to note that black women are predominantly in secretarial jobs while the professional and managerial jobs are occupied mainly by black men. The private sector has most skilled and top managerial positions occupied by white men, while black men occupy largely middle management positions. Black women usually feature as lower-ranking workers since senior and middle secretarial positions are often occupied by white women. The ownership of rural road transportation equipment is almost 100 per cent black male Zimbabwean, although the policy paper mentions only its racial category. Similarly, 50 per cent of domestic capital is said to be owned by black Zimbabweans, when the reality is that these owners are black males.

The papers dwell on policy objectives for indigenising the economy, democratising ownership relations and eliminating racial differences arising from economic disparities. Notably, government does *not* intend to democratise ownership relations with respect to land in the peasant sector, where black women do not have primary rights to land in that half of the country covered by communal land tenure and resettlement leasehold. Women are still expected to depend on marriage to access land for their livelihoods. Discussion of the constraints on indigenisation of the rural economy focuses on the lack of title that men who hold lineage land have to deal with, but not on black women's dispossession from primary rights to the same land, on which they are the major sources of both labour and management. While staunchly refusing to deal with intra-black resource disparities by gender, both government and the black business lobbies have instead focused on acquiring land held by white farmers. The explicit focus on race while ignoring gender and other differentials among blacks, points to the specific interests of male-dominated government thinking on black empowerment and indigenisation. And the embarrassing saga of the Tenancy scheme that led to the allocation of land earmarked for the resettlement of poor Zimbabweans to influential government, party and army officials, was not addressed by the AAG or IBWO either.

Efforts to indigenise the economy have included an emphasis on science and technical education in which black women's participation has been largely confined to secretarial and some agricultural education. On the education issues, the policy papers are silent about the insignificant numbers of women who are science teachers and students, and on the limited access that women have to university education, particularly in engineering and related fields. Their gender-insensitive language does not make these policy documents particularly good reading for women.

The strategies these policy papers have recommended to indigenise the economy focus mainly on industrialisation, economic expansion and increased indigenous private investment and skills development. Existing and past industrialisation has relegated women to unskilled, casual, seasonal, unpaid labour and there is no reason to assume that, under black male leadership, this consequence of industrialisation would change in the future. The policy papers do not regard gender and other inequalities as important issues, worth recognising before defining solutions through indigenisation initiatives.

## Funding indigenous empowerment: savings

Government plans to introduce a savings scheme to create employment and indigenise the economy. The funding for such a scheme is expected to come from reduced government consumption expenditure. But in 1996 alone civil servants struck for more pay, and the Solar Summit cost Zimbabwe's taxpayers over Z$100 million. Notwithstanding the recent endorsement of government policy by the International Monetary Fund (IMF) and its pending but long-deferred release of previously withheld funding for the second phase of ESAP, most Zimbabweans find it increasingly difficult to believe that government has the will or the ability to curb consumption by its bloated and politicised civil service and state officials accustomed to enviable lifestyles funded by taxpayers. Claims that a savings scheme might be funded by reducing government consumption expenditure are unconvincing, when in its first year of operation in 1994, the new compulsory national retirement fund lost nearly all of its incoming funds to peculation by two top officials. In 1994, the chief executive of the National Social Security Agency had already been asked to step down on allegations of misusing NSSA funds and assets such as cars, allowances and personnel.[13]

For over a decade, government has resisted curbing its consumption expenditure despite calls to do so by the business lobbies, civil society, aid donors, the World Bank and the IMF. In view of the stringencies that accompany structural adjustment as it has impoverished them, ordinary people are angry. The government is wary of its survival possibilities if it continues to 'adjust'. President Mugabe has recurrently stated that he is considering abandoning some of the reforms already implemented. Further reforms will necessarily squeeze more (male) members of the middle classes who are more likely to be vocal and politically audible than the poor who have so far borne the brunt of ESAP in Zimbabwe. Given government's concern for its survival, it is very doubtful that public consumption expenditure can be curbed significantly, notwithstanding recent ZCTU-organised industrial action to try to force government to change its spending priorities in favour of the working people of Zimbabwe. Government reaction has been to allege a conspiratorial capital–labour alliance against the state, accusing the ZCTU of wishing to seize political power.

The state's savings proposal is again silent on an important gendered issue: most black women do not have large discretionary incomes, and will not be able to increase the rate and size of their savings, especially under conditions of structural adjustment in Zimbabwe. Therefore, their contribution to the rate and size of national savings will not increase significantly while the present thinking in government prevails. The continuing refusal by different government agencies to deal with gender differences and plan with them in mind will ensure that the 'blanket' planning approach, aggregating everybody and recognising only racial diversity, will yield the usual results of continuing exploitation and disadvantage among those already accustomed to being discriminated against.

## Funding indigenous empowerment: the National Investment Trust

Government planned to transfer its loss-making parastatals and those unimpressively performing companies in which it has shareholdings to the indigenous population through a National Investment Trust (NIT), as part of its indigenisation policy (Zimbabwe 1996a: 10). Siziba (1996) criticised this approach to black economic empowerment, since funding of the Trust was envisaged to take place partly through the paper transfer of existing government shares in parastatals and companies into the Trust, and parastatals would be worth very little – just the size of their market share – without their existing monopolies and with their past management. The objectives of the NIT were to enhance the participation of the indigenous people in the economy and to bring about equity in the distribution of wealth; to mobilise savings and to promote saving among local people (whether indigenous or not is not stated); to develop capital markets and widen the scope of the stock market by assisting indigenous people to acquire shares in locally quoted companies. Warehousing shares in any such Trust is widely viewed as business suicide under a high rate of inflation (Zimbabwe's has recently again risen to over 30 per cent annually). Whether poor 'indigenous people' would have the money or even want to buy units in such a Trust is doubtful, particularly when the majority shareholdings are likely to be held by politically approved economic failures, should such a Trust ever materialise. By 1998, the state was planning to sell many of its share-holdings[14] merely to meet existing deficits.

In the first public flotation of parastatal shares (in Dairibord Zimbabwe Limited) in mid-1997, government initially retained 40 per cent for itself[15] and reserved 35 per cent for existing stakeholders in the dairy industry, with another 10 per cent earmarked for the NIT. Ordinary Zimbabweans, together with private-sector institutional investors, massively over-subscribed for the small minority of shares (15 per cent) made available to them,[16] suggesting their preference for personal ownership over NIT-type 'empowerment'.

## Conclusion

Clearly, the whole process of indigenisation and black economic empower-ment still has to be fully thought out and conceptualised in government circles, which seem to be purposely blind to the internal differentiation of Zimbabwe's black population. Sectoral analyses of the economy do not differentiate the players except by race and one can only conclude that government function-aries are as yet thinking seriously about indigenisation and black economic empowerment only with reference to a limited, predominantly male, political circle. Strong anti-racist initiatives have been accompanied by equally strong tendencies to paper over the differentiation, the experiences and the economic struggles *within* the black population. The debate and discourse on black eco-nomic empowerment and indigenisation are thus suspect and proposed govern-ment solutions about as farsighted as its policy analyses: so far these have left a lot to be desired.

It is therefore necessary, for the future health of Zimbabwe's economy, for the black and white communities to partake seriously in this debate and wrest the discursive initiative from the black business lobbies and the govern-ment – a process which seems to have started in late 1997 following the first of a series of mass industrial actions. Given the previous experiences with land, the War Victims' Compensation Fund, salaries and perks, which highly placed government officials and politicians awarded themselves while pleading shortages of land and cash when the rest of the citizenry demanded the same, it seems that any government-led indigenisation and empowerment programme will probably follow the state's past modes of allocating wealth. The fuzziness of the definitions of indigenisation and black empowerment and the nebulous and questionable instruments for achieving the desired goals, the undifferentiated and superficial analyses of the economy, the participants, their profiles, roles and other-than-racial conflicts in the economy, do not augur well for the empowerment of black people other than a small political fragment of the 'new class' variety (Djilas 1958).

The bulk of the black population will probably have to struggle in the way that Strive Masiyiwa, the peasants and workers, the retrenched, the unemployed and the never-employed in Zimbabwe have done and are still doing. In their struggle for economic empowerment, in the present discourse they can only parlay their loyalties as men or women, blacks, ethnic cronies and political loyalists in order to empower themselves individually.

## Notes

1 Economic Structural Adjustment Programme.
2 *The Herald*, 21 July 1994.
3 Advertisement for the United Merchant Bank, *Sunday Mail*, 27 October 1996.
4 *The Herald*, 21 July 1997.
5 *The Herald*, 11 April 1997.
6 *Zimbabwe Independent*, 25 October 1996 (Muckraker, p. 10).
7 In 1996, twenty-one tenders to supply the PTC were nullified by the state's own Tender Board for not having used approved procedures (*Financial Gazette*, 6 June 1996, p. 1).
8 Fifteen heifers and one bull comprised this slightly belated wedding gift from the Tobacco Trade Association and the Zimbabwe Tobacco Association (*The Herald*, 31 August 1996).
9 'Facts' published by the Zimbabwe Tobacco Association in *The Herald*, 24 May 1996, in response to advertisements by the black empowerment advocate, Roger Boka.
10 *Business Herald*, 17 July 1997, *Zimbabwe Independent*, 18 July 1997.
11 *Sunday Mail*, 5 February 1995.
12 *IBWO Mirror*, vol. 1, 1996, p. 1.
13 The *Financial Gazette*, 23 February 1995, reported on the meeting betwen the Zimbabwe Congress of Trades Unions and the employers' organisation (EMCOZ) regarding mismanagement of workers' pension contributions. An expatriate manager was appointed on contract to head NSSA, and in due course (in 1997) legal process jailed his predecessor.
14 *Zimbabwe Independent*, 17 April 1998, p. 28.
15 Government intends 'to reduce its shareholding to a maximum of 25 per cent in the shortest possible space of time. In the medium term, it expects to divest itself fully of its DZL shares, subject to appropriate market and economic conditions' (*DZL Prospectus*, 1997, p. 9).
16 *DZL Prospectus*, 1997.

## References

Cheater, A.P. and Gaidzanwa, R.B. (1996) Citizenship in neo-patrilineal states: gender and mobility in Southern Africa. *Journal of Southern African Studies* 22, 2: 189–200.

Djilas, M. (1958) *The New Class*. New York: Praeger.

Gaidzanwa, R.B. (1993) Citizenship, nationality and gender in Southern Africa. *Alternatives* 18: 39–59.

Siziba, C. (1996) Indigenising the Zimbabwean economy by 2020. Issues of policy and process. Paper commissioned by VISION 2020, Zimbabwe.

Zimbabwe (1996a) *Indigenising the Zimbabwean Economy*. Harare: Government Printer.

—— (1996b) *Programme for Economic and Social Transformation* (Draft MS).

# Chapter 10

# Exploitation after Marx

*Robert Layton*

There is an assumption prevalent in current Western political thought that Marxist theory has been discredited by collapse of communism, and that a capitalist, free market theory is the only viable one. It is argued here that the interplay of power and cooperation in society can best be understood by combining insights from both paradigms. The argument is illustrated with material from the French village of Pellaport and neighbouring communities, which I first studied for my PhD in 1969 and have most recently re-studied during the summer of 1995. Darwinian theory owes much to the model of market economics and, in some regards, Darwin's theory of evolution can be considered an application of free market principles to nature, subsequently reapplied to social behaviour by socioecologists. The chapter will consider how adaptationist models of social process derived from Darwinian theory can elucidate one of the key defects of Marx's theory. It will, however, also argue that some of Marx's principles must be retained, not only to explain how social adaptations can result in imbalances in the distribution of power, but also to explain why social change sometimes seems to proceed in the linear, cumulative fashion often referred to as 'progress', which plays no part in Darwinian theory.

Karl Marx and Charles Darwin were contemporaries. Marx's *A Contribution to the Critique of Political Economy* was published in the same year as *The Origin of Species* (1859). Their theories of evolution were, however, radically different. Marx worked within the tradition of 'progressive' evolutionists, who assumed that both social and biological change is driven forward by an internal dynamic, whereas Darwin saw evolution as the result of local ecological conditions acting on random genetic variation in a species. Marx identified two processes of 'positive feedback' causing cumulative change in capitalist society. If a craftsman needs to work six hours to earn his subsistence, but the capitalist makes him work for eight, the extra two hours labour earns the capitalist his profit. With this he can buy more labour, or more equipment for his workshop. It is a case of, in Marx's words, 'self-expanding value . . . a monster quick with life' (Marx 1930: 189). The second process which tended to bring about a progressive transformation of the social system was the incentive to reduce labour costs further by introducing machinery. One machine can simultaneously do the work of several people and machines can be run continuously, causing increasing unemployment.

The failure to identify processes of positive feedback in biological evolution is identified by Odling-Smee as a shortcoming in traditional Darwinian theory (Odling-Smee 1995). Organisms consume resources, leave detritus and interact socially with other members of their own species. Hence, Odling-Smee argues, organisms inherit both genes which have survived the effects of natural selection and ancestrally modified environments. Wherever organisms modify their environment, they will modify the selection pressures to which subsequent generations of the same population are subjected. While biological 'niche-construction' may be almost imperceptibly slow, the processes described by Marx can be seen as the social equivalents of 'niche-construction'. In concluding, I shall argue that socio-ecological studies of the diffusion of innovations have failed fully to consider the consequences of innovations transforming the social environment.

The principal weakness in Marx's analysis, from the perspective of this chapter, was his failure to subject the alternative to capitalism he advocated, collective ownership, to a similar analysis. Marx's approach to collective ownership was flawed by his treatment of it as the natural, or original human condition, thereby apparently removing the need to analyse the specific conditions which sustained it. In recent years socioecologists have applied neo-Darwinian ideas to social process. Their work on the parallel between the increase in the frequency of adaptive genetic mutations and the spread of innovations is particularly relevant to this chapter, as is the development of economic and socioecological theories which try to establish the circumstances in which it is in the individual's self-interest to cooperate with others in the management of common property, rather than to compete in its exploitation.

One school of thought, exemplified by Hardin (1968), holds that unless coercion is applied by an authority, the commons are inevitably less well managed than private property. A simple market model is used to support this contention. The other school, exemplified by McCay and Acheson (1987) and Ostrom (1990), draws on aspects of Darwinian theory to argue that individual and collective ownership are both adaptive, but in particular circumstances (that is, in particular social and natural environments).

Hardin assumed that access to common land was normally unregulated (Hardin 1968). He drew on the work of Lloyd, a nineteenth-century writer who proposed a parallel between common grazing land and the labour market. Lloyd's model of commons management can be seen, in retrospect, to depend on the effect of positive feedback or, in Odling-Smee's terms, 'niche-construction'. Lloyd argued that the market was a public good to which there was open access. Where children had to fend for themselves from an early age and there were no restrictions on entry into the labour market, nothing would limit the size of working-class families. The market was flooded with labour and wages fell. It should have been in the working class's interest to restrict the number of children they had, to keep wages high. The difficulty was that if a few families produced many children, the level of wages fell for everyone, and the large families earned more than those who had showed restraint. Large families were transforming the 'niche' in which all workers tried to survive. Since others were not to be trusted, the rational strategy was for all to have large families (Lloyd 1964 [1833]). Lloyd, followed by Hardin, applied the same principle to the commons. If there are no controls over access, self-restraint by some herdsmen will be undermined when others put too much stock on the commons. The 'free-riders' cause degradation of the niche on which all depend, but only they benefit from the higher numbers of stock they have pastured. The rational strategy is therefore for everyone to overstock, destroying the commons' value. Hardin argued that only sanctions imposed by government, or privatising the commons, would enable responsible management. He discounted the possibility of self-regulation among the users (Hardin 1968).

Dyson-Hudson and Smith argued that the Karimojong of East Africa defend grazing land collectively as a 'tribe' because the distribution of grass and water is too unpredictable to justify dividing it into small areas defended by individual lineages. Small fields of maize, however, are defended by the households who cultivate them (Dyson-Hudson and Smith 1978). Netting used the same argument in his analysis of landownership in the Swiss village of Torbel. Grass on the alpine pastures is too dispersed and unreliable to justify the cost and risk of dividing it into fields owned by individual households. Collective management is more efficient. Far from allowing open access, use of the alpine commons is closely regulated by the community. Only citizens of the village are allowed to use it and the number of cattle they can graze is controlled (Netting 1981: 60–7). McCay and Acheson point out that, under the medieval and post-medieval open field system, use of English commons was also regulated by the communities to which they belonged. They argue that the English enclosures were precipitated by conditions peculiar to the rise of capitalism and not by an inherent weakness in commons management (McCay and Acheson 1987; cf. Layton 1995).

Ostrom argues that Hardin's model is not wrong, but lacks the generality Hardin claimed for it. Ostrom contends that the 'open-access' scenario proposed by Hardin is not the only possibility. The application of games theory to study the evolution of social strategies shows how individuals can form stable coalitions based on mutual trust which can avert the 'tragedy' of over-exploitation. Even if the cumulative benefits of cooperation are greater than those of cheating (free-riding), individuals who only interact once will do best to assume the other will cheat and thus avoid the costs of restraint. When individuals interact repeatedly, however, cooperation can become a stable strategy (see Axelrod 1990). Ostrom draws on games theory to identify the conditions most likely to enable successful control of the commons by those who use them. People who interact regularly in a local context, who have developed shared norms and patterns of reciprocity, who can monitor whether their associates are adhering to the agreed level of exploitation, and who can punish free-riders, are most likely to succeed (Ostrom 1990: 184–8).

On the Plateau of Levier, in eastern France, a substantial proportion of land within the territory of each village on the plateau is communally owned. Common pasture and forest still make an important contribution to the income of the village. Co-operative dairy associations have also been active since the thirteenth century. The pattern of land management is very similar to contemporary institutions described by Netting in Torbel (Netting 1981), and derives from the open field system that was once widespread in northern Europe. The evolution of commons management and dairy associations can be linked with two causes of social change familiar to Marx and other nineteenth-century writers: population growth and inflation. Villagers have responded both by mechanising farm production and by transforming the principles by which collective property is managed. Ideas developed in socio-ecological thinking on the diffusion of innovations, which draw attention to the similarities and differences between biological evolution and sociocultural change (Boyd and Richerson 1985; Cavalli-Sforza and Feldman 1981; Durham 1991), help to explain why change has been cumulative and unidirectional rather than displaying a Darwinian adaptive radiation. I explore the effects of feedback which link these processes in order to highlight their impact on the distribution of power which, in turn, determines the ability of villagers to regulate their own lives.

## History of the commons on the Plateau of Levier

The French Jura begins at the Swiss border as a chain of mountains, which give way to a series of limestone plateaux as one travels west. The Plateau of Levier, on which the village of Pellaport is situated, lies west of Pontarlier. An average of 40 per cent of land within the territory of each village on the plateau is communally owned. Common pasture and forest still make an important contribution to the income of the village. The first cooperative dairy associations are recorded in a document written in 1264 (Lambert 1953: 175). The organising principles of the dairy associations appear to have spread from Switzerland to the Plateau of Levier at a time when long-distance trade in France was 'taking off' during the thirteenth century. Two ancient trade routes linking France with Switzerland and Italy border the Plateau of Levier (Braudel 1990: 231). Members of the original associations pooled their milk and took it in turns to manufacture a large cheese which could withstand the rigours of travel to distant towns (see Latouche 1938). Dairy associations have therefore always existed within the context of a market economy.

## The population curve

Reliable population figures for the Plateau of Levier are available from the seventeenth century. Franche-Comté, the ancient province to which the plateau belonged, was held by the Spanish Hapsburgs from 1555 to 1678. In 1639 Richelieu engaged a German duke, Bernard of Saxe-Weimar, to devastate the province as a prelude to French conquest. Saxe-Weimar's soldiers systematically destroyed villages and, inadvertently, brought an epidemic of plague to the region. Documented population densities therefore begin from a nadir in which 'the countryside was so depopulated as to resemble a desert rather than a once-peopled land' (Lebeau 1951: 408). Recent calculations suggest the villages of the Plateau of Levier lost up to 50% of their population at this time (Courtieu 1982–7). Figure 1 shows how the population grew steadily for 200 years, apart from a brief dip at the time of the French Revolution, passing

*Figure 1* Average population of villages on the Plateau of Levier 1590–1990

*Sources:* Courtieu (1982–7), census figures from Institut National de La Statistique et Études Économiques.

the estimated pre-1639 level some time during the eighteenth century and reaching a peak in 1850. After 1850 the French industrial revolution provided an escape route for the day labourers and domestic servants at the bottom of the peasant hierarchy, and population fell equally inexorably until the 1970s, when private car ownership enabled people working in town to commute to work.

The most significant response to the increasing population was the appearance of a 'European marriage pattern' (Hajnal 1965), in which marriage was delayed and many remained celibate throughout their lives. This mitigated the effect of partible inheritance. If only one son and one daughter married, family holdings would not decrease in size. A similar strategy exists in Nepal, where it has been convincingly related to the need to avoid the division of family farms through partible inheritance (see Durham 1991: 83–8). Population growth did not follow Lloyd's prediction because subsistence was tied to a clearly limited supply of family land rather than to an open-access market. While the effects of this strategy on village social structure were less divisive than the consequences of primogeniture in England, it did create discontent among those forced to remain celibate while working on the family farms, and the presence of a small class of agricultural labourers usually living in single-parent households can also be seen in late nineteenth-century household censuses (Layton 1989: 444–6, 1995: 711–13).

As late as 1826, 363 of the 546 associations in the *département* of Doubs were located in the area west of Pontarlier bounded by the two ancient trade routes that border the Plateau of Levier. During the eighteenth century, however, the practice of forming dairy associations spread from the Plateau of Levier into surrounding areas (Daveau 1959: 249), and several strategies were adopted to improve production. Swiss dairymen were hired, bringing with them the knowledge of how to manufacture *gruyère*, a superior cheese to the *vachelin* previously made locally. The practice of taking it in turn to make the cheese in each member's household gave way to production in purpose-built dairies. Originally, each member had kept the cheese made in their house to sell but, during the nineteenth century, the practice of selling cheeses in bulk and distributing the profits to members was introduced (Latouche 1938). Each of these innovations spread through the region in turn. Daveau estimates that almost half of the dairy associations in the neighbouring *département* of Jura had adopted bulk selling by 1896 (Daveau 1959: 282).

Improved husbandry techniques, constantly promoted by local government through its year books and agricultural shows, gradually increased the milk yield of cattle. In the eighteenth century dairy associations ceased production during the winter, when there was only enough milk available for domestic consumption. Two personal records of production, in 1769 and 1778, suggest that a cow's annual yield was then around 500 kilos a year (see Latouche 1938: 778–9). By the mid-nineteenth century the annual yield per cow had risen to between 1,000 and 1,600 kilos (figures in Courtieu 1982–7), but human population growth had outstripped the number of livestock. In 1688, the region including the Plateau of Levier that was to become the *département* of Doubs had a population of 110,900, and 47,689 dairy cattle (0.42 per person). In 1884, the population of 310,827 owned 106,975 dairy cattle (0.33 per person) (Gauthier 1886: 52–4).

Until 1790, management of the commons was the prerogative of the assembly of household heads. In 1625, for example, Pellaport's assembly sold a portion of commons to two individuals, on condition that if it were resold, the purchasers should be 'born, native and originating in the village of Pellaport'. Management was for long hindered by rights of inter-commoning, which allowed adjacent villages to pasture their livestock on the same land. In 1731 and 1746 Pellaport's assembly appealed to the government's representative in Pontarlier to issue a decree forbidding the inhabitants of a neighbouring village from putting diseased cattle on shared commons. Repeated, and eventually successful efforts were made during the eighteenth century to agree the boundaries between the land of adjacent communities. Both these conflicts may be interpreted as responses to an increasing population. Before community boundaries had been agreed the commons were probably an open-access resource. Once community assemblies had gained control they were in a position to avoid 'the tragedy of the commons'.

After 1790 community assemblies were replaced by elected municipal councils. I have no information on how the commons were managed by the council in the nineteenth century, but suppose that the accounts given me by older villagers in 1969, of the system that obtained during their childhood, describe a traditional arrangement. Part of the commons was given over to pasture, part to hay meadow. The meadow was divided into lots. Each person born before 1 January that year was entitled to put one cow on the pasture, and harvest one portion of about 25–30 ares (0. 25–0.3 ha) of meadow. Cattle on the pasture formed a single herd supervised by a hired cowherd. Portions of meadow were allocated at a draw in the village hall attended by the head of each household, who drew one lot for each member of his family. The quality of meadow varied, and the effect of the lottery was to randomise each household's allocation. Since the French army and urban tradesmen relied heavily on horse-power until the late 1940s, villagers who were not themselves farmers could harvest and sell their hay. As one villager explained, 'there were many retired people who had no cows. They scythed their portions, harvested them and sold them at a good price.'

## Mechanisation

The advent of the French industrial revolution unleashed a flood of people from the countryside into the cities. By 1873 the region's agriculture was in crisis:

Complaints about the lack of capital are to be heard almost everywhere but for large and medium-scale agriculture the scarcity of rural labourers and the consequent rise in wages are considerable sources of difficulty and embarrassment. Scarcity of labour is undoubtedly the open wound (*la plaie vive*) in our agricultural system.

(Laurens 1873: 161–2)

The solution to the vanishing rural workforce was provided by machinery. Horse-drawn mechanical mowers and hay rakes appeared in Franche-Comté during the 1880s (Daveau 1959: 275), becoming more widespread between the turn of the century and the First World War. Early machinery was adopted to overcome the rising cost of agricultural labour (a variant on the labour models of Marx and Lloyd!) and, by the end of the First World War, the massive loss of life in the trenches.

Once rural depopulation began the rural and urban economies became caught up in an interactive process in which the effects of positive feedback are clear. The countryside provided the initial urban workforce, but the towns produced the agricultural equipment which made it possible for agriculture to continue without the vanishing hired labourers (OECD 1965: 37). The incentive to improve farming techniques and resource management ceased to be the need to feed a growing local population, and became the desire to participate in expanding urban markets. Rising urban incomes caused general inflation, steadily eroding the value of farmers' income which they attempted to offset by increasing production. The irony of this process is that, while the commons were not treated as an open-access resource, the urban market for dairy produce *was*, bringing about precisely the inflationary effect on the value of dairy produce predicted by Lloyd/Hardin model and ultimately eroding the solidarity of the peasant community.

During the 1880s, when rural depopulation was already in full flood on the Plateau of Levier, European agriculture was first exposed to competition from American beef and cereals. In France as a whole 48 per cent of the population were still cultivators, making them a formidable political force. The government imposed import tariffs on imported farm products to make home-grown products competitive (Tracy 1964: 38ff). The disruption of trade across the Atlantic during the First World War argued in favour of continuing a protectionist policy, and few inter-war French politicians dared advocate alternatives. Inflation again encouraged farmers to improve their income by increasing production, until home markets became saturated and the surplus could not be sold abroad because it was too expensive (Tracy 1964: 187). Although the value of the franc rose between 1931 and 1935, the appearance of the first tractors in the region around Pellaport at this time (Clade 1994: 13) is symptomatic of the continuing decline in the rural labour force. Had it not been for the Second World War, the second phase of mechanisation, known as 'motorisation' (Franklin 1969: 24–6) which began in the 1950s would probably have started ten or fifteen years earlier.

Resolution of the problem was deferred by the Second World War. By the end of the war agricultural production in France had fallen again by 30 per cent (Baum 1958: 16–19). Post-war governments continued to protect French agriculture from foreign competition. The government fixed the price of chemical fertilisers, the price of petrol and diesel was subsidised and farmers were offered loans at low rates of interest to buy new equipment (Baum 1958: 298–300; Franklin 1969: 28–30). Agricultural cooperatives were promoted as a means of maintaining the viability of small-scale *exploitations*[1] (Franklin 1969: 15). Nonetheless, the same cycle of declining incomes and over-production occurred during the 1950s and 1960s (OECD 1965: 21, 83). Elderly farmers were offered improved pensions if they retired in favour of their sons (Tracy 1964: 246). Attempts to implement a more drastic, EC-wide programme to reduce the number of people occupied in farming failed due to popular opposition (Shutes 1993: 135). The persistence of over-production in dairy farming led the EC to impose quotas on milk production in 1984. Each *exploitation* now has a milk production level attached to it and is liable to the 'super-levy', the fine dairy farmers pay for each kilo of milk they produce over their quota (Jurjus 1993: 102).

## Inflation

The effect of increased production on the value of milk can be clearly seen from the seasonal variation in its value. Table 1 plots seasonal variation in the quantity of milk produced on two *exploitations* in Pellaport against the effect on the value of milk which arises from the global change in seasonal levels of milk production. Each year, the total level of cheese production increases and this has a similar inflationary effect, causing the price paid for milk at the dairy progressively to fall (see Figure 2). In order to achieve a constant income, milk production will have to be steadily increased, thus further lowering the price of milk. Just as Hardin and Lloyd noted, it is only necessary for a minority of *cultivateurs* producing cheese to follow this strategy for all to suffer the effect of declining

*Table 1*  Milk values and output

|  | 1935 | 1954 | 1967 | 1975 |
|---|---|---|---|---|
| July value of milk as % of November value | 75% | 85% | 96% | 91% |
| July production of milk as % of November production | | | | |
| exploitation (i) | 483% | 325% | 144% | 178% |
| exploitation (ii) | – | 318% | 178% | 169% |

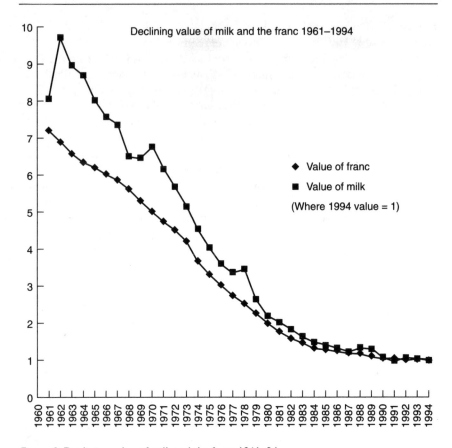

*Figure 2* Declining value of milk and the franc 1961–94

value. All *cultivateurs* must follow suit, or see their income progressively eroded. In 1968 the average price of milk at Pellaport's dairy was 0.4686 francs per kilo and the average annual production per *cultivateur* was 35,775 kilos, giving an average annual income of 16,764 francs. In 1994 the average price of milk at the village dairy was 2.2812 francs per litre and the average annual production per *cultivateur* was 170,646 litres, giving an annual average income of 389,278 francs.[2] A comparison of the price of standard items of agricultural machinery shows, however, that despite an increase in average milk production of 477 per cent, purchasing power has only risen by 31 per cent. A *cultivateur* who had ten cows in 1969 may well have been hesitating whether to invest in this suite of equipment, which would then have cost him 212 per cent of his annual income. Suppose he decided not to increase his herd size and to continue with his existing techniques. Even if he had been able to match the others' improved yields per cow in 1994, the corresponding suite of equipment would now cost him 406 per cent of his annual income. The longer technological change is delayed, the harder it becomes. Chapuis calculated that in the late 1950s, 29 per cent of *cultivateurs* in the Loue Valley (which forms the northern boundary of the Plateau of Levier) were already unable to afford the equipment that would have enabled them to increase production and keep pace with the rising incomes of factory workers (Chapuis 1958: 180). The net effect is a steady decline in the number of *exploitations* as the smaller ones cease production and the family's children seek other employment. Pellaport's dairy cooperative had 45 members in 1945, 31 in 1968 and 12 in 1994.

## Management of the commons in the twentieth century

During the 1950s, existing procedures for managing the commons came to appear increasingly inappropriate. With the disappearance of horse-transport there was no longer a large market for hay and non-farmers were no longer interested in exploiting their rights to the commons. The procedure for allocating portions of hay was based on the number of people in the household but, since the decline of the 'European Marriage' strategy, the number of people per household was falling while the number of cattle rose. The primary aim had become, not to provide for the household's subsistence, but to take greatest advantage of the market for cheese. In the nineteenth century everyone in the village had to some extent been involved in farming but, due to the processes of positive feedback outlined above, agriculture was becoming the occupation of an increasingly specialist interest group within the community.

Although cattle placed on the commons were guarded by a cowherd (generally an elderly villager) appointed and paid by the municipal council, the commons were unfenced and in order to keep his herd from straying into the surrounding fields and forest the herdsman had to keep them together, preventing the animals from spreading out in search of the best grass. There was no supply of water to the commons, and the cattle had to be led back to one of the village cattle troughs at midday. No chemical fertilisers were put on the commons, and no arrangement was made to level molehills or cut back brushwood. Between the First and Second World Wars, the village dairy association had periodically tried to organise work parties to clear brushwood but only some *cultivateurs* played their part and gradually no one was willing to participate.

Despite all these drawbacks, the *cultivateurs* of the village persisted with traditional procedures until they were overtaken by a crisis. In 1954 there was no one left willing to work all day as village cowherd. At that moment, several of the younger farmers announced their intention of forming a new cooperative. The procedures were well-known through the running of the dairy cooperative, and a movement was under way throughout the district to create village pasture cooperatives. An inaugural meeting was advertised outside the dairy. Those who attended drew up a list of statutes based on government regulations for the running of cooperatives and elected a nine-man committee from the thirty-four who joined. Only one *cultivateur* in the village had sufficient land not to need to use the commons. The village council agreed to rent the pasture to the association and provided it with a loan to pay for the 8 kilometres of boundary fence required. Now the *cultivateurs* would only need to find someone willing to bring the cattle to and from the pasture, who would be paid from the annual contribution levied on members of the cooperative. A few years later the cooperative installed a pump to take water to the pasture and bought a machine to spread chemical fertiliser. Members were invited to tender for the job of levelling molehills and cutting back brushwood. Any income they received by working for the cooperative was deducted from their annual levy. In 1967 the municipal council voted to abolish the traditional distribution of hay to each household, and rent the remaining commons to the cooperative.

When I began fieldwork in 1969 membership had declined to twenty-two, but between them the members sent 206 head of cattle to graze on the commons, 73 per cent of the village's heifers and 30 per cent of its milk cows. The continuing decline in the number of *cultivateurs* later prompted the division of the commons between those who remained. In Pellaport the commons were divided in 1979, when membership of the pasture cooperative had fallen to about sixteen. Three reasons were given in favour of the division. No one suffered the risk of disease spreading from one stable's cattle to another's. Each *cultivateur* could decide whether to graze livestock or cut hay on his portion – the land benefits from a rotation between hay meadow and pasture. People looked after the land better when they were solely responsible for their portion. One of my old friends told me in 1995 that milk production from cattle pastured on the commons had doubled since its division. The division took place, however, without privatisation. The commons continue to belong to the village and are rented by the cooperative, but the cooperative's role is now limited to obtaining insurance for the cattle and negotiating the current division, ensuring some flexibility as the relative needs of different *exploitations* change.

When I carried out a comparative survey in 1972, management of the commons was still carried out by the mayor and members of the municipal council in five of the fourteen villages surveyed, while pasture cooperatives had been created in six. In three others the dairy cooperative had begun to rent the pasture from the commune and arrange its management. By 1995, pasture cooperatives existed in all but three communes. Eight villages, however, had divided the commons. Two further villages had divided some sections of the commons, but left the remainder as a single high pasture on which the heifers were placed together.

There are some striking echoes from the old English debate on enclosure in the reasons villagers gave in favour of dividing the commons. Equally, the same question remains unanswered: if division is so much better, why was joint exploitation tolerated for so long? The growth of divisions in the community, resulting in the exclusion of large numbers of people who still had a vital interest in commons, which I argue explains the English case, cannot be extended to the Plateau of Levier (Layton 1995). Villages have kept their democratic organisation and corporate ownership of the commons. The socio-ecological prediction that scarce and unpredictable resources are most efficiently exploited in common, however, has less force as the number of *cultivateurs* declines. The fewer the *cultivateurs*, the larger the patch each will receive, evening out the risk of random variation in patch quality.

## Conclusions

Changes in management of commons during the present century arise from two of the consequences of the feedback processes outlined above: the need to improve the productivity of the land, which in turn feeds back upon inflation, and the decline in the number of *cultivateurs* as inflation takes its toll on the viability of smaller farms. Collective management of local resources is undermined by the strategies which *cultivateurs* adopt in their exploitation of the market, creating a division between the relatively wealthy (powerful) and relatively poor.

The processes by which members of the community adapt to the current social environment can partly be understood in terms of the 'dual inheritance' or 'co-evolution' models which examine the similarities and differences between the genetic and cultural transmission of information within a Darwinian paradigm (Boyd and Richerson 1985; Cavalli-Sforza and Feldman 1981; Durham 1991). Culture has a potential advantage over genetic evolution in allowing new patterns of behaviour to be transmitted more rapidly (within the span of one generation) and more widely (beyond the parent–child relationship) than would be possible through the natural selection of random genetic variation. If vertical transmission (transmission from parent to child) were the only mode of transmission for cultural traits, culture would follow the same lines as genetic transmission. The significance of cultural inheritance increases when it ceases to follow this narrow path. Cultural traits can be transmitted horizontally (between members of the same generation) and obliquely (between generations, but not to the transmitter's own children). Whereas all genetic mutations occur at random, a cultural innovation may be devised in response to a perceived problem, although it is recognised that humans are rarely perfectly informed (Cavalli-Sforza and Feldman 1981: 342). The spread of both technological and institutional innovations can be explained in these terms. New machines are tested by those who can afford them and, if they improve on existing techniques, are also bought by friends and neighbours. Communities experiment with new administrative procedures and, if they are effective, these too spread to neighbouring villages.

The weakest aspect of the 'dual inheritance' approach is the relatively limited attention it gives to processes of feedback or 'niche construction' which transform power relations in the community. Boyd and Richerson argue that the term 'environment' should be restricted to factors such as availability of food, the climate and the actions of predators, writing 'the social behaviour of individuals in a population is *not* part of the environment, *even though behaviour may affect individual fitness*, because it is internal to the evolving population' (Boyd and Richerson 1985: 5, my emphasis). Durham stresses that inequalities of power may compel some individuals to adopt traits which favour the fitness of the powerful but not their own fitness (Durham 1991: 191). The nineteenth-century labourers who worked for farming households without sharing in the family inheritance illustrate this process (see Layton 1989: 445).

The spread of an innovation may resemble the spread of an epidemic (Cavalli-Sforza and Feldman 1981: 33), but this will only apply where the individuals who are susceptible are randomly distributed through the population. Cavalli-Sforza and Feldman recognise that where a large proportion of the population have adopted an innovation, this may put increased pressure on the remainder to follow suit (Cavalli-Sforza and Feldman 1981: 36). The actions of certain *cultivateurs* on the Plateau of Levier who have the resources to increase production oblige others to follow suit or be eliminated from farming. Numerous studies of technological change in the Third World (e.g. Scott 1976) have shown that adoption of an innovation by a relatively wealthy minority may transform the social environment so greatly that it becomes increasingly *difficult* for the poorer to follow their example and the same process applies, although with less force, in the villages of Franche-Comté. The exclusion of increasing numbers from agriculture on the Plateau of Levier has had nothing like the effects seen in Third World (there are no shanty towns outside Pontarlier). Nonetheless, while there was no rural unemployment in 1969/72, in 1995 between 3 and 5 per cent of household heads in the fourteen villages surveyed were unemployed.

Durham's approach comes closest to the one I wish to advance in this chapter. He criticises the 'radical individualism' of Boyd and Richerson's model which causes them to ignore the effects of power and coercion. 'In cultural systems . . . significant evolutionary forces can and do arise from unequal social relations' (Durham 1991: 182). Their model also ignores 'the interaction between cultural evolution and changes in the social organisation of a population, which may be termed its "social evolution"' (Durham 1991: 182–3). But Durham is interested in the way that a status quo characterised by unequal power can coerce the weak into adopting maladaptive traits, not in the way that adopting particular traits can feed back upon the power structure.

I suggest there are two reasons why social change on the Plateau appears to follow a linear trajectory closer to a Marxist model than a neo-Darwinian one. Comparison of the fourteen villages in the survey shows that, at any time, several alternative strategies exist. Diversification analogous to an adaptive radiation is, however, inhibited by the uniform change in the social environment created by inflation in the price of milk, itself the consequence of strategies to increase output. The second cause arises from the wish to avoid the risk of adopting an unfamiliar strategy. Further experimentation is discouraged and the apparently successful innovation spreads rapidly through the local culture. I have analysed this process in more detail, with regard to technological innovation, in an earlier paper (Layton 1973). Hence, I conclude, both the Marxist and the Darwinian approaches to social evolution can contribute to an understanding of contemporary social change.

## Notes

1 The terms *ferme* and *fermier* refer to a rented property and its tenant. Since these terms are locally considered demeaning (and are generally inappropriate, since the land is frequently owned by members of the household or their relatives) I have used the locally favoured terms *exploitation* and *cultivateur* rather than farm and farmer.
2 The unit of measurement changes from kilos to litres in the records. A litre of milk weighs 1.03 kilos.

## References

Axelrod, R. (1990) *The Evolution of Co-operation*. Harmondsworth: Penguin. (First published 1984 New York: Basic Books.)

Baum, W.C. (1958) *The French Economy and the State*. Princeton, NJ: Princeton University Press.

Braudel, F. (1990) *The Identity of France, vol. II: People and Production* (trans.) S. Reynolds. Glasgow: Collins.

Boyd, R. and Richerson, P.J. (1985) *Culture and the Evolutionary Process*. Chicago: University of Chicago Press.

Cavalli-Sforza, L.L. and Feldman, M.W. (1981) *Cultural Transmission and Evolution: A Quantitative Approach*. Princeton, NJ: Princeton University Press.

Chapuis, R. (1958) *Une Vallée Franc-Comtoise, la Haute-Loue*, Annales Litteraires de l'Université de Besançon, 23. Paris: Belles Lettres.

Clade, J.-L. (1994) *La Vie des paysans Franc-Comtois dans les années 50*. Lyon: Horvarth.

Courtieu, J. (ed.) (1982–7) *Dictionnaire des communes du département de Doubs*. Besançon: Éditions Cêtre. (Six volumes, published at intervals from 1982 to 1987.)

Darwin, C. (1859) *The Origin of Species*. London, Murray.

Daveau, S. (1959) *Les Régions frontalières de la montagne Jurassienne: étude de géographie humaine*. Lyon: Institut des Etudes Rhodaniennes.

Durham, W.H. (1991) *Co-evolution: Genes, Culture and Human Diversity*. Stanford, CA: Stanford University Press.

Dyson-Hudson, R. and Smith, E.A. (1978) Human territoriality: an ecological reassessment. *American Anthropologist* 80: 21–41.

Franklin, S.H. (1969) *The European Peasantry, the Final Phase*. London: Methuen.

Gauthier, J. (1886) *Annuaire du Doubs, de la Franche-Comté et du territoire de Belfort, 1886.* Besançon: Jacquin.

Hajnal, J. (1965) European marriage patterns in perspective. In *Population in History: Essays in Historical Demography* (eds) D.V. Glass and D.E.C. Eversley. London: Arnold (pp. 101–43).

Hardin, G. (1968) The tragedy of the commons. *Science* 162: 1243–8.

Jurjus, A. (1993) Farming styles and intermediate structures in the wake of 1992. In *Culture Change and the New Europe: Perspectives on the European Community* (eds) T.M. Wilson and M.E. Smith. Boulder, CO: Westview (pp. 99–121).

Lambert, R. (1953) Structure agraire et économie rurale du Plateau de Levier. *Bulletin de Association Géographes Français* 237–8: 170–8.

Latouche, R. (1938) La fruitière Jurassienne au XVIII siècle. *Revue de Géographie Alpine* 26: 773–91.

Laurens, P. (1873) *Annuaire du Doubs et de la Franche-Comté.* Besançon: Jacquin.

Layton, R. (1973) Pellaport. In *Debate and Compromise* (ed.) F.G. Bailey. Oxford: Blackwell (pp. 48–74).

Layton, R. (1989) Are sociobiology and social anthropology compatible? The significance of sociocultural resources in human evolution. In *Comparative Socioecology: The Behavioural Ecology of Mammals and Man* (eds) V. Standen and R. Foley. Oxford: Blackwell (pp. 433–55).

Layton, R. (1995) Functional and historical explanations for village social organisation in northern Europe. *Journal of the Royal Anthropological Institute (N.S.)* 1: 703–23.

Lebeau, R. (1951) Deux anciens genres de vie opposés de la montaigne Jurassienne. *Revue de Géographie de Lyon* 26: 378–410.

Lloyd, W.F. (1964) [1833] The checks to population. In *Population, Evolution and Birth Control* (ed.) G. Hardin. San Francisco: Freeman (pp. 337–42).

Marx, K. (1930) [1867] *Capital, vol. 1* (trans.) E. Paul and C. Paul. London: Dent.

Marx, K. (1971) [1859] *A Contribution to the Critique of Political Economy* (trans.) S.W. Ryazanskaya. New York: International.

McCay, B.J. and Acheson, J.M. (1987) Human ecology of the commons. In *The Question of the Commons: The Culture and Ecology of Communal Resources* (eds) B.J. McCay and J.M. Acheson. Tucson: University of Arizona Press (pp. 1–34).

Netting, R. McC. (1981) *Balancing on an Alp: Ecological Change and Continuity in a Swiss Mountain Community.* Cambridge: Cambridge University Press.

Odling-Smee, J. (1995) Biological evolution and cultural change. In *Survival and Religion: Biological Evolution and Cultural Change* (eds) E. Jones and V. Reynolds. New York: Wiley (pp. 1–43).

OECD (1965) *Agriculture and Economic Growth: A Report by a Group of Experts.* Paris: OECD.

Ostrom, E. (1990) *Governing the Commons: The Evolution of Institutions for Collective Action.* Cambridge: Cambridge University Press.

Scott, J. (1976) *The Moral Economy of the Peasant: Rebellion and Subsistence in Southeast Asia.* New Haven: Yale University Press.

Shutes, M. (1993) Rural communities without family farms? Family dairy farming in the post-1993 EC. In *Culture Change and the New Europe: Perspectives on the European Community* (eds) T.M. Wilson and M.E. Smith. Boulder, CO: Westview (pp. 123–42).

Tracy, M. (1964) *Agriculture in Western Europe.* London: Cape.

# Chapter 11

# Evading state control

## Political protest and technology in Saudi Arabia

*Madawi Al-Rasheed*

Recently anthropologists have been concerned with the concept of civil society and the prospect of its development in non-Western societies. The rediscovery of the concept is motivated by political changes that have swept 'traditional' societies now integrated into nation-states, most modelled on a Western pattern. The resulting debate has ramifications beyond the specific concept of civil society which touch wider issues at the heart of anthropological analysis and interpretation (Hann and Dunn 1996). Is civil society, the child of the European Enlightenment, an appropriate tool for the analysis of political processes in societies culturally and historically removed from the West? Classically, civil society implies that individuals and groups are free to form associations and organisations independent of the state, which can mediate between citizens and the state (Hann and Dunn 1996: 1). This development is regarded as associated with interaction through market capitalism. With the exception of a few convincing applications in the Middle East (Norton 1995, 1996; Eickelman 1996), anthropologists remain sceptical. Gellner has led denials of its applicability and even the prospect of its appearance in the Muslim world. In his view, the underlying bonds of the Muslim *umma* (community) militate against it because Islam 'exemplifies a social order which seems to lack much capacity to provide political countervailing institutions and associations, which is atomized without much individualism, and operates effectively without intellectual pluralism' (Gellner 1994: 29).[1]

In this chapter I aim to expand our understanding of civil society in Saudi Arabia, here exemplifying the Islamic world although by no means representative of Muslim countries. If we retain a narrow definition of civil society (limiting it to the emergence of independent and formal non-kin-based organisations as buffer zones between the individual and the polity, guarding the individual interests of citizens, regardless of their kin or regional identities, against those of the state), then Saudi Arabia does not pass the test as the formation of such formal organisations is banned under the present regime. However, political protest has been voiced in the last decade through various mechanisms, ranging from the formation of non-kin-based dissident groups, through petitions to the ruling elite signed by a cross-section of society, to the electronic transmission of critical literature, which are the seeds of an emerging civil society. Saudi Arabia, now immersed in modernity, is benefiting from new technologies used for purposes not anticipated by those who introduced them. Here I investigate the changing forms of political protest in Saudi Arabia, applying a historical perspective to highlight the transformation of the means of protest and their evolution over time. I contrast two periods: pre-state political structures and state structures. Pre-state politics was characterised by the fragmentation of authority and the genuine ability of people to contest and challenge their legitimate rulers. In pre-state Arabia and in the context of centralised tribal dynasties, political protest manifested itself in the arena of the tribal *majlis* (council). When this resource was exhausted, groups resorted to the old mechanism of fission and shifting alliances. In contrast, the state era was initially characterised by the state's ability to silence protest and curb its eruption, and by the failure of society to organise effective opposition. However, in the 1990s silencing opposition has become more difficult as a result of increased education, literacy, modernisation and the availability of new technologies of communication, and groups can organise themselves effectively along new, non-kin lines. As long as political parties remain banned, one has to look beyond the rigidity of the Western model to see an emerging civil society on the pages of the opposition press, faxes and electronic mail.

In the Middle East, the wide spread of mass higher education, printing and communication technology (videos, televisions, cassettes, personal computers, facsimile machines and electronic mail) has undermined traditional sources of knowledge and authority and created multiple political discourses and protests against absolutist states. This has led to the intensification of dispute and contest, the polarisation of groups, the consolidation of multiple centres of power (Eickelman 1992), and has marginalised the traditional elite in the emergence of a new category of citizen – educated, urban and computer literate. While such new groups may retain the rhetoric of tradition, they are otherwise immersed in modernity, particularly the new Islamists of the Muslim world, including members of the Saudi Islamic opposition. Their Islamist discourse evokes a vision of society faithful to authenticity and genuine ancient tradition while simultaneously benefiting from modern technology and modern discourses on democracy, human rights, autonomy and equality. Islamist discourse and organisational strategies are both facilitating the emergence of civil society in the Muslim world, contrary to Gellner's assertion that they represent its antithesis.

## Pre-state politics

The central region of Saudi Arabia, Najd, is most interesting in terms of investigating local processes of political centralisation because it had a number of dynastic emirates (*imarah*) with characteristics resembling those of states. The Rashidi dynasty (1836–1921), based in the oasis of Hail in northern

Najd,[2] was established among the sedentary population of the oasis, but included pastoral nomads.

The nineteenth-century founders of the Rashidi dynasty were a prominent lineage drawn from the Shammar, one of the major tribal confederations of north-central Arabia. While the majority of the tribe was nomadic, the Rashidi lineage was settled in the oasis. They assumed the title of *amirs* (princes) whose authority was recognised not only among members of their own lineage, but also among other Shammar lineages. The *amirs* coexisted with Shammar chiefs – known as *sheikhs* – whose influence was restricted to their own lineages. The *amirs*, as heads of the whole tribe, represented it to external powers such as the Ottoman Empire in adjacent areas, the Hijaz and Mesopotamia.

The *amirs* ensured the protection not only of their subjects, but also of vital trade routes into the oases they controlled using an armed force of Shammar volunteers, conscripts from the oases, mercenaries and slaves. This permanent force, paid in cash and kind, enforced the *amirs'* orders, punished transgressors, expanded their domain, and distinguished the *amirs'* leadership from that of the tribal *sheikhs* as leaders with no power to influence people's decisions. While all male members of the tribal section carried weapons, they neither served the *sheikhs'* personal interests, nor enforced their commands. Their voluntary participation in raids and in the defence of their section was a moral duty. In contrast, the *amirs'* armed men constituted a permanent professional force, giving them powers of coercion which tribal *sheikhs* lacked. Centralised oasis-based leadership was thus enforced and maintained.

However, the *amirs* had little control over the economic base of pastoral production. Shammar tribesmen grazed their animals in their traditional tribal territory and their *sheikhs* negotiated with their counterparts for access to other (including non-Shammar) sections' grazing land and wells. The *amirs'* economic power rested on their ability to control and protect caravan and pilgrimage routes within Shammar territory. Their armed force ensured the safe passage of both merchants and pilgrims to the holy cities of Arabia, Mecca and Madina, in return for caravan tolls.

The Rashidi dynasty was complex. It combined the fluid leadership of the Shammar *sheikhs* with the centralised leadership of the Rashidi *amirs*. Economically, the *amirs* depended on an economy combining pastoral nomadism, oasis agriculture and trade. These attributes distinguished the system from the tribal organisation of the nomadic groups. The Hail dynasty was a micro-polity characterised by an urban base, the appointment of local representatives, an independent military force, the generation of surplus and the imposition of taxes.

Fragmented authority and fluctuations in both territory and constituency distinguished this political system from modern states, as a dynasty with centralised power but no single authority. The *amirs* had to accommodate the authority of the tribal *sheikhs* with whom they coexisted. This resulted in tensions stemming from the coexistence of a centralising agency, the *amirs*, and a decentralised political tribal structure and fluid economic base, both militating against a durable polity. The contradiction between political centralisation and the inherently decentralised tribal organisation and pastoral economy generated political protest, managed through *majlis* politics – the negotiation and resolution of conflict within the confines of the *amirs'* council in Hail.

The Hail *majlis* attracted the attention of European travellers who visited the *amirs* in the nineteenth and early twentieth centuries. My description of this institution draws on their accounts and on the oral narratives of the Shammar and the descendants of the Rashidi *amirs*. Early maps of the *amirs'* residence in Hail, Barzan Palace, show its proximity to the oasis market and mosque (Euting 1983). Palgrave claims that the palace site occupied one-tenth of the oasis (Palgrave 1865: 103). In Wallin's (1854: 200) account, the palace was easily distinguished from other houses by its imposing size. It consisted of two courtyards, the first comprising a guest reception room, the *amir's* private rooms, stables, kitchen, prison and a private quarter, while the second held the main entrance overlooking the central square, al-Mishab. The regular public meetings of the *majlis* were held in al-Mishab, opposite the *amir's* warehouses and guest chambers. Maps show a slave market behind the fortified, walled palace.

The arrangement of space reflected the concerns of the *amirs*. The kitchen, the reception rooms and the *majlis* occupied a substantial part of the building. The kitchen was important to prepare meals for *majlis* attendants. These feasts crucially consolidated the *amirs'* leadership and enhanced their reputation as generous rulers, attracting new supporters and enhancing the loyalty of existing ones. The *majlis* received numerous visitors: Hail notables, Shammar and non-Shammar *sheikhs*, and ordinary tribesmen. The amir with his brothers, uncles, and cousins sat on a slightly raised bench, he himself occupying the central place. Often foreign visitors, such as Ottoman and British messengers, were received in the *majlis*, the arena linking the Rashidi dynasty to the outside world and the various external powers which influenced the course of political events in Arabia. Access to the *majlis* was not generally regulated by strict rules; anyone with a case, request or enquiry attended these open meetings.

The *majlis* was an arena for dispute settlement between individuals and groups, ranging from theft and trespassing to murder and vengeance. These disputes were resolved by applying both customary tribal law and the *sharia*, the Islamic legal code. In the latter, the *amirs* were assisted by a *qadi*, Islamic judge, who was often literate and knowledgeable in Islamic matters as a result of studying in Hail, or other centres of Muslim learning. The *qadis* dealt specifically with disputes relating to commerce, marriage, divorce and inheritance. Other cases, especially those involving the nomadic population, were resolved according to tribal customary law. The two legal codes coexisted:

> Where, however, quarrels are not settled by the intervention of friends, the disputants bring their cases to the Emir, who settles them in open court, the *majlis*, and whose word is final. The law of the Koran,

though often referred to, is not, I fancy, the main rule of the Emir's decision, but rather Arabian custom, an authority far older than the Musluman code. I doubt if it is often necessary for the soldiers to support such decisions by force.

(Blunt 1968: 266)

The procedure for dispute settlement was simple:

Someone steps forward and announces that a couple of sheep have been stolen from him by such and such a person. The *amir* promises him that he will see to it that they are given back or replaced, and has the *sheikh* of the tribe to which the thief belongs informed of this with the observation that he must clear the matter up. This simple announcement implies the tacit threat that in case of delay, the *sheikh* in question, together with his tribe, may, at the next year's distribution of grazing grounds, be allotted a region inferior to their previous one.

(Euting in Ward 1983: 467)

The *amirs* apparently sought the cooperation of the tribal *sheikhs* in close contact with their followers and with grassroots knowledge of their behaviour. The tribal *sheikhs* attending the *amir's majlis* were held responsible for returning stolen property and arranging for blood money to be paid in cases of murder. The failure of a *sheikh* to do so resulted in withdrawal of benefits from the whole group.

Settling disputes within the *majlis* thus involved a multiplicity of authorities and legal codes in their successful resolution. Although various accounts indicate that the amir was the final judge, the voices of both *qadis* and tribal *sheikhs* were heard and respected. Above all, participation of the *sheikhs* ensured enforcement of the decisions taken. However, power remained with the *amirs* who, thanks to their armed force, were able to exert pressure on those who did not abide by *majlis* resolutions.

In addition to its role in mediating disputes, the *majlis* was the site of political participation of multiple but equal centres of authority. Here again, *amirs* heading their own lineages and the Shammar tribe were elevated by their noble origin, economic and military power, but were regarded by Shammar *sheikhs* as equal partners. Shammar *sheikhs* regarded *amirs* as their equals by birth and common ancestry. Kinship ties between the *amirs* and the Shammar lineages equalised a relationship which had the potential to develop hierarchically. The *amirs* could not coerce the Shammar *sheikhs* nor could they impose their will on them, but sought their participation in negotiating alliances and cementing loyalty. Decisions to raid other groups to gain booty or territory followed prolonged consultation with the *sheikhs* during their regular visits to the *majlis*. As their participation in raids was essential for the *amir's* campaigns, the latter could not afford to antagonise them.

Direct coercion being inappropriate, the *amirs* resorted to indirect bribery and subsidies to tribal *sheikhs* attending the *majlis* through gifts of rice, sugar, flour, weapons, cash and other useful items. Tribal *sheikhs* also offered the *amirs* gifts of camels and other items drawn from their pastoral economy. The exchange, however, remained unequal. The *amirs* were more lavish, with their greater surplus from raids and conquest within Arabia, and their external relations with the Ottoman governors who occasionally offered them income in return for swearing allegiance to the Ottoman Sultan. However, authority remained diffused in the tribal structure, with no single *sheikh* or *amir* claiming supreme political authority.

The *majlis* was also the arena where political protest was voiced. Realising both their equality with the Hail *amirs* and the inability of the latter to coerce them, the Shammar *sheikhs* and other non-Shammar tribal leaders used the *majlis* to voice their protest against policies imposed on them by the Rashidi leadership, concerning the allocation of pasture and wells, and access to markets in oases under Rashidi jurisdiction, and also complained about raids against their sections, especially if they had paid the protection tax imposed on them by Hail. The *sheikhs* generally used the *majlis* to contest decisions against the interests of their lineages and were occasionally able to revoke them. While the *sheikhs* appreciated strong leadership in Hail, they were intolerant of weak, unjust and hesitant *amirs* who were not able to deliver security, prosperity and lavish subsidies.

Disenchanted tribal *sheikhs* resorted to fission to express their political protest. When *majlis* politics failed, tribal groups opted for the old strategy of shifting alliances. Fission allowed groups to maintain their autonomy and subvert their coercion by central authority. The ability of tribal sections to switch allegiance accompanied the development and consolidation of the Rashidi dynasty. However, its most devastating implications occurred in 1921 when the Rashidi *amirs* came under the attack of a rival dynasty, that of the Saudis, and some Shammar sections demonstrated their protest against their traditional Rashidi *amirs* (weakened by internal strife and competition over leadership within their own lineage), by switching allegiance to the Saudis. The Rashidi dynasty collapsed and Shammar territory was incorporated into the modern Saudi state. In the nineteenth century, the *amirs* were able to deal with such fission by resorting to diplomacy, negotiation and bribery. However, the weakened leadership of the first two decades of the twentieth century had neither the resources nor the skills to control the fragmentation of either their territory or their tribe.

The Rashidi dynasty demonstrates that pre-state Arabia witnessed varying degrees of centralised leadership. Tribal dynasties such as the Rashidis rested on a mixed economy of pastoralism, agriculture and trade, based on tribal organisation coexisting with multiple centres of authority. Although power was concentrated in the hands of an oasis-based lineage with economic and military resources, the exercise of power had to be negotiated with equally important tribal *sheikhs*. The latter had no economic, military or symbolic powers to match those of the *amirs*, yet they were important reservoirs of authority diffused in the tribal structure. Political protest was not silenced for two reasons. First, the mixed economic base militated against the exercise of absolute control over tribal sections. Second, the inability of the *amirs* to communicate effectively with the hinterland disallowed any durable supervision of distant territories and populations within their sphere of influence. *Majlis* politics was the mechanism by which the *amirs* maintained their position and accommodated the interests of their tribe.

## State politics

The emergence of the modern Saudi state in 1932 resulted in the triumph of one dynasty over others in Arabia through conquest assisted by a religious reformist movement, Wahhabism, and external support from Britain (which assumed a more important role in the region after the collapse of the Ottoman Empire after the First World War). The Saudis did not immediately establish the modern state of today (Kostiner 1993). In its early days, the Saudi state is better described as a dynasty, exhibiting characteristics little different from the political systems which had existed in Arabia such as the Rashidi dynasty described above. The major difference, however, stems from the fact that while the Rashidi dynasty was purely a tribal configuration, that of the Saudis was an amalgamation of tribal leadership and Islamic ideology. Saudi political hegemony was achieved through religious reform, which resulted in the Saudis emerging as the central political power and the Wahhabi *ulama* as the only interpreters of faith. The founder of the modern Saudi state, Ibn Saud, adopted the title of first Sultan and later King.

The adoption of this title was accompanied by major political transformations, thus altering traditional tribal dynastic government. The new state moved away from the historical pattern whereby a central power coexisted with other centres. The Saudi state was based from the very beginning on the elimination of other power centres. Prominent tribal *sheikhs* and *amirs* in Arabia were either eliminated or co-opted by this central power. This double process of elimination and co-option began to crystallise in the 1950s when oil revenues started flowing into the state treasury. Armed with enormous oil wealth, the state laid the foundation for an elaborate bureaucratic apparatus, a modern army, an educational infrastructure and an efficient transport network, linking the various regions in the country and facilitating the entry of Saudi Arabia into the modern world. This transformation was strikingly rapid. By the 1970s, the country had already benefited from the latest Western technological innovations at inflated prices. Even more striking was the fact that this material transformation was imposed on a society which did not adjust socially or culturally to the new era.

The race to enter the modern world economically and technologically was not matched by a similar race towards political modernisation. In the 1990s, Saudi Arabia is still an absolutist monarchical state, ruled by a royal lineage assisted by a number of appointed ministers, and a 60-member appointed consultative council, *majlis al shura*, created only in 1992. The country's constitution is the Quran and the law of the land is the *sharia*, the Islamic legal code, as interpreted by the Wahhabi *ulama*. Political parties are banned, freedom of assembly and expression virtually non-existent. The fiscal accountability of rulers cannot be checked in the absence of legitimate channels. The state controls the economy, supervises education, and generally restricts personal rights and freedoms. Political decisions remain top secret and are the monopoly of an elite, often composed of the king and other members of the royal family. Consulting the consultative council remains a formality given its unelected nature and composition.

This political system has made direct protest and opposition to central power difficult. The various tribal and non-tribal groups are unable to resort to the old mechanism of fission, the dominant form of previous protest. Ruling out fission as a mechanism of protest has narrowed the space for local autonomy and directed the attention of discontented groups towards other options within the limitations of the new state.

Despite the sophistication and rapid proliferation of the state bureaucracy, the princely *majlis* remains, quite separate from the formal consultative council, *majlis al shura* created in 1992. The princely *majlis* – a daily meeting held by the king and local governors, often princes of the royal family – is a survival of the traditional tribal *majlis*, at the heart of previous dynastic systems. The idea of the *majlis* has survived but its function, structure and meaning have been transformed with the consolidation of the state.

The *majlis* has lost its past main function as an arena for the free expression of opinions and political participation,[3] although disputes are still settled, and favours and subsidies demanded by the constituency are supplied by the king and the princes. The *majlis* is today a space for gaining loyalty in return for cash handouts, the allocation of resources and the smoothing of the rigidity of the state bureaucracy. Citizens frustrated by the impersonal state apparatus bypass it altogether by demanding the direct settlement of their cases by the *majlis*.

The underlying power structure of the *majlis* has also been transformed, into an hierarchical institution with a single head who makes the final decisions. Its hierarchy manifests itself through symbolic acts of greeting and elaborate seating arrangements, and the presence of armed bodyguards who not only represent the elevated status of the prince, but also ensure his security. Upon entering the *majlis*, attendants greet the prince by kissing his hand, forehead or shoulder, depending on their own standing in the new hierarchy. Kissing his hand is reserved for those of low status, whereas the forehead and the shoulder are reserved for attendants of noble origin. Attendants are then directed to seats reflecting their social status – those of higher standing being seated on the right or left sides of the prince and those of low status further away from the central core of the *majlis*. This hierarchy is also preserved in the rules of the *majlis* dictating who is given the opportunity to speak directly to the prince. Low-status attendants may only hand a letter to the guards who take it to the prince. Anyone given the opportunity to speak, in addressing the prince must follow a formula. While in the tribal *majlis* participants could address the *amir* using first names, today this is replaced by the formula of '*jalalat al malik*' ('Your Majesty' for the king and 'Your Royal Highness' for princes). These symbolic expressions reflect the transformation of the *majlis*' underlying political structure from diffused tribal authority to hierarchical state power.

Given this transformation, political protest has been squeezed out of the *majlis*. Discontented groups within the kingdom resort to modern means of protest, previously unknown in the country because of the availability of traditional mechanisms. The demonstrations and strikes witnessed at various periods in the 1950s, 1970s and 1980s represented a shift towards new strategies. Demonstrations were always dealt with swiftly by the government. Political protest has also been expressed through petitions to the King and other members of the royal family. The most famous petitions were submitted during and after the Gulf War of 1991, and originated from both the religious establishment and 'secular' groups, reflecting discontent among those who previously supported the government.

In the 1990s, we witness the use of the fax machine and electronic mail – technological innovations appropriated by a whole spectrum of discontented groups to voice their political protest. My ethnographic data is based on an analysis of one Saudi Islamist opposition group, the Committee for the Defence of Legitimate Rights in Saudi Arabia (CDLR), which has employed such technological innovations in its struggle against the royal family.[4]

The CDLR was initially established in the capital, Riyadh, in May 1993 by six Saudis, and was immediately banned by the authorities; some of its supporters were arrested, including Dr al-Massari, the son of one of the founders. After his release, al-Massari and al-Faqih established new London headquarters for the Committee in exile. The CDLR started an active campaign to undermine the legitimacy of the royal family armed with the latest telecommunications technology linking them to Saudi Arabia. In addition to smuggling tapes and videos into the country, more recently the CDLR started satellite television broadcasts.

The CDLR relies heavily on fax machines and electronic mail to distribute weekly monitors to their supporters in and beyond Saudi Arabia. Through these channels the London office also receives information from Saudi Arabia, which is redistributed by fax and computer. The CDLR have thus challenged the Saudi state, whose agencies have so far failed to curb these flows of information.[5]

The rise of the CDLR,[6] and other organisations not considered here, needs to be contextualised within the Gulf War and its political, social and economic impact on Saudi Arabia. I have dealt with this context elsewhere (Al-Rasheed 1996, 1997). Suffice it to say that the expansion of the education system was critically important, especially the rise in student numbers in the Islamic and technological universities. During the economic boom of the 1970s and early 1980s, such students were recruited to jobs in the civil service, the oil industry and the religious institutions (graduates of Islamic colleges). However, the decline of oil prices in the 1990s, the heavy cost of the Gulf War and the general stagnation of the Saudi economy have meant that not all recent graduates have been absorbed into work. Today some respond to unemployment by giving their support to the Islamic opposition in return for a promise to ameliorate their economic situation under a regime more sensitive to their needs and concerns.

The number of unemployed university graduates with high expectations is likely to increase, given the demographic characteristics of the country (almost 60 per cent of the population is under the age of 21 and the annual population growth rate 3.8 per cent). This new category of citizen, computer literate and with technological and other valuable skills acquired in the country or abroad, is frustrated by the contradiction of being a national of a very wealthy state with a bleak employment future and no access to legitimate political channels to change his situation. His rising expectations of a secure future have been fuelled by his empowerment through education. Mass education tends to elevate such individuals above traditionally recognised authorities through their command of foreign languages, computer literacy, and scientific skills. Such young individuals have no experience of the historically recent tribal structure even though they may retain a tribal affiliation and identity. Excluded from the circles of princes, their prospects for economic prosperity are limited to patronage networks woven in the princely *majlis*.

This situation triggered a reaction resulting in the formation of the CDLR and other Islamist opposition groups. The educationally empowered individual searches for means to voice his protest. In the absence of alternative and legitimate channels such as political parties or pressure groups, he lends his ears to Friday sermons critical of the government, attends theological debates on the nature of the Islamic state in the centres of religious learning and participates in clandestine group discussions debating political issues, while he continues to communicate and receive messages from exiled and local opposition groups on his personal computer. He eagerly consumes news, broadcast on radio and television.

The long-term impact on society of mass education and the adoption of new technologies to express political protest still needs to be assessed. In Saudi Arabia, this strategy gathered momentum only after the Gulf War; as such, it is perhaps premature to predict the future on the basis of short experience. However, at the moment a number of trends can be observed and documented.

The intensification of Islamist opposition to the regime and the identification of the newly emerging category of the young, literate, educated citizens with this opposition, have definitely contributed to the marginalisation of traditional political and religious authorities in the country. The old tribal groups who retained their elevated status were first marginalised by the centralised state, but today they cease to inspire deference or enjoy their vague authority under the patronage of the Saudi princes. Their old discourse emphasising blood ties, noble ancestry and respect for elderly authority, has waned in the face of new political concepts and ideologies. Today they present no real challenge to the state.

Equally, the traditional Wahhabi religious establishment whose authority crystallised over the last seventy years of Saudi rule find themselves challenged from within and below. The defection of young *ulama* and their support for the new Islamist groups through the Friday sermons, the circulation of critical tapes, leaflets and treatises, demonstrates that a unified religious discourse in support of the government is no longer possible. The old apologist *ulama* are constantly challenged by the young, who have adopted a more vigorous interpretive approach to crucial political questions such as those pertaining to the nature of the state, the status of the monarchy, the accountability of rulers and the importance of advice to government. These young *ulama* have gone beyond theological debates relating to how people should practise 'true Islam'; today they find themselves debating current political affairs, aided by increased literacy and the availability of new technologies of communication among the populace. Their debates are no longer confined to mosques and religious colleges, but propagated to a wider audience thanks to printing, electronic mail, fax machines, videos and cassettes.

What these new technologies allow is a serious evasion of state control. Today political protest cannot be curbed successfully unless it takes the form of an open confrontation with the state through demonstrations and strikes. The state coercive machinery remains intact to deal with such confrontations swiftly and efficiently. Arrests of suspected opponents and the execution of political activists have increased in the 1990s. However, these measures deal successfully only with the tip of the iceberg, but fail to provide a durable solution to the rising tide of political protest, now disseminated through networks of new technologies which cannot be efficiently controlled or regulated by the state.

The functional transformation of information technology from education and entertainment to embodying and facilitating political ends has been remarkable. A university student with access to computers may use them for his mathematical models, but can also receive messages and communicate with political groups in his spare time without even moving out of his department's computer room. In Saudi Arabia, this has given rise to a new brand of a *homo politicus*, who is capable of expressing his political views against central power and away from state control.[7] Access to these new technologies empowers individuals. The question at this juncture is whether this empowerment is illusory or real. While it is too early to give a definite answer based on empirical evidence, my guess is that the new *homo politicus*, by virtue of his command over new technologies can and will develop a consciousness of his real empowerment. Access to information, the ability to make news, influence public opinion and change attitudes are real outcomes of new technologies. How such changes will materialise in real power is not so self-evident. New technologies have become efficient vents for political protest; but its full materialisation and ability to trigger political change depend on other, non-technological variables. The major achievement of this political protest so far has been the politicisation of citizens, long slowed through oil prosperity, generous welfare benefits and efficient state control.

The use of technology for political protest has given rise to a dynamic political life, characterised by the coexistence of a multiplicity of political and religious discourses. Eickelman refers to this as the emergence of a culture of protest, reflecting in the Muslim world and elsewhere the fragmentation of authority, accompanied by the flourishing of multiple centres each with an agenda and a programme for change (Eickelman and Piscatori 1996). In his opinion, two scenarios may result: the intensification of dispute and contest leading to the polarisation of society; or a *modus vivendi* of accommodation and adjustment. It seems that Saudi society has recently moved in the direction of polarisation. Labels such as *islamiyyunn* (Islamists), *usuliuun* (fundamentalists), *ulmaniuun* (secularists), *ghulat* (radicals), *mutagharibuun* (westernised), *muhdithun* (modernists) have regularly made their appearance in everyday parlance and on the pages of both the official and opposition presses. These labels are new classifications gradually replacing conventional identities which in the past revolved around kin and tribe. They allow the categorisation of individuals on the basis of new criteria and discourses. They also capture the emerging new social identities and political orientations.

In the 1990s the Saudi state remains resilient to serious political change and resistant to widening real political participation and introducing legitimate mechanisms for the expression of political protest. The state has done all it can to suppress the development of civil society in its classical narrow definition. But in the 1990s, Saudi Arabia has also demonstrated some characteristics resembling those of the pre-state era of centralised tribal dynasties incapable of controlling their pastoral peripheries yet coexisting with other centres of authority. Today the state finds itself in a similar situation due to its inability to control information and communication.

While fission has not yet occurred, there are indicators pointing to the possibility of a return to the status quo ante, whereby the centralised power coexisted with alternative centres, capable at times of crisis of presenting real challenges to the state. It is hard to predict when this coexistence might erupt into major confrontations, but the proliferation of Islamist opposition groups indicates that this cannot be ruled out. Although these vary in their agendas and the number of their supporters, they agree on important principles: the need for political reform to limit corruption, to expand political participation and to provide for the legitimate expression of overt protest. Unless these issues are seriously considered by the state and its ruling group, the future of the country remains at stake, for new identities are forming and being given new meanings in the new context of mass education, competing discourses and new technologies.

The Saudi case demonstrates that if we continue to adhere to a rigid model which restricts signs of civil society to the formation of formal organisations and associations, then the country is obviously lagging behind. However, if we are prepared to widen our definition, there is a whole range of new mechanisms whereby civility is manifested. Today new technology has created a space beyond state control, which is appropriated by the new citizens. Technology has filled a gap in societies where absolute states continue to rule and where guilds, associations and other non-govermental organisations are banned. People evade state control by using new mechanisms, or transforming old ones to give them new meanings and functions, to guard their interests and bind them together. In this novel area we need more empirical investigation to assess the value of old concepts such as civil society.

## Notes

1 For a critique of Gellner's general theory of Muslim society, see Zubaida (1995). For an assessment of his theorising about the absence of civil society in the Muslim world, see Norton (1995, 1996).
2 Information on the Rashidi dynasty derives from my ethnohistorical research on this polity (Al-Rasheed 1991).
3 As a female researcher, I have no access to the princely *majlis* in Saudi Arabia, which remains a predominantly male arena. My ethnographic data is based on the accounts of those who have attended such meetings.
4 My research on the CDLR started in 1994. Most of the data here derive from the organisation in London.
5 In 1996, Britain rejected al-Massari's demand for asylum under pressure from the Saudi government. The court rejected the proposal to deport him to the Dominican Republic as requested by the Home Office. Instead, he was granted a temporary immigration status 'Leave to Remain in the UK', allowing him to continue his campaign from his north London office.
6 The CDLR publishes a number of Arabic and English communiqués, pamphlets and magazines to disseminate its ideas and political programme. These can be purchased in book shops in London and elsewhere or accessed through the fax machine and electronic mail.
7 *Homo politicus* described here remains male. Saudi women have not yet taken an active role in the political life of the country although during the Gulf War they succeeded in organising an unprecedented demonstration against the ban on women driving. Fifty Saudi women violated the ban and drove their cars to a shopping centre in Riyadh. The demonstration ended when the police arrested the women drivers. With the exception of this daring and couragous act of defiance, Saudi women are still politically inactive.

# References

Al-Rasheed, M. (1991) *Politics in an Arabian Oasis: The Rashidi Tribal Dynasty*. London: I.B. Tauris.

—— (1996) Saudi Arabia's Islamic opposition. *Current History* 95, 597: 16–22.

—— (1997) Le Couronne et le turban: l'état Saoudien a la recherche d'une nouvelle légitimité. In *Les États Arabes Face à la Contestations Islamiste* (eds) B. Qudmani-Darwish and M. Chartouni-Dubarry. Paris: Armand Colin.

Blunt, A. (1968 [1881]) *A Pilgrimage to Nejd, the Cradle of the Arab Race: A Visit to the Court of the Arab Emir and our Persian Campaign*, 2 vols. London: John Murray.

Committee for the Defense of Legitimate Rights in Saudi Arabia (CDLR) (1994) *Matha taqul lajnat al difa an al huquq al shariya fi al jazira al arabiyya*. London.

CDLR (1994) Al-huquq. *Communiques* 1–30.

Eickelman, D. (1992) Mass higher education and the religious imagination in contemporary Arab society. *American Ethnologist* 19, 4: 1–13.

—— (1996) Foreword. In *Civil Society in the Middle East*, vol. 2 (ed.) A.R. Norton. Leiden: Brill (pp. viii–xiv).

Eickelman, D. and Piscatori, J. (eds) (1996) *Muslim Politics*. Princeton: Princeton University Press.

Euting, J. (1983) Julius Euting, 1883-4. In *Hail: An Oasis City of Saudi Arabia* (ed.) P. Ward. Cambridge: Oleander Press (pp. 439–610).

Gellner, E. (1994) *Conditions of Liberty Civil Society and its Rivals*. Harmondsworth: Penguin.

Hann, C. and Dunn, E. (eds) (1996) *Civil Society: Challenging Western Models*. London: Routledge.

Kostiner, J. (1993) *The Making of Saudi Arabia 1916–1936: From Chieftancy to Monarchical State*. Oxford: Oxford University Press.

Norton, A.R. (ed.) (1995–6) *Civil Society in the Middle East*, 2 vols. Leiden: Brill.

Palgrave, W. (1865) *Personal Narrative of a Year's Journey through Central and Eastern Arabia (1862–1863)*, 2 vols. London: Macmillan.

Wallin, G.A. (1854) Narrative of a journey from Cairo to Medina and Mecca, by Suez, Araba, Tawila, al-Jauf, Jublae, Hail and Negd in 1854. *Journal of the Royal Geographical Society* 24: 115–201.

Zubaida, S. (1995) Is there a Muslim society? Ernest Gellner's sociology of Islam. *Economy and Society* 24, 2: 151–88.

# Chapter 12

# Authority versus power

## A view from social anthropology

*Peter Skalník*

## Introduction

Throughout history the tension between authority and power appears essential for the quality of political affairs. Authoritative dictionaries and encyclopaedias such as *Blackwell's Encyclopaedia of Political Thought* are well aware of this tension. Whereas authority is the right to act and make laws, power is understood as an ability to enforce obedience (Miller *et al.* 1991: 34–5). Thus right stands against coercion, recognised ability against force or the threat of it. Legitimacy stands against usurpation and democracy against dictatorship.

The classical Weberian definition of authority is closely related to domination (*herrschaft*) which may be traditional, charismatic or legitimised. Especially charismatic leadership is based on authority of specially endowed personalities such as prophets, military princes, demagogues or party leaders. The state, in Max Weber's understanding, is defined by the means which it monopolises, i.e. physical coercion. Through it the state can dominate, and some people exercise power over others (Weber 1958: 494–5). The prestigious *International Encyclopaedia of the Social Sciences* agrees, in its article on authority written by Robert Peabody, that definitions of this concept vary but eventually concludes that authority is first of all a relationship and not a capacity (Peabody 1968; Bierstedt 1964). Nobody, according to Peabody, refutes de Jouvenel's (1957) assertion that authority is basic to human behaviour. Lasswell and Kaplan (1950) in their influential book equate authority with formal power. Power however remains weakly defined not only there but in all of the literature. Peabody, following Weber of course, argues that it is legitimacy that distinguishes authority from coercion, force, power but also from influence, leadership and persuasion.

My position is different and unambiguous. As I try to show in this chapter, with the help of anthropological data from four different societies, if legitimacy were so crucial then authority would be only a sub-category of power. Authority as legitimate power may perhaps be less inclined to use physical force, while the threat of force would nevertheless remain integral to authority.

I rather view authority and power as fundamentally opposed principles which relate to mutually exclusive 'ideal types' of arrangements of public affairs. In my conceptualisation power is closely identified with the state. State power means that decisions are taken on behalf of the whole society by specific state agencies that rely on the state's monopoly of organised violence. Authority, in contrast, is legitimate without the backing of power, and is voluntarily recognised by all people. Authority in principle does not require state power and domination of some over others (Skalník 1989a: 8). I argue that whenever people have acted with such authority while handling matters concerning human collectivities, the quality of arrangements concerning these has been fundamentally better, decisions were also more durable and truly accepted. In brief, public affairs were dealt with in a more civilised manner than when people wielding mere power represented group interests. While authority is gained by free public support and works by vote or consensus, power is a result of the use or threat of physical force and operates without specific recourse to the people's wishes.

In actual politics, however, both authority and power are present. In everyday political processes the seemingly exclusive dichotomy of power and authority appears much more complex. What matters is the tension between them. The prevalence of authority means that power methods are less prominent and vice versa. Naked power rarely survives, as the famous dictum about the difficulty of sitting on bayonets reminds us. Conversely, pure authority without the power to act is rarely desired. Humanity has struggled throughout the ages for the right mix of both ingredients of politics (Havel 1985).

The above assertions which evidently prefer authority to power must at least be shown valid for some well documented cases so that they can be taken seriously. Otherwise they would be hardly more than somewhat naive value judgements. Here I shall deal with data gathered at different times and places in four societies on four continents during my career as a social anthropologist. They have in common my preoccupation with arrangements and solutions in the realm of public affairs where authority has worked more profoundly and thus better than power, where democratic decision-making methods such as consensus have been preferred to the use of force.

## Ghana

In the Nanumba District of the Northern Region of Ghana, where I have worked intermittently for eighteen years, the interplay of authority and power is very dramatic. The neo-traditional chiefdom of Nanun, whose history goes back at least for three centuries, covers the entire area of the district but also claims sovereignty over its former hunting grounds of Kpasaland which lie to the south-east over the Oti River in the Volta Region. The modern Ghanaian state, following the German and British colonial powers which divided kingdoms such as Dagbon into halves, recognises traditional areas such as Nanun but is unable to accept that they may cross over the modern regional or district borders which do not respect the historically developed boundaries of traditional polities.

Once the traditional authority or *naam* vested in the paramount chief of Nanun, whose title is the Bimbilla Naa (he resides in the Nanumba capital called Bimbilla), started in 1980 to 'enskin' (install) chiefs for Kpasaland – which was settled after the state of Ghana built a highway through it – the predominantly Konkomba settlers opposed themselves to the Nanumba chiefs. In April 1981 after a violent incident in Bimbilla, the Kpasaland Konkomba used force to kill or chase away the chiefs and their Nanumba and Dagomba dependants. The police from Bimbilla were not allowed to restore order in the neighbouring region. Before the Ghanaian state with its army managed to stop the killing, it was a *fait accompli* that Nanumba traditional authority could no longer be exerted in Kpasaland. The imported Western-type state, based on power principles, failed to project its putative authority and instead of promoting a sensitive consensual solution to the conflict between the Nanumba chiefly authority and the Konkomba agricultural settlers, merely imposed a belated and uneasy ceasefire by the sheer power of its army. The historically developed authority of *naam* was weakened after the death of Bimbilla Naa Dasana in May 1981 on the same night as his 'skinmaker' Kpatihi.

Disappointment with the state and lack of authoritative leadership among the Nanumba led in June 1981 to a Nanumba armed counteraction and a spate of killings. Bimbilla was attacked by Konkomba mobilised from all over Ghana. The power principle, this time applied by both parties in the conflict, was no solution, nor was the Ghanaian army intervention and temporary location of an army detachment in Bimbilla.

Perhaps a solution could have been found through the investigation by the state-appointed Commission of Inquiry. However, this commission was suspended once the Ghanaian civilian regime of President Limann was toppled by the coup which brought to power the Provisional National Defence Council headed by Flight Lieutenant J.J. Rawlings (the present President of Ghana) on New Year's Eve 1981. The new regime, self-assured in its fairly well-armed power, called the army detachment away from Bimbilla. The Nanumba–Konkomba conflict was forgotten by Accra for thirteen long years, but not by its local and regional protagonists who never forgot that the state had bitterly failed them both. Their negotiations, promoted by their respective youth associations, continued for several years but due to intransigence on both sides brought no result (Skalník 1987, 1989b).

The arrival of another civilian government in 1993 was a signal for the Konkomba to table more radical demands. This time they asked for their own 'traditional independence' which meant, besides the recognition of their chieftaincy as paramount, also carving out a territory within the Northern Region as their 'traditional' area. When this demand was rejected by the Nanumba and Dagomba neo-traditional representatives and youth, the violence repeated itself in February 1994, on much larger scale, involving seven districts and resulting in some 2,000 dead, the Ghana army again intervening late. The government-appointed special reconciliation committee negotiated a signed declaration committing both sides to the principle of negotiating peace, but in March 1995 there followed another clash resulting in more than 100 deaths. There was until recently no sign of a negotiated solution on the horizon and the next clash might well shake the foundations of Ghana as a modern nation-state (cf. Skalník 1992, 1996). The 'Kumasi accord on peace and reconciliation between the various ethnic groups in the Northern Region of Ghana', negotiated thanks to the Nairobi Peace Initiative led by Professor Hizkias Assefa and signed on 30 March 1996, bypasses the efforts of the Permanent Negotiation team of Nana Dr Obori Yeboah II which was appointed by President Rawlings. It is still to be seen whether this accord is respected by all parties in the conflict (Skalník 1997).

The recourse to power brought neither peace nor coexistence among different political cultures. In my view, a solution will be found only when the state of Ghana accepts that the Nanumba traditional authority has responsibilities for public affairs along with, or perhaps on an equal footing with itself, in what Owusu (1996a, 1996b) has called 'pragmatic pluralism'. Any solution must also recognise the Konkomba as holders of authority in the wider regional and Ghanaian national political fields. That would not mean 'traditional independence', but at least acceptance of semi-autonomous political institutions of a subordinate order whereby the Konkomba would recognise the superordination of Nanumba institutions and the paramountcy of the state in public affairs.

## Slovakia

In northern Slovakia, where since 1970 I have worked intermittently in the two submontane villages of Nižná Šuňava and Vyšná Šuňava (Skalník 1982, 1986, 1993), the state has also acted with little understanding of local conditions. The villagers have traditionally recognised the authority of the Roman Catholic church represented by the local priest who served both villages while the state was an entity beyond village life. With the coming of communist rule, the church and religious belief as such were the targets of suppression. The villagers were invited to form agricultural cooperatives. When they did not respond positively, the state drastically increased the quota of forced supplies of agricultural produce to the state granaries. Eventually, the Nižná village actively resisted by ignoring the pressure and closing its ranks around the priest. The resistance was broken in June 1950 by massive use of force (by the so-called 'people's militia' and the army) against the villagers.

For twenty-four years the village was then starved of development funds until it first succumbed to the cooperative drive and subsequently merged with Vyšná into one unified Šuňava village in 1974. For another fifteen years it seemed that there was harmony between the state and the village: the communist party reigned and the unified agricultural cooperative contributed to public development projects such as water and the sewerage system, and some new public buildings. The highest authority for the villagers old and young, men and women, remained, however, the Catholic church and its local priest, the more so because from 1967 to 1985 the village priest was a man whose wisdom, education and overall moral qualities far surpassed those of the village functionaries of the communist regime.

Once the rule of the Communist Party was toppled in 1989, the old question of autonomous authority of the villagers on the one hand and the distant but powerful state entered a new phase. There was no suppression of religious life any longer but public funds dried up and projects such as the expansion of the school were finished only with enormous effort. The villagers became very disturbed by the return of unemployment which had forced their ancestors into emigration to the United States and Canada. High unemployment rates in the nearby factories, built originally in order to eliminate poverty, were a shock. So the Šuňava villagers were dismayed by the dismemberment of Czechoslovakia at the turn of 1992/3.

The independence of Slovakia was received with somewhat worried faces as the north of Slovakia traditionally considered Prague and Košice rather than Bratislava or Budapest as their points of reference and acceptable centres of both power and authority. The Bratislava-centrism with the ruling crypto-communist-cum-nationalist government foretold a bleak future for Catholic Šuňava. The first free elections in 1990 confirmed the democratic Public Against Violence (VPN) alliance in power, both in the parliament of the federated Slovakia and in the Šuňava village council, while the Christian Democratic Movement came second. But gradually the crypto-communist and populist Movement for a Democratic Slovakia (HZDS) of the present prime minister, Vladimír Mečiar gained the support of the majority of Slovakia's voters. In 1992 Mečiar's movement won the parliamentary elections and confirmed its grip on Slovakia in the extraordinary 1994 election.

In Šuňava the 1994 municipal elections returned to office the former VPN mayor as an independent candidate. This man, who married into the village and was always known as an ardent Catholic and never a communist, had the advantage of being neutral in the rivalry between two parts of the village. His authority was widely accepted among the villagers. Perhaps surprisingly in an all-Catholic village, nearly half the voters had supported the HZDS in the election to the National Council (parliament) of the newly independent Slovak Republic a few months earlier. Fear of the resurgence of pre-war misery may have been behind Mečiar's success, as the HZDS promised to slow the economic transformation and thus preserve jobs which would otherwise have become obsolete. The skilful use of propaganda on state-owned television by Mečiar's regime – presenting successes and improvements as to his credit, but faults and failures as resulting from the opposition or adverse international circumstances – helped reinforce the increasingly widespread view of Mečiar and his movement as saviours of Slovakia and the only acceptable political leadership for the country. If there was in Šuňava a silent majority disagreeing with this view, it shows itself only in passivity and a waiting attitude (possibly an 'outwitting' tactic: Skalník 1989a). The authority of the religious majority of villagers seemed dormant while the power of the state triumphed.

## South Africa

The accession to the South African state presidency of P.W. Botha in 1978, followed by the splintering of the Conservative Party from the ruling National Party (NP), were both symptoms of the realisation that the system of racial domination or apartheid must be revised. The reform was announced in 1982 and the 1983 all-white referendum endorsed a tripartite constitutional system in which whites, still dominant, gave some largely symbolic crumbs of power to Coloureds and Indians. The black majority was left with the system of nominally independent 'Bantustans' as *de jure* sovereign states or autonomous territories within the Republic of South Africa. However, the continuous discontent bordering on civil war in some areas during 1984–6 led to the repeal of the statutes prohibiting the influx of black Africans into cities, and sex and effectively marriage between whites and Blacks. The very hesitant dismantling of apartheid lasted through over ten years (1983–94) of civil unrest: the years before the 1994 general election were very volatile and bloody. Many predicted attempts to seize power by right extremists, the South African army, left extremists within the African National Congress, or even by the Pan-African Congress. But optimistic voices never disappeared from the scene, and visions of civil or racial war were matched by the hope of a bloodless takeover by the winners of free elections. In brief, there was always a chance that people's authority would win over apartheid power, which eventually happened thanks to a series of compromises after very protracted negotiations about every aspect of the first, temporary, post-apartheid constitution. Thousands died, mostly in faction fights and ambushes, through necklacing and explosions, but eventually the election and the transfer of power went peacefully.

I believe that explanations of this quite surprising phenomenon are to be found in the 'common denominators' of South Africa, not in consensus politics or the existence of a morally strong middle class. In my opinion three factors explain the successful South African transition: first, common economic interest; second, the deterrent of bad precedents; and, third, spiritual commonality.

First, South Africa under apartheid had reached a relatively high degree of industrial and infrastructural development which affected every South African, irrespective of skin colour, sex or level of education, either through personal advancement or the prospect (vision) of social mobility. Although the left-wing leaders of the poor black majority called for a more just society through redistribution, people at every point of the social spectrum understood that the South African economy must be kept productive so that the aspirations of South Africans could be, albeit slowly, fulfilled.

Second, the decay of Africa north of the Limpopo, including relatively prosperous countries such as Ivory Coast, Ghana, Uganda, Kenya and Zimbabwe, served as warnings to South African left-wing radicals. The civil wars in Yugoslavia, Rwanda, Somalia and Sri Lanka reminded especially the negotiators of the post-apartheid arrangement that they must do everything to avoid confrontation and bloodshed in South Africa. After his release from prison in 1990, Nelson Mandela proved to be a moderate leader who realised the danger of slipping into violence and an accelerated economic downslide if the transition did not succeed. His personal role as a leader without formal power – until he became president in May 1994 – but endowed with towering authority, was essential.

Finally, and perhaps most important, the whole transition period was marked by the authority of God, the Christian churches and civil society at large. South Africans, with the exception of Jews, Muslims and Hindus, are predominantly Christians. In particular black Christians respected church leaders who rejected apartheid on moral grounds. These leaders, however, never adopted revolutionary theologies advocating militant action by the clergy along the lines of Latin American armed insurgence led by radical priests and monks. Voluntary associations, often with religious affiliations, were also important as holders of authority.

I see the authority of these three South African common denominators as having saved South Africa from armed revolution and its logical consequences. Some critics today argue that a bloody revolutionary purge was necessary because South African society did not change, merely continuing in the same style as before. The 'apartheid-is-dead-long-live-apartheid' mentality goes on. They may be right concerning continuity, but they perhaps do not realise what kind of destruction, which would have afflicted everyone, was actually averted.

At this junction I should discuss the role of power in the long transition (1983–94). It seems quite logical that one of the motivations of the NP leaders (and to some extent of their junior Coloured and Indian partners in the post-1983 constitutional arrangement) was the continuation of at least some privileges which whites had enjoyed for many decades. But taking into account all the repression of dissent during those transitional years, the common denominator of God-fearing always opened a little space for further progress. The crucial role played by the Anglican archbishop of Cape Town, Desmond Tutu, whose authority within pre-liberation South Africa was highly regarded by both his adherents and his opponents, best illustrates the spiritual and moral importance of religious and church authority in the South African equation.

The ostensibly democratic South African system of the privileged minority, including the Boer democracy and British ingredients in the constitution of the

Union of South Africa, enabled the more dynamic de Klerk government to replace the inflexible and hesitant P.W. Botha regime (1978–89); and the NP leadership eventually facilitated the application of the 'one person one vote' principle. The role of the main actor who publicly recognised the tragic error if not crime of apartheid and became the active dismantler of the apartheid regime, cannot be overestimated. De Klerk managed not only to convince the majority of whites to accept a non-racial democracy, but he also gained new authority for his party in retreating from a power monopoly to share power with black political parties.

## Lebanon

By the end of its civil war (1975–90), the state of Lebanon hardly existed. There were two governments, one in West Beirut headed by Selim Hoss (the premiership was reserved for Sunni Muslims by virtue of the unwritten National Pact), which was recognised by Syria. The other was led by army commander Michel Aoun, a Maronite Christian appointed in 1988 by the outgoing president Amine Gemayel because the parliament had failed to elect his successor. After the Syrian troops conquered Aoun's headquarters (the presidential palace in Baabda near Beirut) on 13 October 1990 and effectively ended the war, Aoun (endowed with an admirable mix of power and authority) was exiled to France. Lebanon was further divided into a plethora of warlording, confessionally based militia. The Syrian army, invited into the country in 1976 by the then president Sleiman Frangie to save beleaguered Christians, emerged in 1990 as the strongest armed formation and its supreme commander, Syrian president Hafez Assad, as Lebanon's undeclared but undisputed ruler. His unchallenged power in Syria, which he usurped in 1970, was matched by equally paramount authority which he enjoyed with some, especially but not exclusively Muslim, leaders and groupings in Lebanon.

Real and putative opponents of Syria in Lebanon were eliminated. In 1989, President René Moawad had died in a car explosion. Dany Chamoun, a former presidential candidate and leader of the National Liberal Party founded by his father, ex-president Camille Chamoun, was assassinated, together with his family, a week after the 1990 fall of the presidential palace. The remnants of the Lebanese army, deprived of its commander (Aoun), were united with fractions of disarmed militias and slowly put into the role of order guarantor along with the Syrian army. Most militias were successfully disarmed, but two Shiite formations (Amal and Hizbullah), resisting the Israeli Defence Force and its proxy South Lebanese Army, were allowed to be active in south Lebanon.

Elias Hraoui, who had been elected President under Syrian supervision in November 1989, embraced his role of facilitator of post-war security and national reconciliation with dogged determination. Never at serious variance with Assad's Syria, he concentrated on building up the Lebanese army under the command of the pro-Syrian general Emile Lahoud. The mainly Christian opposition, including Amine Gemayel, Raymond Eddé (leader of the National Bloc) and Dory Chamoun (the new leader of the National Liberal Party), almost all went into Parisian exile. The only authority remaining in Lebanon which was opposed to the Syrian military presence was the Maronite patriarch Butros Sfeir and a number of bishops and other church dignitaries.

The government as executive power remained fairly weak for two years after the war ended. Parliament, lacking legitimacy because no election had taken place since 1972, was enlarged by a number of appointed (non-elected) deputies. The Taif agreement of October 1989, reached by the remaining Lebanese deputies under Saudi and other Arab sponsorship, revised the 1926 constitution and stipulated the principle of political parity between Christians and Muslims, for which the Muslims and the Syrian president had long called. Although the Lebanese president would, as previously, always be a Maronite Christian, the prime minister a Sunni Muslim and the Speaker of the Parliament a Shia Muslim, both parliament and government would have to be composed equally of Muslims and Christians. The 6:5 weighting in favour of Christians (based on the 1932 census) was abolished. A complex system also ensured that different sects and political movements would be represented within each religious grouping as had been the case since Lebanon's inception as an independent state.

The most important post-Taif innovation appeared to be balancing power between the three presidents – of the republic, the council of ministers and the assembly. This balance became all-important once the office of the premier (or president of the council of ministers) was assumed in November 1992 by Rafiq Hariri, a Lebanese-Saudi multimilliardaire. During the preceding years Hariri through his wealth and philanthropic activities gained widely recognised authority as a potential saviour of Lebanon. His good relations with President Hraoui and (dubious) legitimation by the 1992 parliamentary election, along with his undisguised strong personal ambition, drove him into the prime minister's chair. Hariri wanted to reconstruct Lebanon as soon as possible and started to run it as he used to run his own private company. The third 'president', Speaker Nabih Berri, wanting to produce new laws to back up the crucial role of parliament, inevitably collided on almost every issue with Hariri. President Hraoui often played the role of arbiter, but all three 'presidents' had to travel far too often to Damascus to seek mediation from President Assad or his Vice-President Khaddam (widely believed to handle the Lebanon 'portfolio' since he had been minister of foreign affairs in the 1970s).

Prime Minister Hariri's ongoing ability to combine power and authority has rested on first manipulating his original authority in order to gain the premier's office, then as premier using the authority of his promises to reconstruct Lebanon (and specifically the centre of Beirut) as political credit with which to acquire even more power. Three threats to resign (whenever parliament or other politicians stood in his way) confirmed his indispensability and increased both his power and authority. He skilfully cultivated close contacts with Syria, while not neglecting his previous good relations with Saudi King Fahd and French President Chirac. In 1995 Hariri supported prolonging the mandate of President Hraoui for three years, which automatically extended his own mandate as prime minister. Finally, in 1996, he entered the election battle and won a parliamentary seat in Beirut, although he originated from Saida. This not only increased his authority among the Sunni Muslim electorate but also changed the power constellation in the legislature. From October 1996 onwards the Hariri parliamentary bloc has been the strongest and Hariri's reconstruction drive is generally expected to stumble less and less in the cumbersome parliament. Direct Syrian involvement in Lebanon remains problematic, however. If Lebanon's independence and sovereignty do not become real and trustworthy once more, the dream of reconstructing Beirut and restoring a beautiful country once again as 'the Switzerland of the Middle East' with excellent infrastructure and tourist facilities, may not materialise.

Rafiq Hariri is today the most powerful man in Lebanon. His authority, however, has been weakened over his years in the prime minister's office, both because of what appear to be his increasing power ambitions and only relative success in his reconstruction drive. In contrast, Maronite Patriarch Butros Sfeir's authority has been growing steadily in direct relation to his open and repeated public criticism of Lebanon's alleged loss of its democratic character and sovereignty. Sfeir has also been made a cardinal by the Pope, which has further strengthened his moral and political authority. Sfeir and the entire Maronite bishops' conference have repeatedly expressed their displeasure over Syria's continuing military presence (which results mainly from the continuing Israeli occupation of one-tenth of Lebanese territory); and the limitations on freedoms which flow out of laws proposed by the Hariri government. In the latter they were supported by the 1995 Papal Synod on Lebanon which took place in Rome.

Most controversial of these laws so far has been the law on audiovisual media, requiring registration and a concomitant limitation of the number of TV and FM broadcasting stations. Rejection of this law has united the church with journalists and political opponents of the regime both left and right, including some deputies and trade unionists and many ordinary people. By the end of 1996, the authority of democratic principles seemed to stand opposed to the Hariri government, which was accused of insensitivity to these principles. Nonetheless, Hariri himself, speaking in Washington at the opening of the 1996 'Friends of Lebanon' donor meeting, reiterated his adherence to democratic principles and the specific place of Lebanon in the Middle East and the eastern Mediterranean. Hariri also wants Lebanon to join the (south-eastern) Mediterranean partnership linked to the European Union.

I conclude that, in spite of strong Syrian influence in Lebanon, a certain balance of conflicting authorities has enabled political pluralism to continue. The struggle to preserve Lebanon's democratic character has prevented the imposition of naked state power on the traditionally freedom-loving population, especially the Christians. The remaining problem of Lebanese in relation to Arab identity requires separate analysis.

## Conclusion

In the present chapter I have tried to examine four cases of the interplay of authority with power, to show that authority has the potential to outwit power or at least to make power less predatory than it usually is. It is useful and necessary to distinguish between authority and power. But I have argued, in contrast to many (though not all) analysts, that authority is not legally vested or formalised 'authority of power', i.e. legitimated power in the Weberian sense. Instead, its autonomous existence makes authority indispensable in both politics and society. The assertion that authority is 'not vested in particular idiosyncratic individuals but in roles, offices and positions' (*Encyclopaedia Britannica* 14: 699) is not confirmed by the data discussed above. Similarly, the assertion that 'virtually all political systems endeavour to establish the authority of crucial roles and institutions' because 'it is uncertain . . . how long pure authority endures if it is not reinforced by other types of power' (ibid.), does not seem to be valid for personalities and organisations such as Cardinal Sfeir and the Maronite bishops' conference in Lebanon or Nelson Mandela and Archbishop Tutu in South Africa. It seems that personalities may give authority to institutions and roles rather than the other way around.

Moreover, Max Weber argued that authority does not have a rational base and commands are obeyed because they possess authority rather than because of the reasoning behind them, even that the substance of authority excludes rational justification (Kejzerov 1975: 83). Indeed, some of the case material examined in this chapter supports this assertion.

If the chapter has persuaded the reader that the analysis of authority versus power, their autonomous functions, their interrelationship and their differential impact on societies, are legitimate concerns, its purpose is met. The authority of individuals, institutions and ideas should be studied against the background of power in order to understand better the mechanisms whereby states become too sovereign and too eager to fight wars, and to search for ways whereby potentially lethal state sovereignty may be tamed and limited (Malinowski 1944).

## References

Bierstedt, R. (1964) The problem of authority. In *Freedom and Control in Modern Society* (ed.) M. Berger, T. Abel and C.H. Page. New York: Octagon Press (pp. 67–81).
de Jouvenel, B. (1957) *Sovereignty: An Inquiry into the Political Good*. Chicago: University of Chicago Press.

*Encyclopaedia Britannica* (1976) *Encyclopaedia Britannica: Macropaedia*, 15th edn. Chicago: Encyclopaedia Britannica.

Havel, V. *et al.* (1985) *The Power of the Powerless*. London: Hutchinson.

Kejzerov, N.M. (1975) *Moc a autorita. Kritika buržoazních teorií*. Praha: Orbis.

Lasswell, H. D. and Kaplan, A. (1950) *Power and Society: A Framework for Political Inquiry*. New Haven, CT: Yale University Press.

Malinowski, B. (1944) *Freedom and Civilization*. New York: Roy.

Miller, D. with Coleman, J., Connolly, W. and Ryan, A. (eds) (1991) *Blackwell's Encyclopaedia of Political Thought*. Oxford: Blackwell.

Owusu, M. (1996a) Tradition, traditionalists and political transformation: the dynamics of democratization in Africa. Paper presented at the Association for Anthropology in Southern Africa/Pan-African Association of Anthropologists conference at Pretoria.

—— (1996b) Tradition and transformation: democracy and the politics of popular power in Ghana. *Journal of Modern African Studies* 34, 2: 307–43.

Peabody, R.L. (1968) Authority. *International Encyclopaedia of the Social Sciences*, vol. I. New York: Macmillan/Free Press (pp. 473–7).

Skalník, P. (1982) Community studies and limits of representativeness: a socio-ecological discussion on mountain communities. In *Theories and Methods in Rural Community Studies* (eds) H. Mendras and I. Mihailescu. Oxford: Pergamon (pp. 169–89).

—— (1986) Uneven development in European mountain communities. *Dialectical Anthropology* 10, 3–4: 215–28.

—— (1987) On the inadequacy of the concept of 'traditional state' (illustrated by ethnographic material on Nanun, Ghana). *Journal of Legal Pluralism and Unofficial Law* 25–6: 301–25.

—— (1989a) Outwitting the state: an introduction. In *Outwitting the State* (ed.) P. Skalník. New Brunswick: Transaction (pp. 1–21).

—— (1989b) Outwitting Ghana: pluralism of political culture in Nanun. In *Outwitting the State* (ed.) P. Skalník. New Brunswick: Transaction (pp. 145–68).

—— (1992) Why Ghana is not a nation-state. *Africa Insight* (Pretoria) 22, 1: 66–72.

—— (1993) 'Socialism is dead' and very much alive in Slovakia: political inertia in a Tatra village. In *Socialism: Ideals, Ideology and Social Practice* (ed.) C.M. Hann. London: Routledge (pp. 218–26).

—— (1996) The state and local ethnopolitical identities (the case of community conflicts in northern Ghana). Unpublished paper presented at Association for Anthropology in Southern Africa/Pan African Association of Anthropologists conference at Pretoria.

—— (1997) Nanumba versus Konkomba: an assessment of the troubled coexistence. Paper presented at the Pan-African Association of Anthropologists conference, Legon, Ghana.

Weber, M. (1958) *Gesammelte politische Schriften*. Tübingen: Mohr.

# Chapter 13

# Speaking truth to power?

## Some problems using ethnographic methods to influence the formulation of housing policy in South Africa[1]

*Andrew Spiegel, Vanessa Watson and Peter Wilkinson*

## Introduction

> The 'Enlightenment', which discovered the liberties, also invented the disciplines.
>
> (Foucault 1979: 222; in Escobar 1992: 133)

> One cannot look on the bright side of planning, its modern achievements (if one were to accept them), without looking at the same time on its dark side of domination. The management of the social has produced modern subjects who are not only dependent on professionals for [satisfaction of] their needs, but also ordered into realities (cities, health and educational systems, economies, etc.) that can be governed by the state through planning. *Planning inevitably requires the normalization and standardization of reality, which in turn entails injustice and the erasure of difference and diversity.*
>
> (Escobar 1992: 134, emphasis added)

Foucault's recognition of the ambivalent, two-edged nature of the Enlightenment project underpins a central proposition of his work, namely that the discourses and practices of modernity inextricably couple questions of knowledge and power. Escobar (1992, 1995) has built on Foucault's insight to formulate what has become a quite widely recognised critique of development or social planning as a key instrument of what Foucault (1979) labels 'governmentality'[2] – the disciplinary mode more familiarly known in the Anglophone world as 'social engineering', of which housing policy is undoubtedly a part.

In general, the overt intentions of most development programmes, and of practitioners engaged in them, have been to improve some aspect of the material conditions of life for an identified 'target' population. However, from a critical perspective constructed around Foucault's analysis, execution of such programmes appears to involve an apparently necessary process of 'surveillance' of that population by the development agencies concerned. To facilitate what would be regarded as effective intervention, planning processes seem to require a 'mapping' of the lives of those development programmes are intended to benefit. The 'mapping' takes the form of information-gathering through assembly of social, demographic and other 'data' to be used for ends invariably presented by the development agencies as beneficial. Simultaneously, however, such data also become available as a potential instrument for top-down control and manipulation of 'target' populations (Ferguson 1990).

Whether or not it is explicitly articulated, recognition of the 'dark side of domination' embodied in development programmes means that the people identified as potential 'beneficiaries' sometimes resist demands for information, or provide false answers, particularly when they are sought through the impersonal mechanism of large-scale statistically representative surveys. In the face of such resistance, and in acknowledgement of the limited 'reach' of surveys, one response of development agencies has been to turn to ethnographic methods, which appear to offer a less 'distanced' and perhaps more subtle and effective, if also less aggregative or statistically representative, means of collecting certain types of information.

Understanding the surveillance aspect of information-gathering provides a backdrop for recognising the salient and problematic nature of the relationship between knowledge and power in South Africa today. What appears to be a global trend towards forging closer relationships between academic researchers and decision-makers located in both the public and the private spheres has taken a specific and perhaps particularly intense form here, associated with the process of transition to a post-apartheid society.

Prior to the emergence of a 'Government of National Unity' in 1994, many South African academics and intellectuals working in the non-governmental sector were excluded from policy-making arenas, either directly by the political-ideological 'gatekeeping' of the apartheid regime's bureaucrats, or by their own personal decisions not to participate formally in the structures of apartheid government. The present transition, however, has drawn many such previously excluded academics and intellectuals into direct engagement with policy-making processes, and into government apparatuses themselves. One result has been that an earlier period of vigorous critique of development theory and practice within such circles has increasingly given way to a much less critically distanced involvement in the design and implementation of development programmes. We have a sense that the need to concentrate on the immediate 'practical' tasks of project and programme management has demanded suppression of broader theoretical questions and their implications for practice, which previously occupied such people. For those academics or researchers still outside the immediate sphere of policy engagement, however – and for their students – the question of whether, and on what terms, they may choose to enter the terrain remains central. Moreover, given tendencies for ethnographic methods to be deployed, increasingly, as an adjunct to official modes of large-scale data collection, the question is clearly of fundamental import to social anthropologists.

It is in these terms that we cast the object of our present inquiry: can ethnographic methods be used *unproblematically* to try to influence the making of social policy? More specifically, how can we engage with policy discourse in ways that avoid what Escobar sees as the inevitable 'normalisation and standardisation of reality' required by that mode of discourse? Our conclusion, based on our own recent experience in undertaking such a project, is that ethnographic methods *cannot* be used unproblematically for this purpose, and we devote the body of our chapter to an exploration of the various types of problem we have encountered in making the attempt.

## Designing a 'policy-relevant' research project: some methodological assumptions

Our chapter developed out of critical reflection on our own attempt to deploy ethnographic methods to influence the formulation of housing policy in South Africa. Our project began by questioning certain of what seemed to us to be invalid or over-simplistic assumptions about the process of urbanisation and settlement of Africans in South Africa, particularly as these had been incorporated, largely implicitly, in the emerging national housing policy framework (Wilkinson 1993). Our prime concern was an apparent 'homogenisation' and 'normalisation' within the specification of national housing needs, particularly for the African population whose experience of urbanisation was, in our understanding, extremely heterogeneous and fluid, and involved a correspondingly diverse range of needs.

From the outset, then, our research was conceived as an interdisciplinary exercise using ethnographic methods to inform the analysis of, and commentary on, current housing delivery policies in South Africa. To this end, two planning academics (Watson and Wilkinson), both with a specific interest in the field of housing policy, came together with a social anthropologist (Spiegel) to formulate a project entitled 'African population movement in metropolitan Cape Town and its implications for housing policy'.[3]

The project was designed specifically to generate in-depth interview material with a substantial 'ethnographic' content which could then be unpacked to reveal the diversity of household types, 'domestic consolidation' trajectories and associated housing expectations amongst the African population of metropolitan Cape Town.[4] A small, non-random sample of informants in thirty-seven households was interviewed during late 1992 and early 1993.[5] The sample was disaggregated into seven residential areas, identified in terms of different housing types and contrasting settlement histories (Spiegel *et al.* 1996a). In each area, five or (in two cases) six households were selected for interviews on the basis of 'snowball' sampling (Bernard 1989).

Throughout the research process and the subsequent phase of analysis and reporting,[6] we have considered that it is – or should be – important to alert policy-makers to potential lacks of 'fit' between their policies and the realities of social and domestic life that confront Cape Town's African population. Accordingly, a hitherto unexamined assumption, which we now need to explicate, has been that to ring the necessary bells in policy-making chambers all we needed to do was to expose to policy-makers, and to the larger public, the diverse realities of people's domestic situations, of their life trajectories and of their expressed life projects, particularly as these related to housing and domestic 'consolidation' strategies. While continuing to believe that such exposure is important, we now consider it essential to examine critically the questions of whether, and through what specific further effort, such insights can be brought to the notice of policy-makers to influence their discourse in some significant way. We return to these issues below.

A further, more explicit assumption we made was that the most effective way to understand and represent the diverse realities of people's lives was to undertake a relatively detailed, 'micro'-scale 'qualitative' investigation – an essentially anthropological research protocol. The ethnographic product was to be a series of 'stories' that incorporated and commented on respondents' own accounts of their current situations and past histories. We intended that the narratives should capture a sufficient sense of the diversity and differences within the 'target' population to reveal the extent to which its housing needs might diverge from the 'normalised' and 'standardised' assumptions incorporated in current housing policy.

Finally, we were not quite so naïve as to think that simply telling stories would suffice to gain entry to policy-making arenas. We therefore had a (not very clear) idea that we might use – or have others use – the indicative findings of our initial non-representative study to design a more extensive, quantitatively sophisticated survey that would yield the 'representative data' (appropriately gridded and aggregated statistics) needed to translate our stories into 'policy-relevant' conclusions.

We intended that the further exercise should not fall into the trap of mindless 'number crunching' but serve rather to reveal micro-level diversity by quantifying both its extent and its localised incidence. We thus anticipated an extensive multivariate analysis with a range of cross-tabulations offering us purchase on the extent to which variables were interlinked in some sociologically significant, or at least interesting, way. We hoped, therefore, to see our penchant for fine-grained detail reproduced in a statistically representative manner that would satisfy the demand for a properly 'scientific' rationality as seems appropriate, still, in much planning and policy discourse.

More or less explicitly, the above are some key assumptions or expectations that we brought to the design of our research programme. In carrying it out, however, we encountered certain difficulties, to which we now turn.

# Undertaking 'policy-relevant' research: some methodological difficulties

Our difficulties in pursuing the research objectives we set ourselves fall into two broad categories. The first subsumes the specifically ethnographic problems of capturing, interpreting and generalising depth-interview material. Undoubtedly, all, or most, such problems are familiar to social anthropologists: we address them here to indicate the extent to which participants in collaborative interdisciplinary projects may need to examine their methodology explicitly and systematically. In our case, our research design, that had us rely on assistants as fieldworkers, resulted in the planning academics coming to confront such problems seriously only when we set about interpreting the material generated by our fieldworkers' interviews.[7]

The second set of difficulties refers back to the fundamental problem with which we are concerned here: how to engage effectively with policy-making in an attempt to make it more 'beneficial' while attempting to maintain a critical distance from its 'disciplinary' effects. We return to discuss the issue more fully in our concluding section 'Speaking truth to power?'.

## Ethnography and depth-interview material

### Constructing texts, telling stories: 'screening' problems

The very textuality of the 'stories' of people's domestic and settlement experiences we have been able to assemble from our qualitative study presents a specific set of difficulties. They centre on various aspects of our research approach which place distance or 'screens' between ourselves, as researchers, our respondents, as the subjects of our research, and our various, sometimes quite different, audiences.

First – and quite obviously – as 'storytellers' we interpose ourselves between the people about whom we are telling stories and the audience for those stories. In and of itself, this is problematic for, while storytellers might be good, bad or indifferent, they are never simply neutral or transparent conduits for the stories they tell. Since the latter are always *constructed* they are invariably and unavoidably filtered through a particular, perhaps only implicit, cognitive framework.

The conceptual equipment through which we have interrogated our material, and shaped it into stories we can retail to our targeted audience, represents a first 'screen' between that audience and our respondents.[8] This is, of course, not a new problem for storytellers in either the academic or the non-academic mould and, over time, various strategies to deal with it have emerged. Our strategy, at present, is simply to recognise that we are indeed sieving our material through a particular conceptual framework and to attempt to make the elements of that framework as coherent and explicit as possible.

A second possible 'screen' arises from the fact that the primary field research for our project was conducted through interviews and was far less able to rely on personal participant observation of the 'hanging out' kind than at least the anthropologist among us would have preferred. This was of particular concern to him despite dissenting voices from within the discipline acknowledging Bourdieu's argument (in Jenkins 1992: 55) that 'the claim to valid anthropological knowledge may be translated as, "I know, because I was there".' We do not enter this debate here – certainly, the necessity for direct experience or observation is effectively discounted in many other approaches to social research. We note only the existence of objections to our kind of approach.

There are two further, possibly less controversial, 'screening' problems associated with our use of interviews to gather what is conventionally referred to as 'primary' material. The first and perhaps the most obvious of these is that of language. Our fieldworkers conducted their interviews mainly in Xhosa, which they recorded on tape and subsequently translated and transcribed. What they delivered to us was written text which none of us, as non-Xhosa speakers, was able to compare with the original, taped record of the interview. The fact is that we have had to rely on interpretation – and on transcription into written English by English second-language speakers, with all *its* attendant levels of interpretation – to gain access to what is clearly only nominally, by now, our 'raw' or 'primary' material.

The second 'screen' introduced through the use of interviews is linked, but not reducible, to the problems already discussed. It concerns the fact that our interview material reached us in the form of *written* text excluding any detailed sense of either the immediate context or of what Bourdieu would term the 'habitus' that shapes and conditions all such social interactions. Having not, ourselves, generally been party to the interviews, we could not know *directly* how each was contingently and strategically constructed as a symbolic transaction by the people involved. Consequently, we have had to rely on a process of interpolation in order to understand something of how our interviewers' respondents' answers may have been shaped both by how the interviewers asked their questions and, indeed, by what type of person they were asked. It is important to recognise this in order to address the problem, originally posed by Malinowski, which Bourdieu reframes in terms of what he labels 'official accounts' – discursive responses by informants seeking 'to describe the state of affairs which *ought* to happen because the nature of the occasion [and the status of the interviewer?] inspires them to explain (or justify) their behaviour, in addition to (or instead of) describing it' (Jenkins 1992: 53).

In summary, then, a key set of difficulties engendered by our choice of research method has been the various 'screens' interposed both between ourselves and our sources and, in the form of our own interpretive framework, between those sources and our audiences. We are aware that there is nothing novel in this conclusion but would argue that it remains important for researchers using ethnographic methods to recognise the existence of such 'screens'. For it is only then that we can begin to engage in the sort of self-reflexive 'double-distancing' – the 'objectification of objectification' – called for in Bourdieu's epistemological critique of ethnographic methods (cf. Jenkins 1992: 47–52).

## Linking qualitative and quantitative research methods: 'generalisation' problems

As indicated, we had hoped from the start that our research would be used to inform the design of a larger 'quantitative' study, based on a statistically representative survey of African households in the metropolitan area. Such a study was commissioned in late 1994 under the auspices of the then newly formed Western Cape Community-Based Housing Trust (WCCHT),[9] using funds made available by the US Agency for International Development. Our interaction with the demographic researchers contracted by the WCCHT to carry out the survey points to a further set of problems which seem to be endemic to attempts to link qualitative and quantitative research methods.

In designing their study, the WCCHT researchers had access not only to our first attempt at interpreting our case material (Spiegel *et al.* 1994), but also to our interview transcripts. In addition, we were consulted directly at various points in connection with both the formulation of the survey questionnaire and the analysis of the data it generated.

Although constrained by a relatively tight WCCHT timetable – and, perhaps, by some residual scepticism about the utility of playing the 'numbers game' – we assumed that our interactions and contributions would ensure that what we saw as the significant implications of our work would be taken up in the WCCHT study. What we expected, therefore, was that our recognition of the diversity of processes of household formation and settlement among Cape Town's African population would be clearly reflected in the statistically representative results generated by the WCCHT researchers.

Yet, despite the good intentions of everyone involved, we now see that the task of translating our 'stories' into statistically representative 'data' is more complex and difficult than any of us had perceived. Some dimensions of the diversity we detected in our own study are evident in the WCCHT researchers' findings (Mazur and Qangule 1995). But they are limited to what could be incorporated as numerically codable responses to the rigidly structured questions required by survey formats. Consequently, various more interesting 'processual' aspects of respondents' lives which tried to address in our stories – in particular, those relating to explanations of individual urbanisation histories and domestic consolidation trajectories – are simply absent from the data presented in the survey findings.

In part, of course, this may be due to our own failure to communicate clearly to the WCCHT researchers what we considered to be key analytical variables or parameters identified by our work. Hence, the stratification of the WCCHT sample by settlement/housing type and the tendency to use this as the key variable throughout the processing of the data gives that factor an analytical centrality that we had already begun to question when the survey was undertaken. Disaggregation of the survey data primarily in terms of settlement/housing type categories tends to suppress the importance of other variables such as age and sex, which we were then beginning to explore analytically (Spiegel *et al.* forthcoming). To date, then, we have been able to glean little from the WCCHT study that might contribute significantly to the argument we have been trying to make.

Finally, we believe that problems of linking qualitative with quantitative studies go beyond questions of error or omission on the part of the researchers involved. Perhaps it is simply that the richness of the type of biographical and other material generated through open-ended interviews – whatever the 'screening' difficulties might be – cannot be captured effectively through the questionnaire-based survey format. The analytical grid imposed by the necessity for numerical coding of survey data would seem to preclude any really consequential engagement with the textured detail of people's changing lives and cognitive frameworks over time. It may be, therefore, that only ethnographic methods capable of recording 'longitudinally' the diachronic processes central to the phenomena we wish to study are adequate to our primary purpose of achieving 'critical understanding'.

## Ethnography and 'policy-relevant' research

If ethnography is indeed to be our method, we need immediately to address two, probably interrelated, questions about what might be involved in translating ethnographic understanding into 'policy-relevant' discourse. The first concerns the logistical issues that would undoubtedly arise in any attempt to substitute what is, by definition, a time-consuming longitudinal approach for the one-off, 'freeze frame' immediacy of a conventional survey. In general, but particularly in situations of perceived crisis – the 'housing crisis', for instance – policy-makers tend to demand quick responses to their need for information about 'target' populations. They are unlikely to commit resources to research efforts which could take some years to yield results that, ultimately, may serve only to render problematic their preferred or established modes of intervention.

The second question addresses a problem whose existence might be inferred from the last statement, and it is to this, with its implications for power relations, that we now turn.

### Engaging policy-makers: 'entry' problems

A specific difficulty centres on the issue of how to break out of the essentially 'academic' and discursive realm of critical understanding and into the 'practical' realm of policy-making. The latter is, of course, always and already, a realm of *discourse.* Yet the discursive community which occupies it is, in many ways, distinct and isolated from that engaged in the practice of academic research. If we wish to gain entry to the discursive community of policy-makers, we need actively to construct ways of making our voice heard in their circles.

We have, therefore, to ask whether there are ways of using stories such as ours, first, to transform policy-makers' perceptions of what constitutes the problem they are dealing with and then to provide them with the basis for introducing policy changes that will begin to address the sort of complexities our work has uncovered. Do we need always to return to the mode of statistically representative surveys and analysis to be effective? It is at this point that we find ourselves having to admit that we have not yet managed to resolve the problem: we have still to find a mechanism through which to translate our understanding into conclusions that policy-makers might take as relevant.

Entry into the discursive community of policy-makers is not, however, limited only by factors such as 'styles' of discourse or the mode of information assembly. Any strategy to gain such entry must be formulated in terms that take account of the interests and predispositions of those policy-makers we might wish to address, and by whom we would want to be heard. In other words, we need to recognise that access to any arena of policy formation is not uncontested. It is, in fact, an arena of power, guarded by what are often very powerful gatekeepers whose interests may lie primarily in preserving or extending the symbolic capital and status they have already accumulated in that field. For them, the introduction of new, or qualitatively different, discursive frameworks may well be interpreted as a threat. If that is the case, they are likely to be resisted.

Recognition of this immanent or overt politics in which policy – and, per-haps, all – discourse is embedded returns us to the overarching concern we voiced in our introduction. What we asked there was how we might engage with the policy-making process in ways that allowed us to avoid any need either to suppress our own critical faculties or to frame our participation in the very mode of 'normalising' and 'standardising' discourse we have identified as lying at the core of the problem of current policy. Is this possible? Or is the two-edged nature of social planning and policy-making so fundamental a part of the 'governmentalising' thrust of the state that we are damned if we do – the sin of commission, of acting effectively as agents of the state – and damned if we don't – the sin of omission, of failing to act at all, even when our activism might empower the state's subjects?

## The politics of engagement with policy discourse

There are clearly no easy answers to the dilemma encountered in any attempt to address policy-making. It is possible that such a project is irretrievably doomed because, as Appel (1993) suggests regarding South African education policy, the disjunctures between policy and academic discourses are embedded in power relations.[10] In grappling with the dilemma, however, we have found two possible but divergent approaches along which to address it, and a third that throws further light on those two in turn. All are drawn from the work of prominent critics of Foucault. The first derives from Michael Walzer (1986) who questions the usefulness – indeed, the morality – of what he sees as Foucault's fundamental nihilism. The second comes from Barry Smart (1986) who attempts to build, somewhat more sympathetically, on what he sees as Foucault's important insights into the nature of modern 'governmentality'. The third, which offers refinements to the other two, is Nancy Fraser's (1989) use of Foucault to understand the 'politics of need interpretation'.

Walzer suggests that we should reject the essentially nihilistic implications of Foucault's 'radical abolitionism' – his (somewhat blurred) commitment to 'the dismantling of the whole thing [the "disciplinary society"], the fall of the carceral city, not revolution but abolition' (Walzer 1986: 60) – precisely because it leaves us with no alternatives to pursue, no new structures, no new codes for behaviour. Foucault's commitment, Walzer argues:

> . . . if it is serious, is not anarchist so much as nihilist. For on his own arguments, either there will be nothing left at all, nothing visibly human; or new codes and disciplines will be produced, and Foucault gives us no reason to expect that these will be any better than the ones we now live with. Nor, for that matter, does he give us any way of knowing what 'better' might mean.
>
> (1986: 61)

Walzer's position is reinforced by Fraser when she argues that:

> Because Foucault has no basis for distinguishing, for example, forms of power that involve domination from those that do not, he appears to endorse a one-sided, wholesale rejection of modernity as such. Furthermore, he appears to do so without any conception of what is to replace it.
>
> (1989: 32–3)

What lies at the heart of what Walzer calls Foucault's nihilism? For Walzer it is Foucault's refusal to recognize the difference between liberal and authoritarian (or totalitarian) state forms. For Fraser it is his disregard for power that is not domination. For both, therefore, Foucault's politics can only ever be either that of 'a small reform here or there, an easing of disciplinary rigour, the introduction of more humane, if no less effective, methods' (Walzer 1986: 60), or that cast in a 'radical abolitionist' mould.

Both authors offer opportunity for a more substantial engagement with the politics of reform than does Foucault. For Walzer it comes when the state takes a liberal democratic form which is, at least potentially, capable of 'good' or at least 'better' (that is, more benign) government. In this view, there is both the possibility and the need to engage the state actively on the terrain of the 'rule of law' – that arena in which the legitimate 'reach' of disciplinary institutions and their effects can be scrutinised and held to account. There may, therefore, be defensible grounds for seeking to 'improve' the state's social policies by questioning or contesting the grounds on which they are based.

For Fraser it comes from recognition that, whatever form the state takes, there are locuses of, and struggles over, power that always oblige the state to reconceptualise its relation with its subjects. In this view there is always good reason, particularly from those (including academics) engaged in what Fraser calls 'expert discourse', to challenge the state and thereby to contest its policies, hopefully with the result that they will change for the benefit of the state's subjects.

Whichever reason leads us to deem it right to confront state power in the policy arena, however, we must still recognise that doing so does not, in and of itself, solve the problem of *how* to engage in such efforts to improve policy outcomes.

Smart's interpretation of Foucault's politics offers another possible approach to the dilemma. Smart accepts that Foucault omits '[any] recommendation or direction for action, an answer to the question "What is to be done?"' However:

> The omission is a logical consequence of Foucault's method and associated analytical focus rather than a sign of political obduracy, both archaeology and genealogy [Foucault's methods of 'discourse analysis'] standing in opposition to unitary bodies of theory or globalizing discourses which seek to integrate diverse 'local' events within a totalizing frame in order to prescribe particular practices and thereby realize specified effects.
>
> (1986: 166)

In Smart's interpretation, Foucault deliberately intended consistently to refrain 'from the articulation of policy alternatives to the programmes and practices which were the object of critique in the respective genealogical analyses of the present':

> A central political objective of [Foucault's] work has . . . been to assist in the creation of conditions in which particular subject groups, for example patients or prisoners, can express themselves and act, rather than to pro- vide a theory about 'madness' or 'delinquency' from which specialized social agents or functionaries ('social' workers) may derive guidance for their acts of intervention. Indeed, in respect of the latter, Foucault has argued that in effect his project has been to 'bring it about that they

> "no longer know what to do", so that the acts, gestures, discourses which up until then had seemed to go without saying become problematic'.
>
> (Smart 1986: 167)

It may be possible to construct what Smart labels a 'politics of truth' around this conclusion. Indeed, it could provide some sort of rationale for our intuitive sense that what we have been engaged in, one way or another, is an effort to make the work of policy-makers in the housing field *more difficult, more problematic* than it already is, precisely by contesting the easy assumptions on which their discourse has, so far, been based.

We have, however, yet to work fully through the implications of this possibility – which, arguably, could represent the moment at which the *disciplines* (using the word advisedly) of anthropology and planning must part company. Despite pressures both from within and without the academy, it may be sufficient for anthropological discourse to remain primarily oppositional and within the limits of critical analysis, rather than seeking to enter the realm of 'totalizing' discourse within which, according to Foucault, prescriptive statements *must* be framed. But the same can clearly not apply to planning whose very *raison d'être* remains, of course, exactly such prescription – in expert discourse mode. Yet we also need to recognise that neither expert nor oppositional discourse is homogeneous.

We see, then, that our initial assessment was correct: there are, indeed, no easy answers to the dilemma of how – or whether – to address the Janus-faced character of policy-making in the modern state. This is so even if we are willing, with Walzer, to recognise that that state can, in different historical and geographical contexts, take a variety of forms embodying different balances between its 'disciplinary' and its 'benign' aspects. Following Fraser, we need to appreciate that needs discourses are disaggregable and that, in the politics of discursive contestation, 'struggles over cultural meanings and social identities are struggles for cultural hegemony, that is, for the power to construct authoritative definitions of social situations and legitimate interpretations of social needs' (1989: 6). Ultimately, then, *any* response to demands for policy engagement involves a difficult political choice whose efficacy, by its very nature, cannot be guaranteed.

## Speaking truth to power? A tentative conclusion

> In large part, it must be admitted, knowledge is negative. It tells us what we cannot do, where we cannot go, wherein we have been wrong, but not necessarily how to loosen these constraints or correct these errors.
>
> (Wildavsky 1979: 401)

For their part, anthropologists and sociologists have been relegated, or have relegated themselves, to a residual role in the implementation of projects:

they have been employed very largely as pathologists, picking over the corpses of defunct development enterprises and performing intricate structural-functional autopsies. The pious hope that these will advise future planning efforts is usually frustrated by the reluctance of policy makers and planners to learn from the testimony of the negative case.

(Robertson 1984: 294)

From very different starting points, Wildavsky (a policy analyst) and Robertson (an anthropologist) seem to reach similar, or at least broadly convergent, conclusions about the relationship between critical analysis and policy-making processes. In the policy field, they seem to say, valid knowledge ('truth') generally only emerges *post facto*, after the event. It is constructed retrospectively from studies which examine what happened when a particular policy was applied in a particular context. At best, as an optimistic reading of Wildavsky might suggest, policy-makers are willing to learn from such codified experience and hence retrospective policy analysis can play a corrective or 'feedback' role in producing better policy outcomes. At worst, as in Robertson's unambiguously pessimistic view, policy-makers and planners are, as it were, congenitally disposed to ignore cautionary tales and will continue to frame their interventions in terms of the hegemonic discourses of 'developmentalism'. 'Power', in other words, may more often than not choose to remain deaf to the 'truth' – if, indeed, the two terms can be separated at all.

Even if we accept that some justification exists for seeking to 'speak truth to power' – as our interpretation of Walzer's position suggests – questions must remain over how or whether we will be heard by policy-makers. All we may finally be left with, then, is to subscribe to some version of Foucault's 'politics of truth' and to take on the essentially subversive role assigned to 'critique' within it:

In Western culture the social and human sciences have increasingly constituted the 'true' discourses which have provided reasons, principles, and justifications for objectifying and subjectifying practices through which people have been classified, examined, trained, 'divided from others', and formed as subjects. . . . It is on the assumed scientificity of such discourses and the effects of power 'linked to the institution and functioning of an organized scientific discourse within a society such as ours' that both 'conservative' and 'progressive' prescriptions and programmings of behaviour have been predicated. One of the principal objectives of Foucault's analysis is to contest 'the scientific hierarchization of knowledges and the effects intrinsic to their power' implied in the above – not by constructing a higher, more general and more powerful theory, but by developing critiques of both objectifying and subjectifying forms of knowledge, action, and their respective effects, in order to reveal and thereby reactivate the various forms of subjugated knowledge and local

criticism of 'an autonomous, non–centralised kind . . . whose validity is not
dependent on the approval of the established regimes of thought'.

(Smart 1986: 167)

As already indicated, we suspect that many contemporary ethnographers probably feel comfortable with a commitment to contesting the general 'disqualifi-
cation of low-ranking, local, and popular forms of knowledge ("*le savoir des
gens*")' (Smart 1986: 164) by the hegemonic discourses of scientism. Indeed,
as Pamela Reynolds[11] has remarked: 'Rationalities always dissolve when one
has sufficient detail' – which we might interpret as a reasoned response to
the ways the messy 'detailed' realities which people necessarily confront in
their daily lives always and everywhere tend to spill over the normalising and
standardising boundaries of 'rational' policy discourse. Certainly we all have
considerable sympathy with such a view. Yet, naggingly, the 'practical' question which Foucault apparently chose to avoid – 'What is to be done?' –
remains.

Finally, therefore, despite our real and continuing reservations, we would
argue that we have to accept the need to move beyond the realm of critique
in order to canvass or lobby for the formulation of 'better' policy. It may be
that the imperative this implies bears particularly strongly on people, like ourselves, working within the present South African context. The broadly based
and long-suppressed popular demand for a process of fundamental 'reconstruction and development' in our country cannot be ignored by anyone
who professes to even the most limited form of engagement with issues outside
the academy.

Yet our ambivalence and uneasiness about any attempt to 'speak truth to
power' remain – not least because of our perception that, for some academics
or researchers in the current climate, recognition of the inherently problematic
nature of such efforts is either unimportant (in the face of the opportunities presented by policy engagement) or simply absent (perhaps as the consequence of a
failure or inability to reflect critically on their own practices). We believe that
maintaining a critical distance from the decision to enter the terrain of policy
discourse allows one to grasp the otherwise unanticipated difficulties and consequences that that decision may entail. If the 'bright side' of the South African
state, its 'benign' aspect, is indeed ascendant at present, our objective is surely to
ensure that it remains so and therefore to work towards the goal of popular
empowerment. If, as may be the case, its 'dark side of domination' has already
re-emerged as the imperatives of effective government take hold – that is: pre-
dictability, order, the capacity to 'deliver' the benefits of development, in a
word 'disempowerment' – then our objective is to work against that tendency.
We have written the above to provide a platform from which to carry that work
in whichever direction changing circumstances demand.

# Notes

1  Versions of our paper were presented at the annual conference of the Association for Anthropology in Southern Africa, Grahamstown, Sept. 1995, at seminars in the University of Cape Town (UCT) Education Faculty, Nov. 1995, and the University of the Western Cape Department of Anthropology and Sociology, May 1996, and at the annual conference of the Association of Social Anthropologists of the Commonwealth, Harare, Jan. 1997. We acknowledge comments received there and from David Coplan and Jim Ferguson but accept responsibility for the ideas expressed.

2  For Foucault, 'governmentality' is a peculiarly modern mode of exercising power which has 'as its target[,] population, as its principal form of knowledge[,] political economy and as its essential technical means[,] apparatuses of security' (1979: 20). Moreover, government operates through, and alongside, 'a whole complex of *"savoir"'* − knowledge of the art of government - which, with statistics as its key science, 'makes it possible to quantify the phenomena specific to population' (1979: 20, 17).

3  The study was conducted under the auspices of the Urban Problems Research Unit, UCT. We acknowledge financial assistance from the Centre for Science Development, Human Sciences Research Council (and Spiegel from the Wenner-Gren Foundation), but bear full responsibility for views expressed here. We also gratefully acknowledge the assistance of interviewers Anthony Mehlwana and Ayanda Canca.

4  By 'domestic consolidation' we mean the process through which a household consolidates its resources in order to stabilise and improve its domestic situation. The usage should not be confused with the way the term is used in housing policy discourse to describe an essentially *physical* process of incrementally building a formal house over a more or less extended period of time.

5  The field research was conducted by two UCT graduate students. They used open-ended interview schedules. One (who did the majority of interviews, occasionally accompanied by Spiegel) was a social anthropology student, the other a student in the city and regional planning programme. In the case of the anthropology student, a sense of 'ownership' of the project - he used interview material in his own dissertation - may have resulted in the delivery of more useful and better developed material than that delivered by the planning student, for whom the work was little more than a vacation job.

6  We have already published various papers based on the material (Spiegel *et al.* 1996a, 1996b, forthcoming).

7  The reason we selected this mode of generating material lay in the time constraints on us as principal researchers with full-time teaching commitments. (This was despite an appeal by the anthropologist among us, at research design stage, that we build in periods of personal field-based research.) The interviews were conducted by graduate students using an open-ended interview schedule that we prepared in advance and piloted and revised with the interviewers' assistance.

8  The possessives and the commercial metaphor are used here deliberately: we acknowledge the influence of Bourdieu's critique of *homo academicus* and his analysis of the struggles over symbolic capital and status which endemically traverse the academic 'field' (see Jenkins 1992: 119–24).

9  Watson sits on the board of this Trust.

10  'Trying to move politics [as policy-making] with academic theory is like using a walnut to crack a sledgehammer' (Appel 1993: 229).

11  Personal communication, 31 August 1995.

# References

Appel, S. (1993) Chalk and cheese: reflections on educational policy. *Perspectives in Education* 14, 2: 229–38.

Bernard, H.R. (1989) *Research Methods in Cultural Anthropology*. Newbury Park, CA: Sage.

Escobar, A. (1992) Planning. In *The Development Dictionary* (ed.) W. Sachs. London: Zed Books.

—— (1995) *Encountering Development*. Princeton, NJ: Princeton University Press.

Ferguson, J. (1990) *The Anti-Politics Machine*. Cambridge: Cambridge University Press.

Foucault, M. (1979) *Discipline and Punish: The Birth of the Prison*. New York: Pantheon.

Fraser, N. (1989) *Unruly Practices: Power, Discourse and Gender in Contemporary Social Theory*. Cambridge: Polity Press.

Jenkins, R. (1992) *Pierre Bourdieu*. London: Routledge.

Mazur, R. and Qangule, V. (1995) African migration and appropriate housing responses in metropolitan Cape Town. WCCHT, Cape Town (mimeo).

Robertson, A.F. (1984) *People and the State: An Anthropology of Planned Development*. Cambridge: Cambridge University Press.

Smart, B. (1986) The politics of truth and the problem of hegemony. In *Foucault: A Critical Reader* (ed.) D. Couzens Hoy. Oxford: Basil Blackwell.

Spiegel, A., Watson, V. and Wilkinson, P. (1994) Domestic fluidity and movement patterns among Cape Town's African population: some implications for housing policy. Paper presented to the Africa Seminar, University of Cape Town.

—— (1996a) Devaluing diversity? National housing policy and African household dynamics in Cape Town. *Urban Forum* 7, 1: 1–30.

—— (1996b) Domestic diversity and fluidity among some African households in Greater Cape Town. *Social Dynamics* 22, 1: 7–30.

—— (forthcoming) Women, difference and urbanization patterns in Cape Town, South Africa. *African Urban Quarterly* 11, 1.

Walzer, M. (1986) The politics of Michel Foucault. In *Foucault: A Critical Reader* (ed.) D. Couzens Hoy. Oxford: Basil Blackwell.

Wildavsky, A.B. (1979) *Speaking Truth to Power: The Art and Craft of Policy Analysis*. Boston: Little Brown.

Wilkinson, P. (1993) Housing need and housing policy in South Africa: a critical response to the strategy response adopted in the de Loor Report. In *The de Loor Task Group Report on Housing Policy for South Africa: Some Perspectives* (ed.) D. Dewar. Cape Town: The Urbanity and Housing Network, UCT Working Paper No. 1.

# Chapter 14

# Machiavellian empowerment and disempowerment

## The violent political changes in early seventeenth-century Ethiopia

*Manuel João Ramos*

## Machiavelli and political theology

In an article recently published in *Social Anthropology*, the journal of the European Association of Social Anthropologists, anthropologist Adam Kuper has proposed a stimulating approach to the study of power relations in what he refers to as pre-colonial political systems in Africa (Kuper 1995). He looks for, and quite convincingly seems to find, traces of a 'distinctly Machiavellian style' both in the strategies and in the principle formulations of two pre-conquest South African leaders in the early nineteenth century: Shaka, chief of the Nguni–Zulu, and Moeshoeshoe, of the Sotho–Tswana. Although, as Kuper reminds his readers from the start, Machiavelli's work and ideas are 'culturally specific', it wouldn't be inappropriate to study 'exotic situations' through a Machiavellian perspective: 'Machiavelli, it seems, may be read with profit as a comparative sociologist, as one might read Weber or Durkheim' (Kuper 1995: 1, 12). More specifically, a 'realistic, cross-cultural political anthropology', interested in understanding strategies for grabbing and keeping power in different cultural contexts would greatly benefit from incorporating Machiavelli's very general law of politics: 'that the prince must use every means to secure his position, for rivals and enemies will be doing their best to undermine him, and moreover each regime has its intrinsic fault lines, which they will exploit' (Kuper 1995: 12). Clearly, then, an evaluation of the potential of conceptual tools like the notions of 'empowerment' and 'disempowerment' in fields covered by the political anthropologist might be enriched by being coupled with such a lucid analysis of the 'power game' as Machiavelli's is. More to the point of the present proceedings, the acts and discourses of self-empowerment, the situations of disempowerment and the ambiguities of empowering strategies, could usefully be read within a Machiavellian framework, and understood as strategies for grabbing and keeping power, and as conditions where it might be gained or lost, globally affecting the overall system.

Kuper's proposal is quite an appealing one, even if he doesn't really care to make it heuristically convincing. The author doesn't advance any arguments for preferring a Machiavellian point of view to a Voltairean, Hobbesian, Dantean or even a Averroistic, or Aristotelian one, for instance. Furthermore, he doesn't suggest anywhere in the article how the substitution of Weberian or Durkheimian models for a Machiavellian one, or else their mutual complementarity, would lead to a more 'realistic, cross-cultural political anthropology'. Still, the fact that his proposal has, above all, a strong rhetorical foundation shouldn't prevent us from welcoming it. Interestingly, in areas other than strict politics, social psychologists have been for some time dealing with, and categorizing, what they view as specific 'Machiavellian' behavioural and personality types: these refer to the deceptive attitude and decisional behaviour of personalities strongly attracted to leadership, as they are expressed in particularly ambiguous, critical social contexts, where swift and informal individual action is favoured (Christie and Geis 1970). There would also seem to exist a psychological foundation to the characteristic trait of the 'Machiavellian personality' – the ability to suspend any ethical constraints over one's actions and decisions while retaining the capacity of manipulating other people's constraints within a group ('High/Low Machs', see Drory and Gluskinos 1980: 83–5). This use of Machiavelli's ideas, as detailed in *The Prince*, gives us a valuable hint to what can be the proper setting for Kuper's anthropological reading of that Renaissance political analyst: the power game constitutes the interface between collective structures and individual actions, or, as Barth (1959: 2–3) has put it, the systematic individual manipulation of social relations that leads to the (re)creation of institutional groups and to the accretion of individual authority.

Curiously enough, Kuper's contextual option – the study of the 'power game' in two traditional African sovereignty systems – reveals a unexpected degree of kinship between Machiavellian political thought and some pages of Frazer, in the *Golden Bough* and the *Magical Origin of Kings*.[1] In fact, consideration of psychological motivations and of the (frequently deceptive) individual action within the collective system are undoubtedly important forming traits of both the 'prince' and the 'magician-king'.[2] In the field of studies on traditional ('pre-conquest') African sovereignty systems, recent theoretical production has been largely inspired by an active reappraisal of Frazer's ideas on political theology – to the point that Luc de Heusch (1987a: 269, 271, 1987b: 46–56) defines his views, and those of colleagues such as Alfred Adler and Jean-Claude Muller, as decidedly 'neo-frazeréen'. If for no other reason, Kuper's choice – to analyse, under the rhetorical cloak of a Machiavellian framework, the individual roles and 'styles' of leaders and usurpers within two such traditional systems – deserves more than passing attention: his *Social Anthropology* article, where he explicitly embraces a 'Machiavellian' position, can also be seen as suggesting an alternative to 'neo-frazeréen' models of African sovereignty, like de Heusch's, where attention to the 'power game' have been clearly under-stressed – but an alternative that can still be understood within a Frazerian inquiry into the (both mystical *and* mystifying) nature of power and *authoritas*. In this short chapter, therefore, I propose to test some of the features of a Machiavellian interpretation of a pre-colonial African sovereignty system,[3] but in a situation where the attribution of a 'exotic' quality is not as clear-cut as in the ones researched by Kuper. In fact, Christian Ethiopia in the late sixteenth and early seventeenth centuries, as can be perceived through the writings of a group of missionaries belonging to the Society of Jesus,[4] is an interesting case where the 'exoticism' of its sovereignty and religious system was, in some measure, brought on as a negative function of a project of (failed) transformation of the Monophysite *Negusa Nagast* (the Ethiopian king of kings) into a Catholic 'prince'.

The story of the confrontation between two Christian models of political and religious sovereignty, and the failed substitution of Monophysitism for Catholicism, was filled with misunderstandings and tragedy. Even if the Jesuitical accounts demand that systematic attention be given to the fact that they voice a explicitly non- (and anti-)Monophysite perspective of the events, met with disturbing silence on the Ethiopian side, there is still a possibility of evaluating the possibilities and limitations of a Machiavellian grammar in relation to empowerment/disempowerment issues in this 'situation'. Three themes in particular can be inspiring:

1   the Machiavellian assumption that political action and political strategy (the power game) should be seen as autonomous and in dialectical relation with ethics and ideology;
2   the suggestion that individual and informal political action and power relations become most influential in periods of crisis, instability and change, when institutional, traditional means of government seem to crumble;
3   the idea that the use of force and violence becomes a legitimate instrument of power when political life stops functioning.

Machiavelli is generally seen as a founder of the Western ideological concept of a secular, lay state. Can he, then, be of use to the political anthropologist, especially when such systems as the ones that go under the general notion of sacral sovereignty are considered? According to a dichotomous view of the political theory, power and legitimacy can be seen as deriving either from social or from supernatural sources. Machiavelli himself is rather obscure about this matter, but this difficulty could be somewhat overcome by accepting de Heusch's (1987: 218, 256–60) (neo-Frazerian) view that political science is a mere part of the history of religions, and that a secular state is only a special case within a more general context. If this is the case, Machiavellian analysis can fruitfully be taken into consideration when we deal with political practice as autonomous from, but interdependent with, political and religious ideology – for, after all, power and legitimacy can be seen as deriving both from social *and* from supernatural sources.

Up to 1974, according to a peculiar system of priestly sovereignty, evoking both Semitic and African ideological models (Haberland 1965: 71ff), the Ethiopian rulers were supposed to derive their legitimacy and right to rule directly from God through the dynastic line of Solomon: Christlike, they had explicit priestly and jurisdictional functions.[5] But, from a papal point of view, this was rather an unacceptable heresy: thus, the Portuguese project of converting the *Negusa Nagast* was particularly cherished by Ignatius of Loyola, the founder of the Society of Jesus, whose members saw themselves as the 'soldiers of the Pope'; and great care was put into the appointment of a Jesuit patriarch for Ethiopia.[6] This project was, in fact, the result of an active joint effort of the Roman papacy and the Portuguese crown (Brodrick 1946: 237–8) – at the height of a counter-Reformation reaction in south-western Europe that favoured the right of spiritual precedence of the Roman Pope over national monarchies and churches.

To understand the contours of the confrontation between two Christian, yet quite distinct, political theologies (Roman Catholic and Monophysite), which gave discursive body to a internecine civil and religious crisis of great dimensions in Ethiopia, it is useful to start by very briefly evoking the European background of expectations and images about this East African nation (James 1990), that, in connection with the legend of Prester John, led to a Portuguese presence in Ethiopia.

### From *Presbyter Johannes* to *Negusa Nagast*

Prester John, as the utopian-like description of his Indian kingdom in the early medieval Latin letters clearly show,[7] was a very potent image of a Christ-mimetic priestly king, intimately connected with the concept, common in western European medieval traditions, of the 'king of the last days' or '*Endkaiser*', who would, in alliance with a western sovereign, emerge from the Orient to conquer Palestine and free Jerusalem from Muslim hands – this pious act would be a prophetical sign of the end of the world and, simultaneously, of its apocalyptical renewal, with the coming of the New Heavenly Jerusalem (Gosman 1983: 270–84). A temporal ruler, he was also a minor priest, a 'presbyter' in a religious hierarchy headed by the patriarch of St Thomas. This Christian utopia was itself inspired in the Syriac Christian traditions that attributed the conversion of an Indian king and his family to the missionary zeal of St Thomas Didymus, who offered the king a palace in Heaven (Slessarev 1959: 80ff; Ramos 1997a: 208ff). In the course of five centuries and up to the seventeenth century, we can witness the transformation and eventual eclipse of the Christ-mimetic character of the Indian priestly king reigning over a perfect society (Ramos 1997a: 1–11, 1997b).

The ideological background of the Iberian discoveries was highly ecumenical. To 'discover' (i.e. to 'uncover') the world was to cast the light of true faith upon the darkness of ignorance and evil that subjected non-Christian humanity

(Barradas de Carvalho 1983: 529ff; Randles 1966: 3ff). In the Portuguese case, travel around African coasts was also conceptualised within a crusading project which meant to a large extent the penetration of the continent through its water courses (Randles 1960: 20–7); these were thought to be connected, in some unknown ways, to the sources of the Nile (through a central African lake), and consequently to Prester John's kingdom – the West African rulers were often treated as his vassals. At the same time, envoys of the Portuguese king were sent by land to East Africa, with letters to 'Preste João das Índias'.

The idea that had come down from the medieval *Letter*, of an alliance between Prester John and a western sovereign (now the Portuguese king), was to be kept alive in the Portuguese–Ethiopian diplomatic epistolary, and in Portuguese strategic military writings: the conquest of the Holy Land, and the destruction of the Muslim world are frequently suggested or proposed in the documentation. But, by the first half of the sixteenth century, the Ethiopian *Negus* was publicly and officially contacted and the discrepancies between the Ethiopian nation and the magnificent kingdom described in the *Letter* were highlighted by Portuguese writers. In fact, reality seemed to have played a terrible trick: how could a black king, living permanently in a tent, ruling over a poor barbarous and schismatic people in a mountainous wilderness, be the magnificent Prester John? Hereticism, poverty, evil ways and uncivilised, improper customs, Jewish and Arabic influences were to be held as definitive proofs of the inadequacy of the identification between the self-styled author of the *Letter* and this African ruler. This inadequacy became manifest when in 1541, in an ironical inversion of expectations, a small Portuguese expeditionary force was sent to rescue young *Negus* Galawdevos' weak armies from defeat at the hands of the Somali invaders (in 1541–3). Just a few years later, the first Jesuit missionaries landed in Ethiopia with the prospect of converting the Monophysite Christians and their emperor, whom the Portuguese, like most Europeans, still insisted on calling Prester John (Ramos 1997a: 171ff).

In respect of the documents that refer to the Portuguese influence, and specially those that detail the Jesuit missionaries' endeavours to convert the Ethiopian Monophysite court to Catholicism, and to obtain the emperor's submission to the Roman Pope, some words of warning should, at this stage, be given. Ethiopian and Arabic documentation almost entirely omits explicit references to the doings of the Jesuits and to the influence of the Catholic community: but in fact, there is reason to believe that the absence of references to the Catholics and the Jesuits in contemporary texts like the royal chronicle of Susinyus express an obvious intention of obscuring part of the memories of this apostate emperor's times (since this chronicle was written or rewritten in his successor's reign).[8] But one must nevertheless add that the European (i.e. Jesuit) writings of the late sixteenth and early seventeenth centuries that report, and most probably overestimate, their own social and political importance within the imperial court and the Christian core of Ethiopia, must be treated with great care.

The Jesuit missionaries claimed they played an extensive role in Susinyus' imperial self-empowering actions (his bid for power). The vision they expressed in innumerable letters and accounts, on which we must rely to try to reconstruct the history and purpose of this relationship, served more than anything to self-legitimise – in the eyes of their European readers (especially the Pope, and the Portuguese crown and Church leaders) – their own presence and identity as a specific group within Ethiopian society, with declared self-empowering interests in the Ethiopian court.[9] What can, then, be extracted from the documentation?

## The Ethiopian political crisis and emperor Susinyus' steps towards legitimacy

Let us rapidly consider the events that surrounded a particularly dramatic moment of the history of the Ethiopian empire. This moment came when Susinyus, the ruling *Negusa Nagast* proclaimed, in an imperial decree in 1624, his conversion and public submission to Pope Urban VIII (Teles 1660, IV: XXVII). Moreover, it ordered that all Christians should convert to Catholicism, and Monophysitism was to be abolished, prohibited and punished with death. Such institutions as polygamy, divorce, annual baptism, circumcision, marriage of the clergy, celebration of the Sabbath were thus made illegal. This unfortunate decision, that eventually caused a general popular rebellion and a bloody civil war (Abir 1980: 211ff), must be viewed, in Machiavellian terms, as a misjudgement and a grave mistake in the political action of an emperor who asserted himself as a tyrant (Machiavelli 1984: IX). Had he succeeded though, this might not only have resulted in the consolidation of his rule, but also in the general recognition of the influence, and indeed power, of a cultural and religious minority: the group of Portuguese migrants and of Catholic converts, and their Jesuit leaders.

Ethiopia, under Christian Amhara rule had been, since the Somali invasion in the middle of the sixteenth century, in a state of social and political turmoil. The traditional system of interdictions that governed the *Neguses'* lives is known to have relaxed. Even if they still ritually ate alone, and refrained from touching the ground directly, they no longer hid behind curtains and veils during ceremonial sessions. The ritual conditioning rules of imperial succession had also evidently been softened: the custom of imprisoning the heirs to the throne in a mountain fortress, *Amba Gueshem*, had been abandoned by the sixteenth century (Pais 1945, I: X). The fragility of traditional political relations in the administrative chain caused by wars and other external circumstances was also visible. In itself that constituted a vicious circle: as it weakened, the central Amhara stronghold came under increasing warring pressure from the Somali Muslims, and immediately after from the Galla (the nomadic Oromo pastoralists). Modifications in the centralised administrative and military structure of the empire were reported: namely, the creation of the king's personal guard and a drafted army imposed on the feudal class as a parallel and alternative force to the armies raised by each of the lords and chiefs, in order to reduce the dependency of the *Negus* on the feudal class and the landowning monastic orders (Abir 1980: 152–4; Pennec 1996: 143–5, 160ff). Naturally, this favoured a situation of increased antagonism between the emperor and the nobles and the Church. The emperor kept making extensive use of his privilege of appointing and substituting chiefs and governors throughout the empire, and restrained their independent action in the military campaigns. As a result, by the beginning of the seventeenth century the feudal lords were losing many acquired privileges, giving way to the development of a full-fledged autocratic tyranny. The conditions for this development, that Machiavelli analysed in his work *The Prince*, had been fulfilled.

By 1604, when the *Negus* ZaDinguil died, the political and military situation in the Ethiopian Highlands had become very tense; a hard-fought succession struggle followed, between Dingil's weak son Yakob and a young cousin of a previous *Negus*. This pretender, Susinyus, who was later to be enthroned under the name of *Negus* Seltan Segued, as a young man, led a nomadic raiding life and knew Galla/Oromo politics quite well. When he came forward with his claim to replace the appointed emperor Yakob, he had a very good chance of winning the succession conflict. Although his legitimacy was questionable (being only the cousin of a previous *Negus*), he presented better credentials as an opponent of the Galla invaders, as an experienced fighter (familiar with Galla war tactics) and as an alliance maker, than Yakob (Pereira 1892: I–XXX; Abir 1980: 194–6). His steps towards legitimacy took various forms: he apparently succeeded in sustaining Galla invasions and imposing himself as a warlord against other factions, he managed the conversion to Christianity of some Galla and Aggaw groups, and was symbolically enthroned in the old capital of the ancient Aksumite kingdom (Pais 1945, I: XII).

Institutionally legitimated as an (indirect) descendant of King Solomon of Israel, the usurper Susinyus maintained his power by opposing the feudal class, by reducing the influence of the clergy (especially the monastic clergy and the Egyptian Coptic patriarch, the *Abun*), and by trying to succeed both as a warrior and a pacifier. His long reign was a continuous succession of wars and struggles against internal and external enemies. In this context, the empowerment of the small Portuguese/Catholic community, and the group (of not more than twenty at any time) of Jesuit priests, became instrumental for Susinyus. To counterbalance the Ethiopian clergy's power, to obtain Western weapons and military assistance and to introduce foreign technologies seemed to be the pre-conditions to securing a radical political reform in the sovereignty system (see S.B. Chernetsov, in Pennec 1996: 143). He also frequently exploited the tribal factions of the Galla-Oromo, attracting some peripheral groups as allies. In this privileged relation with groups of foreigners, he followed the Machiavellian precept of finding feeble allies to counter stronger adversaries and not losing control as a legitimate congregator of a multi-fractured society (Machiavelli 1984: III; 1983: II, 4).

But it is important to note that the Portuguese military help the Jesuit priests promised was conditional on the prior conversion of the emperor and his Monophysite subjects to Catholicism, as well as the immediate abandonment of the traditions mentioned earlier. When, in a very dramatic moment, Susinyus accepted imposing the forced conversion on Monophysite Ethiopians, making public his decree, and a Jesuit patriarch was appointed by the Roman Pope to Ethiopia, he made a most grievous mistake, one against which Machiavelli very explicitly warns 'princes': he failed to give priority to his relation with the 'people', the mass of Amhara and Tigrean farmers (Machiavelli 1984: IX). A fact that the Jesuits, shall we say 'Machiavellianly',[10] were careful to omit, was that in any case the Portuguese were by this time unable to bring forward any assistance (the Portuguese were no longer an important power in the Indian Ocean region: Abir 1980: 185–7). One could wonder whether, had Susinyus received the military and technical help he requested, the country would not have plunged into one of the most extensive civil wars recorded in imperial Ethiopia. But, as it was, the forced conversion resulted in a string of rebellions and bloody battles that eventually precipitated the erosion of Amhara rule in Ethiopia. Although it pacified both nobles and clergy, the eventual abolition of the imperial decree and the abdication of the emperor altered this situation only minimally.

Fasilidas, the emperor's chosen son, expelled or sentenced to death the Jesuits, the Portuguese-Ethiopian families and a unknown number of Catholic converts (possibly in the order of the thousands: Coulbeaux 1929: 245–6; Pennec 1996: 170ff; Teles 1660: 352–66). He nevertheless approved the changes introduced by his father, under Jesuit influence, in the political-administrative system: for the first time in the Solomonid dynasty the empire had a fixed capital, and the *Negus*, like a true Renaissance 'prince', was living in a (Western-style) palace. Until then, the emperors were ritual roamers who underlined by their cyclical visits and displacements their bond with the various territories and peoples. They presented, wherever they went, a visual model of imperial power and administration in the form of the institutional dis-position of the tents in the camp. As a direct consequence of this immobility, the emperor and the Amhara Christian groups lost control of most of the empire. Ethiopia became for the next two centuries a patch of independent small chiefdoms, subjected to the southern Galla-Oromo invaders (Levine 1974: 78–86; Abir 1980: 231–3).

By Machiavellian standards, the process of fragmentation of the empire had its key turning point in the expressed antagonism between Susinyus and the feudal class, the Church and the Highlands Christian farmers. Moreover, the failure either to expand or even to hold by force the imperial control over the Cushitic and Muslim groups of the lowlands in the south accelerated this fragmentation. Had he succeeded in military terms against these last groups,

Machiavelli would suggest (Machiavelli 1984: XXIV), there would be a chance to maintain imperial power. As it was, the crumbling power of the emperor was turned against a feeble, easily disempowered group that was used as a scapegoat to salvage the unity of the Christian Monophysite section of Ethiopian society.

## Worlds apart – the fate of Ethiopian–Jesuit relations

A Machiavellian focal point seems most appropriate to understand the reported events – in the reign of Susinyus – and the doings and motivations of a number of actors. But, again, one should stress that political actions, the dynamics of power, the use of force, etc., are always submitted to the general ideological principles that structure society, even though they leave open various options, various possible modes of political action. Machiavelli was aware of this fact, when he reminded his reader that politicians must take great care to play their game without publicly breaking any ethical rule or forgetting the overall importance of the systems of beliefs and representations (Machiavelli 1984: XVIII; 1983: I.12–13). Let us accept that the general definition of African sacral kingship structures – projects of cosmic tyranny coupled with an extreme fragility of the king's power as expressed by his ritual duties and prohibitions – applied, at least partly, to imperial Ethiopia (Haberland 1965: 71; de Heusch 1983: 23–8). If that was so, it is clear that, momentarily at least, the institution of sacral sovereignty became unbalanced, for there were no means of institutionally controlling the ruler. In a situation where the ritual and institutional constraints that helped limit the emperor's power had been relaxed, and where he emerged as a sort of tyrant, it is interesting to note that more and more insistently he resorted to the use of force, and to an erratic and illusory empowerment of marginal groups, alien to Ethiopian society, as a tool to restrict the opposition of important areas of the Ethiopian *civitas*.

Susinyus was thus favoured with both an accumulation of personal power and freedom of political action, in a situation where the institutional system had been relaxed and the empire threatened by the outside. The forced conversion and the condemnation of traditional customs – which was an evident *fuite en avant*, to use the French expression – can be considered as a manifestation of the tyrant's will to assert his power. These actions can be understood as leading to an abortive creation of a new system of sovereignty, inspired by a Western Latin political and religious model (Abir 1980: 231), which proposed to reinforce the absolute temporal powers of the emperor, even if it strongly limited his ritual Christ-mimetism (i.e. his priestly functions), through his submission to the Roman Pope. The political intentions behind the conversion to Catholicism – as a means to reduce the controlling power of the traditional clergy – seem to have been largely misunderstood by the Portuguese Jesuits, whose missionary zeal consequently led them to disregard and to abruptly try to suppress essential traits of the Monophysite Ethiopians' faith and culture

(Abir 1980: 224–6). This action backfired and eventually resulted in persecutions against the Catholics.

What happened next was most enlightening. Because it was denied the institutional control of the ruler's power, Ethiopian society – 'the people' – adopted the use of violence and rebellion broke out in a conservative reaction to changes imposed from a top that showed insufficient results in defending the country from external threats (by then, the main influx of Galla-Oromo peoples). The obvious misunderstanding and symmetry of intentions and expectations that characterised relations between the Jesuits and Susinyus must also be reviewed. The emperor's political motivations can be interpreted as a personal, desperate attempt to save and renew the empire. That is, to revive the lost glorious days of the dynasty, three centuries before, by empowering a minority seen as culturally and religiously exogenous. As to the Jesuit priests who successively started the process of converting the emperor and his family, and were behind the already mentioned submission decree, their motivations seemed to be an equally desperate attempt to save not the real empire of Ethiopia, but an imaginary one. In due course, the Jesuit fathers found to their own expense that Ethiopian reality resisted fitting this imaginary picture.

In the writings of the Jesuit missionaries, for whom the conversion of the Ethiopian ruler and the search for the sources of the Nile were two interrelated obsessive goals, it is clear that the Ethiopian reality posed a difficult conceptual problem: like other travellers before them, they retained the designation of 'Prester John' as the valid title of the *Negus*; they confronted Ethiopian social and physical reality having the medieval *Letter* in their minds, and were eager to convert Ethiopia so it would conform to the Indian (utopian) model. Partly Christian but heretical, African but in some important ways Asiatic (with Semitic kingship structures, with Semitic language and writing systems), degenerate but visibly 'civilised' since the Aksumite period, Ethiopia was, in the end, to be declared a true monstrosity by the Jesuit writers.

The Jesuits seemed to have modelled their political action upon the account of the conversion of the Indian king by St Thomas, as well as by the papal perspective of spiritual and temporal supremacy over emperors and kings. The ardour that the Jesuit Pero Pais put into planning and building a Western-style church and palace for Susinyus, and his influence in the *Negus*' decision to found a fixed capital, are important hints that the Jesuits were enacting the legendary relation between patriarch of St Thomas and Prester John. As already mentioned, the *Negusa Nagast*, like Prester John in the legend, had priestly functions within the Monophysite Church. So, the Jesuits seemed to conceive that occupying the position of the *Abun*, the Egyptian Coptic patriarch, meant that they could rule over the Ethiopian emperor, because they were representatives of the Catholic Pope. In particular, the Jesuit Afonso Mendes, the appointed Catholic patriarch who arrogantly insisted on the public act of submission of Susinyus to him as the representative of Rome, visibly failed to understand the particular institutional relation between the *Negus* and the

Coptic patriarch he thought he came to replace. This specific act seems to have been the dramatic turning point which marked the reversal of the course of the emperor's political action, and the apparently systematic disempowerment and persecution of the Catholic minority.

In fact, submission of the emperor to the *Abun* (or for that matter to the Jesuit patriarch) was a concept strange to Ethiopian Christian ideology. The *Abun* was a foreigner, a representative of the Alexandrian Coptic Church, that had no hierarchical supremacy over Ethiopian Christianity or over the *Negusa Nagast* who ruled over Christians, Jews, Muslims and pagans alike. Like the *Abun*, the emperor was also considered a foreigner. Their relation was that of two structurally opposed representatives of foreign civilisations: the *Negus*, who held the title of 'lion of Judah', was the 'son of the kings of Israel' (Haberland 1965: 25–33); and the *Abun* was the representative of the eunuch, the slave of the legendary queen Candace, who introduced Christianity to Ethiopia (Teles 1660: XXVIII). So, in the Ethiopian perspective, there was little reason to see the emperor, descendant of Menelik, the older of Solomon's sons, submit to a representative of the westerners, the *ferenjoch*, descendants of Adrâmi, the young Byzantine half-brother of the first sacred king Menelik, referred to in the *Kebra Nagast* (Budge 1932: 122). As to the attacks on circumcision, polygamy, yearly ritual baptism, etc., and the supreme Jesuitical heresy of affirming that Christ had two natures, these were felt by most as absurdities and pure devilish malignity (Pereira 1892: 259).

Fasilidas, Susinyus' son, aimed at easing the enormous tensions between Amharic and Tigrean groups (both Monophysite Christians), and to achieve this he opted to sacrifice the Catholic minority. He managed to repair the damage caused by his father's 'mistake' (as Machiavelli would put it), but this act of disempowerment was of limited efficacy, for it could not prevent the actual ebb of imperial, and generally Christian, rule over Ethiopian affairs – now dominated by Galla-Oromo influences.[11] Symmetrically, in the perspective of the disempowered Jesuits, Prester John was finally dead (Lobo 1971: 786–9). The tentative identification between Prester John and the Ethiopian ruler came to be actively denied in their writings: not, as before the persecution, as an ambiguous precondition for their pretensions to self-legitimation in European courtly and ecclesiastical circles (especially in their confrontation with the Dominican order, in Italy and the Iberian peninsula), but in definitely negative terms, as the discursive reflection of the violent disempowerment they suffered, from 1631 until their final expulsion.

## Final note

A purely dichotomous perspective that promotes the interpretation of a situation or discourse in terms of asymmetry and conflict between dominating and dominated groups, may fruitfully give way to an awareness of the logical dependence between opposition and communion as defining any kind of social and

cultural interaction. In the particular case presented here, we are primarily dealing with a quantity of literary documents produced by the Jesuit missionaries,
with mainly self-legitimising intentions. In order to categorise the conflicting
and uncontrolled Ethiopian reality, they systematically characterised it as in a
state of progressive demonic 'otherness'. But this quality of 'otherness' was
both a function of an historical attribution of 'sameness' (the identity between
the realm of Prester John and Christian Ethiopia) and a embittered recognition
that, in their disempowerment, the Jesuits were themselves being demonised
and categorised as alien in Ethiopian eyes. This 'exotic situation' gives us a com-
pelling example of the consubstantial quality of a relation where 'sameness' and
'otherness' are overlapping categories.

So, to understand, in a 'Machiavellian-Frazerian' perspective, Emperor
Susinyus' actions during the above-mentioned civil and religious crisis, it
seems important to reassess his relation with the Jesuit missionaries – his
'feeble allies', as Machiavelli would put it. Luc de Heusch's view of the relation
between the African sovereign and an essentially lineage-structured society is
here of little use: Ethiopian historical reality does not conform to the simplifying idea that a structurally egalitarian society, teleologically guessing the dangers
of sacralising central power – the simultaneously sacred and evil character of the
sovereign – creates a overwhelming system of ritual and ideological constraints
to limit his power (de Heusch 1987a: 271, 291). Luc de Heusch's interpretation
of the mystical power of the sovereign – the source of his/her sacrality – does
not, unfortunately, incorporate an element that nevertheless seemed obvious to
both Machiavelli and Frazer: the quality of mystification as a source of the
power game. As to Adam Kuper, his unawareness of the importance of the
ritual and ideological constraints through which the leader's actions must be
perceived, seems a unnecessary weakening of his Machiavellian perspective,
and one that Machiavelli himself wouldn't probably have approved of.

Ethiopian history and literature, from Menelik I in the *Kebra Nagast*, and the
traditions about Queen Candace, to the imperial chronicles of Galawdevos and
Susinyus, to Menelik II's and Haile Selassie's biographies (or even the 'red'
Mengistu Haile Mariam's presidency), offer us recurrent examples of how
imperial power in Ethiopia conceived political and cultural reforms, and solutions for both exogenous and endogenous crisis, through a carefully planned
association with foreigners, namely Europeans (the *ferenjoch*). This feature
should alert us to the possibility of conceptualising the mythical and historical
usurpers' self-legitimising actions and their preferred alliances with groups evidently marginal to Ethiopian society, during periods of social crisis, in more
general terms: political action is certainly autonomous from but also interdependent with ideological, ethical and theological constraints; these two contextual levels interact within a cyclical structure where normally polarised
elements – in this case, the *Negusa Nagast* as a figure of perfect social identity
or 'sameness', and the European Jesuits as figures of malignant alterity or 'otherness' – are momentarily associated as a precondition to envision a (cyclical)

renewal of society and of the imperial institution, which warrants their perpetual interdependence.

This feature, which Radcliffe-Brown (1952: 18, 20) has in another context described as an 'association of contraries' or an 'union of opposites', seems not only widespread in African sovereignty systems but determinant in their formation and continuity (for a comparative review, cf. Gomes da Silva 1989). Behind the confrontational rhetoric that percolates from the discourses of social-political domination and disempowerment, we recognise an equally relevant play of the elements that speak of recognition, identity, 'sameness'. In the case of the 'realm(s) of Prester John' as in many others, it is only when we take notice of the whole ontological and relational process that we understand the effectiveness and strength of the pulleys that hold opposing categories together.

# Notes

1 One could, naturally, direct at Kuper's proposal the same sort of reproach that Adler (1982: 265) directs at Evans-Pritchard: that he empties the ritual content of the institution of sacral sovereignty, reducing it to a system of competition for power.

2 Compare Machiavelli's praise of the deceiving qualities of the 'good prince' and the simplicity of the people (Machiavelli 1984: XVIII), with Frazer's view of the magician's and king's use of imposture (namely their voluntary misuse of the laws of causation) to acquire and accumulate personal power, that reverts to the general good of society - the 'credulous fellows' (Frazer 1920: 82–3; 1978: 80–1, 109).

3 In truth, a historical conjuncture in an African non-colonised nation.

4 Itself an ecclesiastical 'corporate group' recurrently perceived or identified as politically Machiavellian, in the same cultural context as the one that produced *The Prince*: one should note that the Spanish-Italian Jesuit elite was born in such houses as the Medicis, Borgias and Gandias, abundantly depicted in Machiavelli's work; Saint Francis Borgia, kin and descendant of Machiavelli's 'prince' Cesare Borgia, was in fact the third General of the Society of Jesus.

5 According to the 1947 Constitution of the Ethiopian state, 'the Emperor's person is sacred, his dignity is inviolable and his authority indisputable'; traditionally, the emperor is said to 'shine like the sun; his majesty fills men with awe and they recognize that the divine power is in him' (Bureau 1992: 24).

6 To the point that the original draft of the Society's *Constitutions*, which forbade its members to accept any ecclesiastical dignities higher than that of simple priesthood, was modified in order to accommodate the designation of a Jesuit patriarch for Ethiopia (Brodrick 1946: 237).

7 See the compilation of the *Epistola Johannes Presbyter*, with inclusion of the Latin versions of interpolations in Zarncke (1879: 909–24).

8 See text and translation in Pereira (1892–1900). On the comparison between the Ethiopian version (brought to Europe by James Bruce), and the abridged version by Pero Pais in his *História*, see Pennec 1996: 153–60.

9 It is never possible to assert that, when a specific group is said, in a particular set of documents, to exert a dominant role, or when it puts forward an 'empowered' discourse, that this necessarily reflects a dominant status at the level of social structure. The making of a self-empowering discourse can frequently be a tacit recognition of a disempowered condition.

10  As a personality disposition, Machiavellianism is intimately connected with a high capability of ingratiation in interpersonal relations (cf. Pandey and Rastogi 1979).

11  These populations, ignorant of centralised political models, seemed to have preferred maintaining the imperial administrative structures in place, and simply encroached themselves on the emperor's court, as controlling agents (Abir 1980: 234–5; Levine 1974: 80, 82).

## References

Abir, M. (1980) *Ethiopia and the Red Sea – The Rise of the Solomonid Dynasty and Muslim-European Rivalry in the Region*. London: Frank Cass.

Adler, A. (1982) *La Mort est le masque du roi: la royauté sacrée des Moundang du Tchad*. Paris: Payot.

Barradas de Carvalho, J. (1983) *A la recherche de la specifité de la renaissance portugaise*, vol. II. Paris: Fondation Calouste Gulbenkian.

Barth, F. (1959) *Political Leadership among Swat Pathans*. London: Athlone Press.

Brodrick, J., SJ (1946) *The Progress of the Jesuits (1556–79)*. London: Longman Green.

Budge, E.A.W. (1932) *The Queen of Sheba and her Only Son Menyelek I*. Oxford: Oxford University Press.

Bureau, J. (1992) Éthiopie: images et reflets. In *Le Roi Salomon et les maîtres du regard: art et médecine en Éthiopie*. Paris: Réunion des Musées Nationaux (pp. 23–4).

Christie, R. and Geis, F.L. (1970) *Studies in Machiavellianism*. New York: Academic Press.

Coulbeaux, J.-B. (1929) *Histoire politique et religieuse de l'Abyssinie*. Paris: Paul Geuthner.

de Heusch, L. (1982) *Rois nés d'un coeur de vache: mythes et rites bantous*. Paris: Gallimard.

—— (1987a) *Écrits sur la royauté sacrée*. Bruxelles: Editions de l'ULB.

—— (1987b) L'Inversion de la dette (propos sur les royautés sacrées africaines). In *L'Esprit des lois sauvages: Pierre Clastres ou une nouvelle anthropologie politique* (ed.) Miguel Abensour. Paris: Éditions du Seuil (pp. 41–57).

Drory, A. and Gluskinos, U.M. (1980) Machiavellianism and leadership. *Journal of Applied Psychology* 65, 1: 81–6.

Frazer, J.G. (1920) *The Magical Origin of Kings*. Cambridge: Trinity College.

—— (1978/1922) *The Golden Bough. A Study in Magic and Religion* (abr. edn). London: Macmillan.

Gomes da Silva, J.C. (1989) *L'Identité volée: essais d'anthropologie sociale*. Bruxelles: Editions de l'ULB.

Gosman, M. (1983) Otto de Freising et le Prêtre Jean. *Revue Belge de Philologie et d'Histoire* 61: 271–85.

Haberland, E. (1965) *Untersuchungen zum Äthiopischen Königtum*. Wiesbaden: Franz Steiner Verlag.

James, W. (1990) Kings, commoners, and the ethnographic imagination in Sudan and Ethiopia. In *Localizing Strategies: Regional Traditions of Ethnographic Writing* (ed.) R. Fardon. Edinburgh: Scottish Academic Press (pp. 96–135).

Kuper, A. (1995) Machiavelli in pre-colonial Southern Africa. *Social Anthropology* 3, 1: 1–13.

Levine, D. (1974) *Greater Ethiopia: The Evolution of a Multi-Ethnic Society*. Chicago: Chicago University Press.

Lobo, J. (1971) *Itinerário e outros escritos inéditos* (ed.) M. Gonçalves da Costa. Porto: Livraria Civilização.

Machiavelli, N. (1983/1531) *The Discourses of Niccolò Machiavelli*, 2 vols. (trans.) L. Walker. London: Routledge & Kegan Paul.

—— (1984/1532) *The Prince* (trans.) P. Bondanella and M. Musa. Oxford: Oxford University Press.

Pais, P. (1945) *História da Etiópia*, vols 1 and 2. Porto: Livraria Civilização.

Pandey, J. and Rastogi, R. (1979) Machiavellianism and ingratiation. *Journal of Social Psychology* 108: 221–5.

Pennec, H. (1996) La mission jésuite en Éthiopie au temps de Pedro Paez (1583–1622) et ses rapports avec le pouvoir Éthiopien. Troisième partie: le temps de la victoire (1612–22). *Rassegna di Studi Etiopici*, vol. xxxviii, 1996 (1994). Roma-Napoli (pp. 139–81).

Pereira, F.E. (1892–1900) *Chronica de Susenyus, rei de Ethiopia*, vol. 2. Lisboa: Imprensa Nacional.

Radcliffe-Brown, A.R. (1952) The comparative method in social anthropology. *Journal of the Royal Anthropological Institute* 81, 1–2: 15–20.

Ramos, M.J. (1997a) *Ensaios de Mitologia Cristã: A Preste João e a Reversibilidade Simbólica.* Lisboa, Editora Assírio and Alvim.

—— (1997b) Origen y evolution de una imagen Cristo-mimética: El Preste Juan en el tiempo y el espacio de las ideas cosmológicas europeas. *Politica y Sociedad. Revista cuatrimestral de Ciencias Sociales* (Facultad de Ciencias Politicas y Sociologia – Universidad Complutense de Madrid) May–Aug. Agosto 25: 37–44.

Randles, W.G. (1960) Notes on the genesis of the discoveries. *Studia* 5: 20–46.

—— (1966) Sur l'idée de découverte. In *Aspects internationaux de la découverte océanique aux XVe. et XVIe. siècle: travaux du cinquième colloque international d'histoire maritime, Lisbonne 14–16 Sept.* (eds) M. Mollat and P. Adam Paris: SEVPEN (pp. 17–21).

Slessarev, V. (1959) *Prester John. The Letter and the Legend.* Minneapolis: University of Minnesota Press.

Teles, B. (1660) *História geral da Etiópia a Alta ou Preste João.* Coimbra: Manoel Dias – Impressor da Universidade.

Zarncke, F. (1879) Der Presbyter Johannes. *Abhandlungen der Philologisch-Historischen Classe der Königlich Sächsischen Geselschaft der Wissenshaften* (Leipzig) 7: 827–1039.

# Index